Development
in Infancy

Development in Infancy

SECOND EDITION

T. G. R. Bower
University of Edinburgh

W. H. Freeman and Company
San Francisco

Project Editor: Pearl C. Vapnek
Designer: Sharon Helen Smith
Production Coordinator: Bill Murdock
Illustration Coordinators: Cheryl Nufer and Richard Quiñones
Compositor: Vera Allen Composition
Printer and Binder: The Maple-Vail Book Manufacturing Group

Library of Congress Cataloging in Publication Data

Bower, T. G. R., 1941–
    Development in infancy.

    (A series of books in psychology)
    Bibliography: p.
    Includes index.
    1. Infant psychology.   2. Cognition in children.
I. Title. II. Series. [DNLM: 1. Child development.
2. Cognition—In infancy and childhood. 3. Perception—
In infancy and childhood. WS 105.5.C7 B786d]
BF719.B68 1982   155.4'22   81-12544
ISBN 0-7167-1301-2   AACR2
ISBN 0-7167-1302-0 (pbk.)

Printed in the United States of America

Contents

Preface to the Second Edition

I am delighted my publishers have decided that a second edition of this book is worthwhile. In the preface to the first edition, I expressed the hope that it might stimulate new research and new questions. Whatever the book's causal role, it is gratifying to see new research and new questions appearing at an ever increasing rate. Some of the more outrageous speculations of the first edition now seem positively conservative, particularly in the light of recent discoveries in the social field. I am pleased, too, that theorizing, which in the first edition in many cases depended on one study, now has stronger foundations. I regret only that in some cases the data (e.g., on neonate reaching) arrived too late for inclusion in this revision.

The main novelty in this revision is theoretical. I have tried to reach a compromise here between the metatheory of the first edition and the metatheory of my two subsequent books: *A Primer of Infant Development* (1977) and *Human Development* (1979), both published by W. H. Freeman and Company.

I would like to thank my publishers for giving me this second chance to express a theory, Pearl C. Vapnek for sympathetic editing, and Dr. Jennifer Wishart for help with just about everything.

I dedicate the book to infants everywhere, the hope of the future, in particular to the six thousand or so who have complainingly and uncomplainingly passed through my laboratory in the last seven years.

September 1981   *T. G. R. Bower*

Preface to the First Edition

I think it is generally agreed that infancy, the period before language, is one of the most critical segments of human development. During infancy the basic human motor skills are established, perceptual development is virtually completed, and the roots of the cognitive skills that will grow into a human intellect are laid down. Despite this, it is only comparatively recently that infancy as a field of study has truly burgeoned. In the last ten years our methods for the study of infants have become much more precise. The questions we can ask of infants have become much more detailed, and the answers we received have surprised many of us. Infants are capable of many things we would not have expected and at the same time show incapacities we would never have suspected. In this book I have tried to present the methods currently used to get information from infants as well as some of the results obtained through using these methods. I have tried to show how infants can be capable of things we thought beyond them. I have also tried to elucidate the processes whereby infants develop those capacities they must develop, particularly cognitive capacities. My concern throughout has been to show the importance of the psychological environment of the developing infant in speeding up or slowing down his attainment of fundamental cognitive skills. I believe that infancy is the critical period in cognitive development—the period when the greatest gains and the greatest losses can occur. Further, the gains and losses that occur here become harder to offset with increasing age. If this book can stimulate some practical work on these problems, I shall feel well rewarded. I also hope that students who read this book will gain insight into the dynamic interactive process that is called development in infancy. I hope it will stimulate readers to ask new questions and get new answers. Only with the help of new questions and answers can we finally come to comprehend development.

September 1973   *T. G. R. Bower*

Development in Infancy

1
Introduction

Psychology, during most of its history, has been primarily concerned with studying the origins and development of human knowledge and skill. The early philosopher–psychologists who posed many of the problems that still concern us tried to explain how certain kinds of knowledge were acquired in the course of development. Being philosophers more than psychologists, they did not trouble to examine human development, but rather preferred to assume that the newborn human infant knew certain things but not others, or perhaps knew nothing at all. They then tried to see if they could plausibly convert their invented infant into a human adult like themselves. With little constraint on speculation, it is no wonder that theories about the nature of the human infant abounded and gave rise to fierce controversy that was quite innocent of any empirical constraint. The main controversy was between the *nativists* and the *empiricists*. Nativists argued that human knowledge and human skill were built into the structure of the organism. Knowledge could be compared to the arrangement of our ribs—it was something we had because we were human beings rather than fish. Skill could be compared to breathing—it was something that happened inevitably, given the structure of human brains and bodies. Empiricists, by contrast, argued that human knowledge developed selectively as a result of specific encounters with certain types of environmental events. Human skills developed as behaviors were modified through successes or failures in coping with problems posed by the environment. These two theories of development, which could hardly have been more different, had very different social philosophies associated with them. Nativists tended to be pessimistic as far as the perfectibility of man was concerned. The unskilled and ignorant were held to be so, simply because they were born unskilled and ignorant. Their lack of competence was held to be a characteristic comparable to eye color or skin color. Competence or incompetence was something peculiar to a person's native endowment and quite beyond the reach of any human intervention. Empiricists, to the contrary, would say that the unskilled and ignorant were unskilled and ignorant because their environments had denied them the opportunity to develop skills and knowledge; if environments were sufficiently modified, ignorance would disappear and the whole community could share a general high level of competence. To this day these social philosophies heat the emotions to the extent that rational discussion becomes a near impossibility.

The philosopher–psychologists who began the debate on the origins of human knowledge did not do experiments, partly because they thought experiments were unnecessary. Even after psychology had become an experimental science, the study of development still remained nonexperimental for many years; this was particularly true of the study of development in infancy. Furthermore, most early techniques of psychological investigation depended heavily on verbal instructions and verbal reports from subjects. It is only in the last twenty years or so that the techniques necessary for studying nonverbal humans—infants—have been brought to a level where we can begin to ask and answer questions bequeathed to us three centuries ago.

In the meantime the debate has not stood still. There has been a recent series of attempts to argue from indirect evidence that human knowledge and human skill are inherited and that environmental intervention can hardly change the developmental process at all. For example, there has been a somewhat acrimonious debate about IQ scores. IQ tests are made up of items such as those shown in Figure 1.1. It has been proposed that scores on such tests are primarily determined by inherited factors. The evidence in favor of this view is derived from statistical manipulations of the IQ scores of individuals who are more or less closely related. The details of these procedures are given in numerous readily available sources and need not be discussed here. The point to emphasize is that, on the basis of IQ test scores taken from adults and older children, it is argued that the IQ differences shown among individuals are entirely a function of inherited structural differences and have nothing to do with life histories. This hypothesis about development claims that different experiences make no difference in IQ scores. This hypothesis, however, cannot be tested without actually studying the course of development. Since relevant experiments have simply not been done, arguments over the hypothesis are premature at this point. The nativist hypothesis cannot be accepted or rejected with the information presently available.

A second line of research, which is of a much higher caliber, has also been cited to give some indirect support to the nativist hypothesis. The recent explosion of knowledge in genetics has shown how information that is coded in molecular structures within the fertilized egg controls the sequence of chemical events that will result in the development of a complete, complexly differentiated organism. Development under genetic control is now understood as a physical process controlled at the molecular level. According to this line of thinking, development is a complex *physicochemical process,* requiring no reference to any concepts more abstract than those of physics and chemistry.

As long as geneticists stuck to simple physical structures, there was little in their work to disturb psychologists, most of whom have always felt that theories of knowledge, skill, and intelligence were safely beyond the compass of physics and chemistry. The growth and success of genetic studies on mental retardation, however, have shown that this is not necessarily the case. There have been many attempts to help mentally retarded children by giving them special training and special help and experiences; many environmental modifications based on diverse psychological theories have been tried in an attempt to solve the problem of mental retardation. However, the most suc-

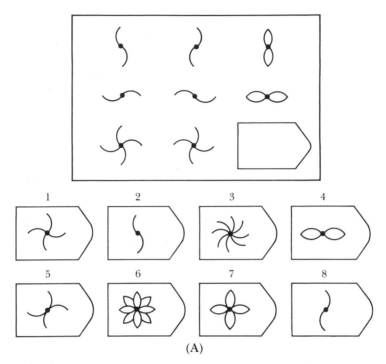

(A)

FIGURE 1.1   Sample IQ items. (A) Raven's progressive
matrices: The subject must choose the missing part from the
eight given alternatives. (From The Raven Progressive Matrices,
1958, Set E. Reprinted by permission of the Executors of the late
Dr. J. C. Raven.) (B) Seguin Form Board: This is a performance
test in which the subject must replace the pieces in the correct
holes as quickly as possible. (C) Stanford–Binet Intelligence
Scale: The items shown are included in the 9-year-old test items.
(Reproduced by permission of the publishers, Houghton Mifflin
Company.)

cessful modification yet discovered did not stem from psychology but
rather from a discovery in biochemical genetics. This discovery concerned a type of mental retardation known as phenylketonuria or
PKU. Persons afflicted with PKU, one of the most severe forms of
mental retardation, used to become imbeciles, unable to care for themselves. Special training did nothing for PKU afflictions. It was then
discovered that persons with PKU lack the enzyme that converts phenylalanine, a protein, to tyrosine, a slightly different kind of protein.
In the absence of the required enzyme, phenylalanine is converted to
phenylpyruvic acid; the buildup of phenylpyruvic acid is associated
with the occurrence of mental deficiency. If a child who lacks the

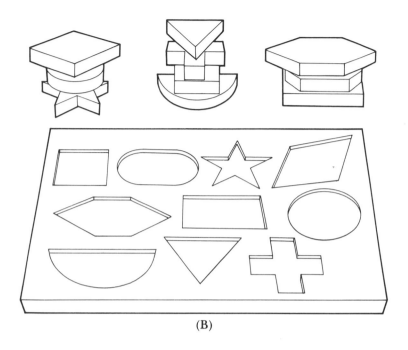

(B)

(a) Bill Jones' feet are so big that he has to pull his trousers on over his head.

(b) In an old graveyard in Spain, they have found a small skull which is believed to have been that of Christopher Columbus when he was about ten years old.

(C)

proper enzyme is given a diet low in protein and therefore low in phenylalanine, there is no buildup of phenylpyruvic acid. As a consequence, there is no mental deficiency, and the child's development is approximately normal. This minor biochemical modification produces significant benefits that no environmental modification had ever been able to produce.

Some environmentalists may be tempted to argue that such a modification is indeed an environmental modification. This is true if *environment* is used in a broad sense, but to psychologists *environment* means the psychological environment, the world as experience, a world of successes, failures, attempts to comprehend, emotional changes, and the like; in the traditional arguments between nativists and empiricists, *environment* has not meant the physicochemical environment. To pretend otherwise is simply dishonest.

The empiricist position has had to suffer other embarrassments. Perhaps the major obstacle to any development of the empiricist theory was the inability of developmental psychologists to demonstrate that human infants could learn at all. It is central to empiricism as a general philosophy that development be accomplished by learning, as a result of the organism's successes and/or failures in coping with its environment. It seemed a direct contradiction to empiricism that infants should develop manifestly while showing no change in behavior that could be related to the success or failure of the behavior. Learning—the adjustment of behavior in accord with its success or failure—seemed to be beyond the capacities of infants in their first year; infants nonetheless develop an enormous amount during the course of their first year. The apparent fact of development with no possibility of learning directly contradicted the empiricist point of view that development can only be generated by learning. That fact of course is a fact no longer: it has been demonstrated that infants on the first day of life can learn. Indeed, it has been claimed that humans can learn better in infancy than at any later age (Lipsitt, 1969). This advance, however, has not been accomplished without some cost to the general empiricist point of view. Learning in infants now appears to be a much more complex process than ever seemed likely before.

Psychologists use very simple paradigms to study learning. In the standard paradigm, the experimenter establishes a contingency between one of the behaviors of the organism and some event in the world around it. In the most famous of all learning situations, the organism, a pigeon, pecks on a key. As a result of circuitry built in by the experimenter, food is presented for a short time after the pecking behavior occurs. Pecking is called the *conditioned response* or *CR*. The food is referred to as the *reinforcement*. If the organism learns in this situation, the rate of occurrence of the CR increases.

There are various possible ways of presenting reinforcement. If reinforcement is presented every time the CR occurs, we have a *continuous reinforcement* or *CRF schedule*. We might also have a schedule in which every *n*th response, say the fifth or tenth, is reinforced; this is referred to as a *fixed ratio* or *FR schedule*. Analogous to the FR schedule is the *fixed interval* or *FI schedule,* in which reinforcement is made available only at fixed time intervals, say every 30 seconds.

Responses made during the fixed interval produce no reinforcement. There are also *variable ratio* or *VR schedules,* in which the number of responses required to elicit reinforcement varies from reinforcement to reinforcement. In addition, there is the *variable interval* or *VI schedule,* in which the interval during which reinforcement is not available varies from reinforcement to reinforcement. These schedules have different effects on the rate of occurrence of a CR. The measure taken with all of these schedules is a *rate measure.* If the rate of occurrence of a CR is higher when the CR–reinforcement contingency is operating than when it is not operating, then we have evidence that the animal has detected the contingency and learned that its response produces the reinforcement. Our evidence of learning thus depends on performance of the CR, which obviously depends on the animal being motivated. If an animal is not hungry, we would not expect it to perform for a food reinforcement. In animal learning experiments, it is usual to ensure performance by starving the animal to 80 percent of its normal body weight prior to the experiment. Any such manipulation is obviously out of the question in the case of human infants. A few studies have used food reward supplementary to normal diet as a reinforcement with infants. However, a more standard practice has been to use exciting visual events to motivate performance.

The effectiveness of reinforcement is obviously critical in experiments like these. If the reinforcement is not effective in motivating infants, there is no possibility of demonstrating that they can learn. Accordingly, experimenters vied with one another to devise exciting visual events, human jack-in-the-boxes, Times Square light displays, and other complex events that were presented as reinforcements; in most cases, however, these efforts were to little avail. Even CRF, the simplest of all schedules, produced learning in only a few cases in a few laboratories. Analysis of these successful cases does not indicate any obvious common factor in the reinforcements used. Experiments using a single flashing light were as successful as experiments using a human jack-in-the-box or something equally complex. However, a closer analysis of the successful experiments does show a common factor. The more successful experiments either did not use CRF at all or quickly shifted from CRF to a more complex schedule, regardless of whether the infants had learned during the CRF phase. This is puzzling since it seems to imply that the schedule rather than the reinforcement is the motivating factor. The nature of the reinforcement was seemingly unimportant, whereas the nature of the schedule was important. What is it about a schedule of reinforcement that can be more motivating than a reinforcement itself? The answer seems to be that the schedule can pose problems to the infant and that problem solving is the true motivation for human infants in a learning situation. Problem solving seems a most unlikely form of motivation to attribute to infants; however, there are a number of experiments that make this conclusion inescapable.

Consider an infant in the situation described by Papousek (1969). The infant can turn on a light by moving its head to the left. Most infants of 2 to 3 months will succeed in turning on the light several times within a quite short time. Their rate of leftward head turning will then drop back to a level that is insufficient to serve as a criterion of learning. The rate will not pick up again so long as the left-turn/light-on contingency is operative. Suppose the experimenter changes the contingency to right-turn/light-on. Sooner or later the infant will make a left turn, and the light will not go on. We then see a burst of leftward head turns, followed by detection of the right-turn/light-on contingency, as shown by a brief, high rate of right head turns, which will then subside. This second rate will also stay low if the contingency is unchanged.

If the contingency is changed again to a left turn followed by right turn to switch the light on, the rate of right turning will increase after the first trial on which the light does not go on; the rate of left turning will also increase, and finally the infant will produce a left turn followed by a right turn and switch the light on. After a brief burst of left–rights, the rate will subside, until the contingency is changed. The change produces a burst of activity, ending when the correct combination of movements is discovered. In such procedures, infants have been brought to master quite complex series of movements, such as right–right–left–left. Every time the contingency is changed, the activity rate of the infant goes up. Examination of the behavior shows that the activity is not random. The infant seems to be testing hypotheses and trying out sequences of movement in order to discover which one operates at the moment. When the correct sequence is discovered, it is tested a few times and then dropped. Behavior, or hypothesis testing, only picks up again when the previous sequence is shown to be inadequate.

It is quite obvious from the behavior of the infants that the light source is not the motivating factor. While hypothesis testing is going on, even after the first success, the infant barely looks at the light. A scant glance is made to check whether the light is on or not. After the confirmatory glance, the infant may manifest behavioral signs of plea-sure and joy, but these signs are displayed with no attention to the light, which is obviously not the cause. It thus seems that the pleasures of problem solving are sufficient to motivate behavioral and mental activity in young infants. If a learning situation is interactive, the infant will demonstrate that it can learn; if the infant's only motive is the prospect of reward, then it will not demonstrate that it can learn. Many of the original experimental failures must thus have resulted because of failures to engage the motivational system of the infant adequately. The parameters of this motivational system have not been fully explained. We do not know, for example, whether the infant will continue to work at an insoluble problem or how successes in problem solving affect motivation in solving other problems. These questions are still to be answered.

This solution to the problem of learning in infants does nothing to bridge the gap between nativists and empiricists. If anything, the gap is sharpened. One can see the possibility of some relations between hunger and biochemical processes in the brain. Problem solving is something else, however, with no conceivable molecular equivalents at this point in intellectual history. At this time, problem solving is a factor in a psychological environment that cannot be reduced to a physicochemical environment. At the same time, demonstrations of learning in infants as complex as those recently carried out should not bring pure joy to the heart of a dedicated empiricist. Learning at this level requires a great deal of information that must be built into the structure of the organism as surely as is the structure of its hands. Consider the experiment of Siqueland and Lipsitt (1966), which was carried out with infants in their first day after birth. The researchers were able to establish a head-turning response to one side when a bell was sounded but not when a buzzer was presented. Thus, as bell and buzzer alternated, the infants came to make a head turn in the appropriate condition only. After that discrimination was made, the experimenters reversed the contingencies; if an infant had learned bell–right head turn/buzzer–no head turn, they were now required to forget that and learn bell–no head turn/buzzer–right head turn. All of the infants were able to make this discrimination reversal in very short order. Indeed, they did it with a facility unsurpassed by any nonhuman primate. Consider, then, what this implies in terms of information that the infant must bring to the learning situation. First of all, the infant must be able to discriminate between bell and buzzer.

TABLE 1.1   Contingencies in the Siqueland and Lipsitt (1966) experiment

Stimulus	Response	Condition
Bell	Left head turn	Not reinforced
Bell	Right head turn	Reinforced
Buzzer	Left head turn	Not reinforced
Buzzer	Right head turn	Not reinforced

The infant must be able to identify a bell and identify a buzzer so as to know which is being presented on any trial so that it can perform the appropriate response. The infant must likewise be able to discriminate and identify head turns to the right and head turns to the left. Further, it must be able to detect the relationship among stimulus (bell or buzzer), response (turn to right or left), and reinforcement. This is complicated enough, as Table 1.1 shows, but these experimentally induced complications are not the only complications in the situation. Suppose an infant is in a bell–head turn/buzzer–no head turn situation. Suppose that after the bell sounds, the infant turns its head to the right and is then reinforced. At the moment the bell sounds, it is highly likely that the infant is aware of other stimuli, such as the room lighting, the texture of his diapers, outside noises, the clicking of equipment, and various other stimuli that must be present. When the infant turns its head to the right, it probably also turns its eyes left; also there are probably foot and hand movements going on before, after, or simultaneously with the head movement. One might ask why the bell and the head turn should be linked with the reinforcement event, rather than with any of the other stimuli or responses occurring prior to the reinforcement? The infant must have extremely precise selection mechanisms to allow this detection to occur as rapidly as it does. The parameters of the selection mechanisms, however, are relatively unexplored in infants. It seems likely that the major constraint is temporal; only those stimuli and responses that occur within a short interval before the reinforcement enter into the selection process. Beyond that limit, the infant must use analysis over time. Thus, if an infant has the set of events shown in Table 1.1 entered for selection, it could find out which one produced reinforcement simply

Head
Left   0°
Right

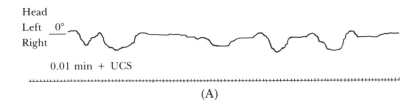

0.01 min + UCS

(A)

Head

Left
       0°
Right

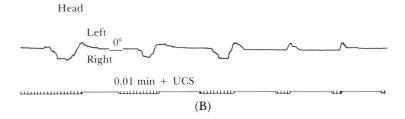

0.01 min + UCS

(B)

Head
Left   0°
Right

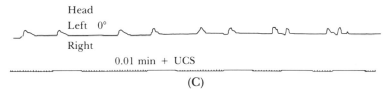

0.01 min + UCS

(C)

FIGURE 1.2   (A) The rate of activity at the beginning of a conditioning session. (B, C) As the session progresses, activity becomes increasingly differentiated; the gross movements of the early stages drop out and are replaced by very precise movements. (After "Individual Variability in Learned Reponses in Human Infants" by H. Papousek. In R. J. Robinson, Ed., *Brain and Early Behavior.* New York: Academic Press, 1969. Courtesy of Developmental Science Trust.)

by testing each combination in the list. The fact that something like this does go on is attested by the high rate of activity customary at the beginning of conditioning sessions (see Figure 1.2). It is as if the infant tests out all possible responses for their potential efficiency. All of these capacities—stimulus identification, response identification, stimulus–response selection—must be built in before learning takes place. These capacities must have developed, without benefit of learning, in the intrauterine environment before the infant's actions had any consequences.

Since learning depends on such a complex of innate capacities and since as we have seen it is reversible and apparently does not lead to any permanent changes, there is a tendency to see learning as a consequence of development rather than as a causal factor in development. Processes of development produce the possibility of learning, but learning itself does not produce development; the effectiveness of the organism in a learning situation is seen as depending on innate mechanisms that cannot be modified by events in a psychological environment. On the surface, there is some measure of support for this since learning ability seemingly declines with age. Apparently, it becomes progressively more difficult to demonstrate learning in infants as they grow older. If the infant becomes less able to learn during the process of development, it seems unlikely that learning can be the causal mechanism in development. In opposition to this view, Watson has argued that the observed decline in learning ability is a function of prior learning experiences.

> Imagine a living thing whose behavioral repertoire is such that it provides no possibility of eliciting rewards from the external world. Rewarding stimulus events could be experienced but could not be produced. With the provision of a benevolent environment, the organism would survive but not learn in the sense of acquiring behavioral adaptations which produce rewards. I propose that in certain ways this situation is descriptive of the human infant's first three months of life. Furthermore, these first few months might well be termed a period of "natural deprivation" of learning experiences, the elimination of which may have desirable long-term intellective consequences. [Watson, 1966a]

Watson argues here that the observed decline in learning ability results from lack of opportunity to learn. In pursuit of this hypothesis, Watson has carried out experiments where infants were given early learning opportunities in hopes that their later learning would be greatly facilitated. Papousek (1967) has conducted similar experiments that support the hypothesis that early learning opportunities affect later learning (see Table 1.2). Such studies suggest that learning ability, initially shaped via innate mechanisms, can decline if it is not exercised. The development of learning ability thus seems to depend on an interaction between an innately generated set of mechanisms and the opportunity to use these mechanisms in a psychological environment—an environmental effect that is not learning in the strict sense. We shall see this pattern repeated again and again in development.

However, there are other changes in infant learning patterns that

TABLE 1.2   Comparison of the conditionability of two groups of infants at approximately the same age. (Group A = infants subjected to condition-ing procedures from birth; Group B = infants subjected to conditioning procedures from the age of 3 months. Comparison shows that early learn-ing opportunities greatly facilitate later learning.)

Group	Mean Age (Days) at Beginning of Test	Mean Trials to Criterion
A	107.54	94.63
B	105.92	176.23

Source: Papousek, 1967.

do not fit with such an analysis. Young infants seem able to detect and utilize a contingency between any response and any reinforcement event. This is not true of older infants. Thus, it has been demonstrated that young infants will suck a pacifier or turn their heads to switch on a display light; 9-month-old infants are very reluctant to do this, but they will push the display with their hands. This seems to indicate a change in the parameters of the response–reinforcement selection mechanism; there is the addition of a spatial constraint so that re-sponse and reinforcement must be spatially as well as temporally con-tiguous. Similar changes seem to occur in the stimulus–reinforcement selection mechanism: infants begin to ignore stimuli that are spatially unconnected with the reinforcement. These changes go on through-out the first year or longer and change the possibilities of learning. Whether these new constraints are endogenously generated like those operative immediately after birth, or whether their acquisition is de-pendent on interaction with the psychological environment, is some-thing we cannot decide at the moment. It is hoped that this book will elucidate the nature of the built-in constraints, their relation to learn-ing, and the relation between learning and development.

In the following chapters we shall look at the development of some of the precursors of learning; we shall begin with the mechanisms of stimulus detection, localization, and identification. The central theme to which we shall constantly return is the role of experience in de-velopment. The two generalized hypotheses, nativism and empiricism, have already been introduced. We have already looked at learning as a prototypal mechanism for the empiricist and found this approach wanting. Learning seems to depend on very elaborate mechanisms that are not themselves the result of learning; further, learning is itself subject to environmental modification by way of some process other than learning. These observations are reason enough to call into question any extreme nativist position, just as the unlearned constraints on learning must restrict any extreme empiricist position.

2
Space Perception

Perception of radial direction by the nose
The role of time differences in olfactory localization
The developmental problems associated with localization
Proximal and distal stimuli • Auditory localization
Proximal stimuli involved • The problem of growth
Possible patterns of development of auditory localization
Methodological problems in testing
Results of experiments

Few topics in the history of experimental psychology have excited as much interest and controversy as has the origin of space perception. For a long while, the topic of space perception was the battlefield where the empiricists and nativists confronted one another with their respective theories. The battle was fought at a very general level; data on human adults was set against data from newly hatched chicks. It is no wonder that Boring (1942) dismissed the controversy as sterile; it produced nothing— not even, as we shall see, a clarification of the developmental problem of space perception.

Human adults live and move in an organized world of three dimensions. We can locate the distance of objects, detect their radial direction or position to our right or left, and determine their height relative to our own. We do this primarily with our sense of sight, which can register all of these variables. Radial direction, however, can also be picked up by the ear and even by the nose, though crudely.*

The perception of radial direction by the nose exemplifies the problems of space perception. If we take a blindfolded observer and place an odoriferous source object in front of him, he can tell us whether the object is straight ahead, to his right, or to his left, and can indicate its precise position with an accuracy of 3.5°. This seems commonplace enough until one inquires into the processes involved in making the judgment. The molecules that produce the sensation of smell diffuse in all directions from the odoriferous source. They impinge on the sense receptors inside the nostrils whenever air is drawn through the nostrils (see Figure 2.1). The nose is well supplied with odor receptors, distributed fairly evenly over its internal surface. The process thus far seems simple enough, but the problem begins when we ask: Where is the right–left–straight-ahead dimension in the nose? What is the structure that registers the rightward or leftward position of the stimulus source? Indeed, there is none. All of the receptors in each nostril are stimulated equally when air is drawn over them; the position of the source of stimulation makes no difference to the process of stimulation within each nostril. The nose therefore has no right and left of its own. How then do we register right–left position with our noses?

The crucial clue, suggested by Mach (1885) nearly 100 years ago is that, although we have but one nose, we have two nostrils, side by side in the radial plane. This anatomical fact has some interesting consequences for the process of odor localization. Consider the situation shown in Figure 2.2A. A subject is facing an odor source that is straight ahead of him. The molecules producing the sensation of odor are diffusing from the odor source. When the subject breathes in, a large number of molecules is simultaneously displaced, with an increasing concentration passing through each nostril over time. At each point in time the concentration in each nostril is the same. Contrast this situation with that in Figure 2.2B, where the stimulus source is on the right. The right nostril is nearer the stimulus source than

---

*Both of these senses can also be used for distance perception. The abilities involved have been studied very little in adults and not at all in infants; they will therefore not be discussed here.

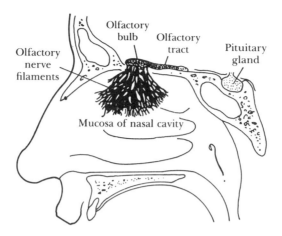

FIGURE 2.1 Drawing of the nasal cavity and olfactory structures. The nose is to the left, and the back of the mouth is to the right. The diagram exposes the interior of the nasal cavities and shows roughly how the olfactory membrane is spread out in the mucosa of the cavity. (After *Fundamentals of Neurology* by E. Gardner. Philadelphia: W. B. Saunders Co., 1947.)

is the left nostril. When inhalation begins, an increasingly intense concentration of molecules again passes through each nostril; but in this case a given intensity of concentration is reached in the right nostril before it is reached in the left nostril. Since there is a threshold below which no odor is sensed, this means that the right nostril is effectively stimulated before the left nostril. In the reverse case, where the stimulus source is placed on the left, the left nostril would be stimulated before the right nostril. Unless the source object is straight ahead, one nostril will be stimulated before the other. The order in which stimulation occurs (right before left or left before right) corresponds, of course, to the position of the source object (to the right or to the left). The amount of the difference between stimulation specifies the separation of the object from the straight-ahead position; the greater the separation, the longer the time lag between stimulation of each nostril. The time of onset of stimulation in each nostril can thus specify the position of the object.

The question arises as to whether this stimulus specification is used by subjects. An ingenious experiment by Békésy (1969) shows that it

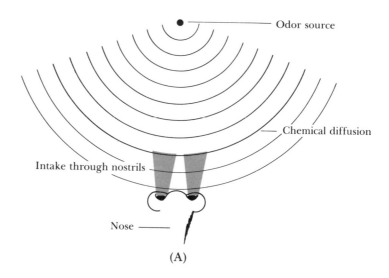

(A)

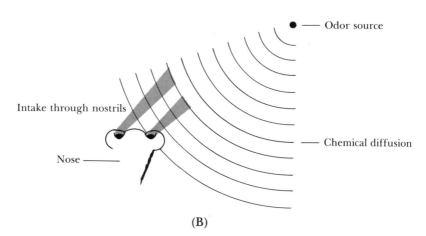

(B)

FIGURE 2.2   (A) Odor source straight ahead. At any one time, the concentration of molecules passing through each nostril is the same since both nostrils are equidistant from the odor source. (B) Odor source on the right. Because the right nostril is nearer to the odor source than is the left nostril, the concentration in the right nostril at any one time is greater than the concentration in the left nostril.

is. Békésy used tubes to deliver odors to each nostril separately. The arrival time at each nostril could be varied. When the odors arrived simultaneously, subjects indicated that the perceived position of the odor source was straight ahead. When the right nostril was stimulated first, the subjects localized the odor source on the right; the greater the lead of right over left, the further the odor seemed to be from a straight-ahead position. When the left nostril was stimulated first, the odor source seemed to be on the left. Békésy thus demonstrated that differences in the time of stimulation of each nostril is the stimulus dimension that specifies for adult subjects the position of an olfactory source.

The student of development will perceive the problems that are associated with this demonstration. Does the time-difference dimension specify position of an olfactory source to the infant? Or does the infant, stimulated in the right nostril and then the left, simply perceive a double odor source with no particular spatial position attached? This is a specific question, but it is representative of the general question of whether infants perceive the world in distal terms or whether they perceive the proximal processes (the processes at the sense organ) that mediate the distal perception in adults.

Olfactory localization in infants has attracted relatively little attention from investigators, but some relevant data have been gathered in the course of studies of olfactory preference. Young infants can apparently turn away from unpleasant odors, smoothly and efficiently. They do not go left when the stimulus is on the left or right when it is on the right. Such observations have been made on infants in the first day of life—indeed in the first hours of life—and it would seem that the capacity to locate position on the basis of olfactory time differences is probably built into the structure of the organism (Engen et al., 1963). The *proximal/distal transduction rule* would seem to be incorporated at an age at which learning could hardly have affected the requisite structural modifications. We are therefore justified in concluding that the capacity to localize the positions of olfactory sources is innate (see also Yonas and Pick, 1975).

Our auditory system, from the point of view of space perception, is similar to our olfactory system. We can locate the radial direction, the position to the right or the left, of a sound source. We do this despite the fact that there is no right and left within the ear (see Figure 2.3). The solution to the problem, as we might expect, lies in the fact that we have two ears. Sound is carried from a source by waves of pressure change. Consider what occurs when one sound source is

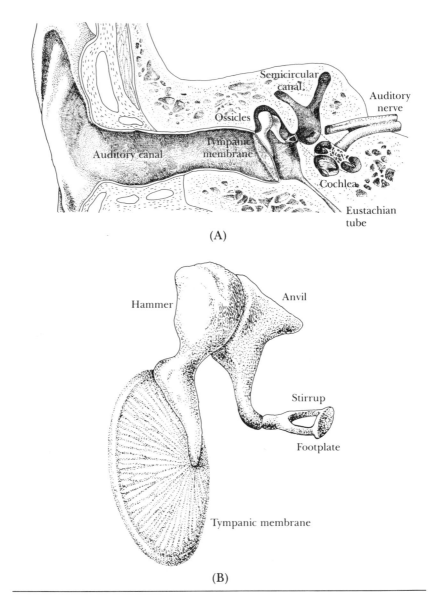

(A)

(B)

placed straight ahead and one is placed to the right (see Figures 2.4A and 2.4B). Sound waves from the straight-ahead source will reach both ears simultaneously; the waves from the source on the right will reach the right ear slightly before they reach the left ear. There is thus a *time difference* in the onset of stimulation at the two ears. The more a sound source deviates from the straight-ahead position, the more one ear will lead over the other, thereby relaying precise infor-

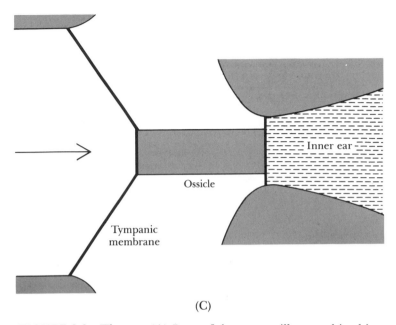

(C)

FIGURE 2.3   The ear. (A) Parts of the ear are illustrated in this somewhat simplified cross section. Between the eardrum (tympanic membrane) and the fluid-filled inner ear are the three small bones (ossicles) of the middle ear. The auditory nerve endings are in an organ (not shown) between the plate of bone that spirals up the cochlea and the outer wall of the cochlea. (B) Three ossicles transmit the vibrations of the tympanic membrane to the inner ear. The footplate of the stirrup, surrounded by a narrow membrane, presses against inner-ear fluid. (C) How the ossicles act as a piston pressing against the fluid of the inner ear is indicated by this drawing. Pressure of the vibrations of tympanic membrane are amplified 22 times. (After "The Ear" by G. von Békésy. Copyright © 1957 by Scientific American, Inc. All rights reserved.)

mation about the location of a sound source (see Figure 2.5). This information is supplemented by two other dimensions of stimulation—*phase differences* and *intensity differences*. Phase differences are a special kind of time difference; sound is propagated as a series of pressure changes, which have a characteristic variation in intensity over time as they pass a fixed station point. Simple sounds have a characteristic wave shape (see Figure 2.6).

A sound source that is straight ahead is equidistant from the two ears. This means that the momentary pressure change at any one point in time will be the same at the two ears. This is not so if the

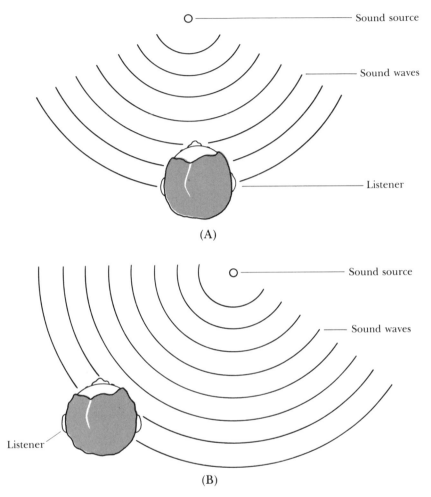

FIGURE 2.4 (A) Sound source straight ahead. The sound reaches both ears simultaneously. (B) Sound source on the right. The sound reaches the right ear first.

sound source is on the right or left. If the source is on the right, for example, the left ear will be receiving the input that the right ear received fractions of a second earlier. This phase difference between the two ears is precisely correlated with the amount of deviation from the straight-ahead position.

There are limitations on the utility of phase differences. Sounds differ in frequency. This means that the rate at which the pattern of pressure changes repeats itself varies from sound to sound. High-pitched sounds repeat their characteristic wave with a high frequency;

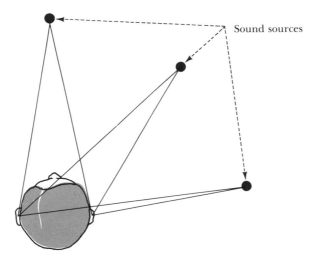

FIGURE 2.5 The more a sound source deviates from the straight-ahead position, the greater is the time difference in onset of stimulation at the two ears.

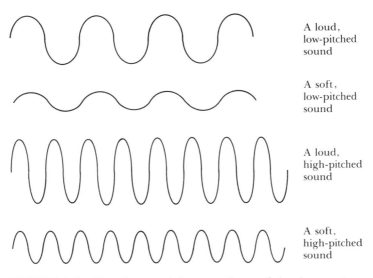

FIGURE 2.6 The characteristic wave shape of simple sounds.

low-pitched sounds repeat with a low frequency. The consequences of this phenomenon for the detection of phase difference at two fixed points (our two ears) are shown in Figure 2.7. Some high-frequency waves will be in the same phase at the two ears when the source is far from straight ahead. In adults it has been found that phase differences are only reliable up to 600 hertz, a range that corresponds quite well to the distance between an adult's ears (Stevens and Newman, 1936).

Intensity differences are produced whenever a sound source is located to the right or left. There are two causes for the intensity difference. The first is simply that intensity decreases with distance. The intensity at the ear farther from the sound source will of course be weaker than the intensity at the nearer ear. The second cause of intensity difference is the presence of the head, which blocks off some of the sound that would reach the farther ear, thereby enhancing the intensity difference. Intensity differences increase with deviation from the straight-ahead position and reach a maximum when the sound source lies on an imaginary line drawn through the two ears. Physiologically speaking, intensity differences are equivalent to time difference, since a lower intensity produces a slower traveling neural signal than does a higher intensity.

In summary, then, there are three dimensions of stimulation at the ears—time differences, phase differences, and intensity differences. These vary with the position of a sound source and thus specify the position of the source to a perceiving organism. There is ample evidence that adult humans can and do use all of these variables to locate sound sources (Stevens and Newman, 1936) We can now ask whether the same is true of infants.

Before looking at the experimental data, such as they are, we must consider the additional problem of growth. As mentioned, the distance between the ears is critically important in determining the amount of the time, phase, and intensity differences produced by sound sources in various locations. The distance between an infant's ears is not the same as the distance between an adult's ears. Interear distance approximately doubles between birth and adulthood, which has some considerable consequences for auditory localization. Location of a sound at the straight-ahead position—specified by zero time difference, zero phase difference and zero intensity difference—is of course unaffected.

Direction of differences specifying position to one side or another is likewise unaffected. A sound on the right will stimulate the right ear first and will be louder at the right ear, regardless of interear

A (Rising phase)

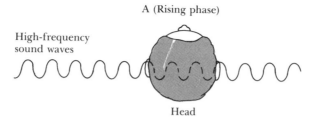

High-frequency
sound waves

Head

B (Falling phase)

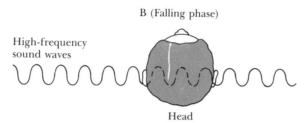

High-frequency
sound waves

Head

FIGURE 2.7 High-frequency waves may be in the same phase on reaching both ears even though they originated from a point well off the straight-ahead position. (A) The sound wave is in the rising phase on arrival at both ears. (B) The sound wave is in the falling phase at both ears.

separation. A sound on the left, likewise, will stimulate the left ear first and will be louder at the left ear, regardless of interear separation. However, the size of the differences specifying precise position off the straight-ahead position is very much affected by the interear separation. The time difference produced at the infant's ears by a sound in any given location will be less than that produced at the adult's ears by a sound in the same location (see Figure 2.8).

What does this imply about the development of auditory localization? The first implication is that the newborn infant probably cannot localize a sound source in any and every position. To do so, the infant would have to be equipped with structures to translate the time differences produced by its head size into distal locations. These structures would, howver, become useless as the infant's head grew and would have to be continuously recalibrated during growth. It would seem uneconomic to build in structures of such limited utility. It is not impossible that such structures and such a pattern of development could have evolved, but it seems rather unlikely. On the other hand,

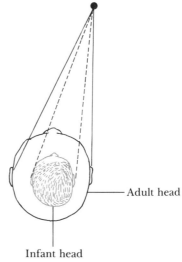

FIGURE 2.8 Because of the difference in head size, the time difference in arrival of a sound at the two ears is less for an infant than for an adult.

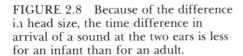

Adult head

Infant head

it would seem quite likely that the newborn is equipped with sufficient structure to tell it when a sound is straight ahead. Such a structure could remain *invariant* during growth since the proximal information specifying straight ahead is not affected by growth. The same structure could serve at any age, since the information it would have to pick up (zero difference between the input at the two ears) would not change during growth. For the same reasons, it seems quite likely that the infant knows when a sound source is on the right or left. The qualitative information specifying sound on the right or sound on the left remains invariant throughout growth. If the infant has these two capacities, then the missing quantitative information could be calibrated in quite easily. This process would require:

1. The ability to recognize when a sound is straight ahead—an ability that could be built in.

2. The ability to detect when a sound is on the right or left, which could also be built in.

3. The ability to turn the head so as to bring sound sources that are off to one side into the straight-ahead position.

4. Some source of metric information about the extent of head movements.

5. Sufficient learning ability to associate the stimulation received prior to head movement with the amount of head movement required to center the sound source.

This is a fairly formidable list of abilities. If all were present, the infant could learn to calibrate the position of sound sources by making the appropriate precalibrated head movements.

The two positions outlined so far have attributed to the infant some or a great deal of built-in structure. It is of course possible that the infant could be born with no built-in structure. In this case the newborn would presumably hear two identical sounds when presented with a straight-ahead sound source and two different sounds when presented with a sound source to the right or left. Before any other development could take place, the infant would have to discover that the two perceived sounds come from one source. How the infant would do this is by no means clear. After this discovery, learning mechanisms—possibly similar to those described above—could fill in the missing capacities.

How would one test these three hypotheses? Each hypothesis makes different predictions about the behavior one can expect from a newborn infant who is presented with sound sources in various locations. What would the last hypothesis (the extreme empiricist hypothesis) predict about the behavior of a newborn infant presented with a sound to its right? Should the infant turn toward the sound, look toward the sound, or make any other localizing responses? On the empiricist hypothesis, the infant might as well turn or look to the left as to the right, and it might well do neither. The empiricst hypothesis makes the same predictions exactly in the case of a sound presented on the left. Indeed, the predictions are the same for a sound presented in the midline. The empiricist hypothesis predicts that there should be no differences in behavior that are correlated with differences in the site of stimulation.

By contrast, the modified nativist position (the second hypothesis presented above) makes quite specific predictions about differential behavior correlated with differences in the location of a sound source. The modified nativistic hypothesis claims that the newborn knows when a sound source is straight ahead and when a sound source comes from the right or left; the infant does not know, however, how far to the right or left the source may be. When an infant is presented with a sound on the right, the modified nativistic hypothesis predicts that the infant should make its localizing responses to the right only. Localizing responses to the left should occur only for sounds on the left; sounds from the straight-ahead position should elicit localization responses to the straight-ahead position. According to this hypothesis, the localizing responses to any position except the straight-ahead position should be imprecise in the newborn and should gradually become more precise with experience. In contrast to this modified approach, the extreme nativist hypothesis (the first hypothesis we described) predicts that localizing movements should be precise from the outset.

Before reviewing the experimental data that are currently available, we must make two methodological points. The first concerns the conclusions we could draw from one possible outcome of the experiment outlined above. Suppose the distribution of localizing responses to varying sound sources were essentially a random one; in other words, responses to the right occurred just as frequently when the stimulus was on the left or straight ahead as when it was on the right. This outcome would be in accord with the predictions made by the extreme empiricist hypothesis. We must then ask whether such an outcome could be taken as proof of the empiricist hypothesis and as disproof of the two nativistic hypotheses. As stated, the answer must be no. If such an outcome were observed, nativists could still hold to their position by arguing that the observed response patterns resulted, not from any deficiencies in the auditory system, but from deficiencies in the response system. They could argue that the infant knows where a sound is but does not know how to get its head or eyes or hands to the sound. This is a plausible argument and certainly cannot be dismissed a priori. What experimental modification would allow one to dismiss it? If we could show that the motor system was precisely controllable, we would wipe out the objection. If it could be shown that localization of visible targets was precise, while localization of audible targets was not, one could not take refuge in arguing hypothetical looseness in the motor system, since such looseness would necessarily result in imprecise motor behavior in the visual situation. Thus, to validate the claim that auditory localization is imprecise, two *converging* experiments would be necessary.

The problem outlined above is one that will recur. Any experiment that relies on precise motor behavior to index perpetual function in infants runs into the problem that infant motor behavior is not precise. The motor system is subject to growth processes more than is any perceptual organ. It is a wonder (a wonder to which we will return) that the infant's motor responses are as accurate as they are. Why then do we do experiments that involve this fragile system? Why not make use of discrimination methods, as Munn (1965) has recommended? One could surely teach an infant to make a conditioned response to a sound source presented on its right; after the response was established, one could then introduce a nonreinforced sound source on the left. If both sound sources were presented successively in random order, with only responses to the sound on the right being reinforced, the infant could learn to respond only to the sound source on the right. We know that infants can form such conditioned discriminations. Surely this way of studying the perceptual capacity would be more satisfactory than relying on the necessarily unreliable motor localizing responses. One could even use an *habituation decrement experiment* (see Figure 2.9). One could present a repetitive sound source on the right, wait until the infant showed no more response to the sound, and then shift the sound to the left and see whether the habituation was reversed. We know that young infants show habituation to some stimuli and recovery from habituation when the stimuli are changed. If these effects could be demonstrated with change of position of a sound source, would this not indicate the capacity we want to study?

Unfortunately, the answer to both these questions must be no. Neither the conditioned discrimination nor the habituation decrement experiment can, by their very nature, tell us anything about auditory *localization*. Suppose an infant could form a conditioned discrimination between a sound on its right and a sound on its left. What would this tell us? It would tell us that the infant could differentiate between a sound on the left and a sound on the right, *on some basis;* it does not tell us *what the basis is.* The infant could differentiate on the basis of spatial position, which is what we are interested in, or it could differentiate equally well on the basis of the succession of sounds at its two ears, with no localization at all. Discrimination experiments cannot tell us the *basis* of a discrimination; they can only tell the fact of a discrimination. They do not tell us whether the discrimination is made on the basis of the distal stimulus differences (which is what we are interested in) or on the basis of the mediating proximal stimulus differences (see Figure 2.10). If we are interested in the distal perception, in this case the location of a sound source, we must use a distally oriented response—in this case a localizing response.

This is not to say that discrimination methods have no place in the investigation of localizing responses. Suppose we found by the use of localizing responses that infants could not localize sound sources. This could result from inability to pick up the proximal stimulus difference, as E. J. Gibson (1969) might argue, or from an inability to interpret or decode the perceived proximal stimulus differences. At this point a discrimination experiment would be appropriate and would decide between these two positions.

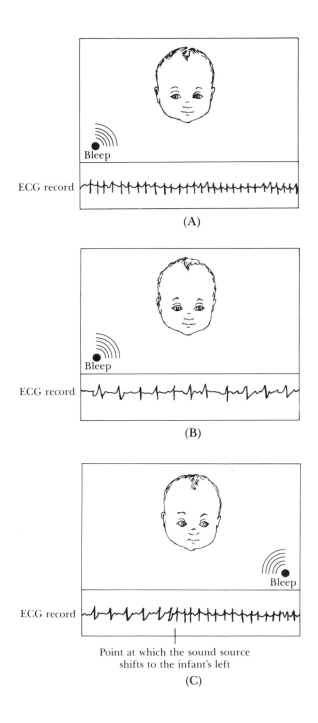

(A)

(B)

Point at which the sound source
shifts to the infant's left

(C)

FIGURE 2.9 *(facing page)* Habituation decrement experiment. (A) Introduction of a repetitive sound source on the infant's right causes it to look to the right. The infant's heart rate also increases. (B) After a time, the infant becomes *habituated* to the sound; the infant ceases to look in the direction of the sound and heart rate is normal. (C) If, however, the sound source is shifted to the left, the infant shows renewed interest and heart rate again increases. This recovery from habituation has been taken by some to be evidence of the ability to localize sound. This assumption is questioned in the text.

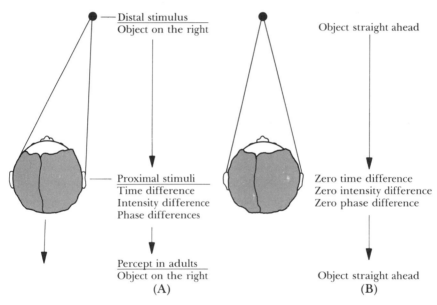

FIGURE 2.10   An infant could discriminate between these two distal presentations on the basis of the proximal stimuli (time difference, intensity difference, and/or phase difference) without being aware of the object being (A) to the right or (B) straight ahead. If all we have is a discriminatory response, there is no way we can determine whether it is made on the basis of perception of the distal or proximal stimulus differences.

The points covered in this lengthy digression from auditory localization are important and will recur. Let us see if they illuminate the existing data on auditory localization. The first experiment outlined above has actually been done; moreover, it was done with an infant subject who was less than 2 minutes old by the end of the experiment. Wertheimer (1961) was fortunate enough to obtain access to a delivery room to carry out his experiment. His subject was delivered without anesthesia (an important point), and the birth was free from trauma. Having thus obtained an optimal subject, Wertheimer presented a series of sounds, randomly to the right or left of the subject. Over the initial period, before boredom set in, the subject correctly looked in the direction of the sound source. Recall the predictions made by the various theories outlined above. The empiricist theory predicted random localizing attempts; this position is therefore refuted by these results. There can be no doubt that the initial localizing attempts of this infant, tested almost at the moment of birth, were nonrandom and were in fact accurate in direction. Were the responses accurate enough to decide between the extreme and the modified nativist positions? Wertheimer does not tell us how accurate the localization was.

This result has been replicated by a number of experimenters who have supplied us with more data on early auditory localization. It is now clear that, by a few days after birth, infants are capable of more than right–straight-ahead–left discrimination; degrees of rightness and leftness can be discriminated. The way in which this is manifested is quite fascinating and has considerable implication for research technique. Essentially, these results show that if a major effort is required to fixate a sound source—a head movement *and* an eye movement— then the more effort required, the less likely are infants to make an orienting response (Macfarlane, 1977). The technical implication of this is that studies of auditory localization should not use extreme stimulus positions if they wish to demonstrate localization. An experiment that used only extreme positions might conclude, erroneously, that newborns cannot localize sounds. An example of this kind of error is the study by McGurk et al. (1977), which used only stimuli 90° off the midline, a position minimally likely to elicit looking behavior. As a result, the researchers concluded, unjustifiably, that infants 2 to 8 days old cannot localize sounds.

Additional complications for research technique have also been introduced in studies that used the human voice as a stimulus. Quite soon after birth, bottle-fed infants will begin to turn their heads away from a voice source, while breast-fed infants continue to turn toward a sound source. These opposed behaviors are surely the result of the differential link between the voice source and food in the breast or bottle situation. The breast is always on the same side as the voice in breast feeding, while the bottle is normally in the opposite direction during bottle feeding. As soon as the infant learns this, use of a voice stimulus could indicate—or, rather, might be interpreted as indicating—that the infant's auditory localization is totally inaccurate, again a conclusion that would be quite unwarranted (Alegria and Noirot, 1978).

Lastly, Turkewitz et al. (1966) found that looking responses to sound sources, like looking responses to light sources, are a function of the intensity of the stimulus. If the stimulus is very intense, looking away is more likely than looking toward—a clearly adaptive response (see also Butterworth and Castillo, 1976).

As far as the decision between extreme and modified nativist theories is concerned, studies of older infants have indicated that the latter hypothesis is more likely to be correct. Thus, Bechtold and Salapatek (1976) found that eye movements of 2-month-olds to peripherally presented auditory targets are less precise than their movements to visually presented targets. Indeed, Gesell et al. (1934) claim that visual orientation to an off-center sound source is not perfectly accurate until the age of 5 months, a result that would seem to support the modified nativist hypothesis. However, the qualifications on any result indicating inability must be borne in mind. Gesell did not show that the lack of accuracy prior to 5 months is due to lack of accuracy within the auditory system; the inability could just as well have resulted from deficiencies in the visual–motor orienting system, particularly since the auditory target in Gesell's experiment was visible.

These objections do not apply to a more recent experiment demonstrating essentially the same developmental effects. In this experiment the same infants were run in two conditions (Bower and Wishart, 1973; Wishart et al., 1978). In one condition the infants, in full illumination, were presented with an object either straight ahead or 30° to the left or right. The infants were allowed to reach for this visible target. Their hit rate in each position gave a measure of the accuracy of visual–motor coordination. In the other condition the infants were run in complete darkness. An object was presented in the same three positions; this time it was a noise-making object. Hit rate here gave a measure of accuracy of auditory–motor coordination. The motor coordination required in both cases was the same. If the auditory system is less precise than the visual system in registering the

TABLE 2.1   A comparison of auditory–motor localization and visual–motor localization in infants under 6 months of age

Object Position	Success Rate (Percent)	
	Auditory–Motor	Visual–Motor
30 ° Left	48	100
Middle	92	96
30 ° Right	33.5	100

position of objects, auditory–motor behavior should have produced a lower hit rate than did visual–motor behavior. Since the same motor behavior is required in both conditions, lesser auditory–motor accuracy could not be explained away by postulating sloppiness in the motor system. The results showed that, at positions off the midline, auditory–motor accuracy was less than visual–motor accuracy below the age of 6 months (see Table 2.1).

What data there are on auditory localization would thus seem to support the hypothesis that detection of a straight-ahead sound source (specified by stimulation that is invariant during growth) is an unlearned ability of the human infant. Detection of positions to the right or left (also specified by stimulation that is invariant during growth) similarly seems to be present before any learning could have occurred. Precise localization to the right or left (which can only be specified by variables whose precise "meaning" is changed during growth) is not present at birth and seems to develop during infancy. We cannot say at the moment whether it is calibrated in the way outlined above. Despite its easy accessibility and despite the classic nature of the problems posed by auditory localization, there are still not enough data available to allow us to describe the development precisely.

3

Radial Localization by Eye

The complexities of localization by ear and nose fade into insignificance when compared with the complex localizing capacities of the eye. The human eye can pick up location in three dimensions, with a precision beyond that of the other senses and with a set of structural peculiarities that would seem to contradict any precision in localization.

At first sight, the problem of right–left or radial localization would seem to be less for the eye than for the ear and nose. The eye has an extended, two-dimensional, sensitive surface—the retina—and a focusing structure—the cornea and lens—that ensure that the ordinal relations between objects are preserved in their projection on the retina. As Figure 3.1 shows, an object on the right is projected onto

FIGURE 3.1 Ordinal relations between objects are preserved in their projection on the retina. Of course, the retina is a two-dimensional surface; the projections of the objects are represented as three-dimensional for ease of identification.

the left half of the eye, an object straight ahead is projected into the center of the eye, and an object on the left is projected onto the right half of the eye. The relationship in the external world (right–center–left) is preserved on the retina, albeit in reverse order (left–center–right). Where then is the problem of radial localization? The problem begins as soon as we begin to wonder how an observer can localize the radial position of an object relative to himself rather than relative to other objects. If we assume that the eye is fixed in the head, there is obviously no problem. An object that stimulates the center of the retina is straight ahead of the observer's face; an object that stimulates the left portion of the retina is on the observer's right; and an object stimulating the right half of the retina is on the observer's left.

A mechanism for translating position of stimulation on the retina into position in the external world would not be at all complex, if such conditions held. The mechanism would merely have to assign fixed labels to retinal positions in order to identify the external directions corresponding to these positions. A very simple neural structure, such as that described by Sperry (1959) for the frog, would suffice. Unfortunately, the human eye is not fixed in the head. It can move. Figure 3.2 shows what happens on the retina when the eye turns from fixating the straight-ahead object to fixating the object on the right. After the eye movement has taken place, the object on the extreme right stimulates the center of the retina, while the other two objects (the one that is physically straight ahead and the one that is physically on the left) stimulate the right half of the retina. If a mechanism to

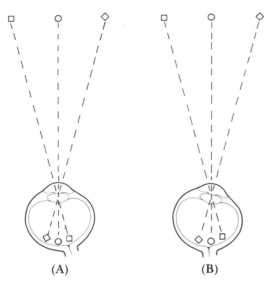

FIGURE 3.2 The results on the retina of a
change in fixation. (A) The eye is fixating on
the object in the center. (B) The eye is
fixating on the object at the right.

assign fixed labels were in operation, the observer should see the
object that is actually on the right but that stimulates the center of
the retina as being straight ahead; the object that is actually straight
ahead would be seen on the left; and the object that is actually on the
left should be seen at the extreme left. This, of course, does not occur
in human adults. Objects are seen to stay in the same fixed position
when the eye moves—a phenomenon referred to as *position constancy.*
Position constancy is the primary problem for theorists of visual perception of radial direction. It is obviously a very significant problem;
yet this problem has received almost no theoretical or experimental
examination in this century. The experimental sources usually cited
in connection with position constancy date from the 1860s. Indeed,
the accepted theory of position constancy must be the most durable
theory in psychology. In essence, this long-lasting theory states that
position constancy is attained by combining retinal-position information with eye-position information. For every site of retinal stimulation, there is a distal, external direction that is specified by the
position of the eye at the moment of stimulation. Thus, an object that
stimulates the fovea, the zone of clearest vision located in the center
of the adult eye, will be seen as straight ahead as long as the eye

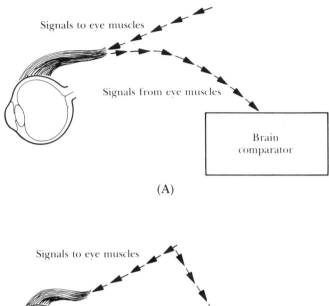

(A)

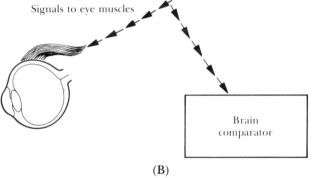

(B)

FIGURE 3.3   Two theories (A and B) of perception of eye movement. (After *The Analysis of Sensations* by E. Mach. New York: Dover Publications reprint, 1959.)

position is registered as straight ahead. An object that stimulates the fovea while the eye is turned 10° to the right will be seen as lying 10° to the right (see Figure 3.2). An object that stimulates a retinal site 10° to the left of the fovea when the eye is turned 10° to the right will be seen as lying straight ahead. Since the position of objects is not given by a system of fixed retinal labels alone, but rather by a combination of retinal labels and eye-position information, changes in eye position (provided they can be registered) will not result in changes in the perceived position of objects.

This theory of position perception and position constancy depends on the combination of two separate sources of information—infor-

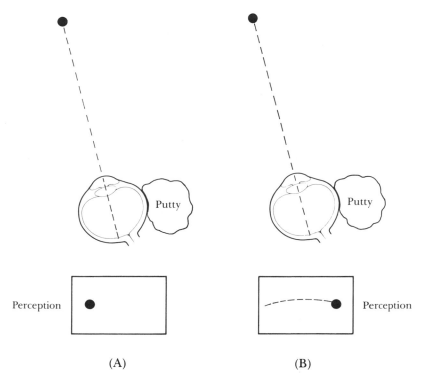

(A)   (B)

FIGURE 3.4   Mach's (1885) experiment. (A) The eye is looking to
the left. (B) The eye is attempting to look to the right.

mation about the site of retinal stimulation (and its labeling) as a given—as something that required no further explanation. The topic that really excited the nineteenth-century investigators of position perception was the nature of our source of information about eye position. Two opposing hypotheses were put forward. One argued that we are aware of eye position as the result of feedback from stretch receptors in the eye muscles. The other hypothesis argued that we are aware of the output to the eye muscles, or the innervation signals that produce movement. The two theories are illustrated in Figure 3.3. At first sight the two theories would seem to produce identical predictions in any situation. One assumes awareness of innervation for movement; the other assumes awareness of the consequences of movement. Since innervation for movement is normally followed by movement and its consequences, there would seem to be no way of differentiating the two theories. Mach, however, created an artificial situation to clarify the matter (see Figure 3.4).

> Let the eyes be turned as far as possible towards the left and two lumps
> of moderately hard putty firmly pressed against the right side of each
> eye-ball. If, now, we attempt to glance quickly to the right, we shall
> succeed only very unperfectly owing to the unperfectly spherical form
> of the eyes, and the object will suffer a strong displacement to the right.
> Thus the mere will to look to the right imparts to the images at certain
> points of the retina a larger "rightward value," as we may term it for
> brevity. [Mach, 1885]

A second critical experiment is even easier to try. Simply look at a
scene and gently move your eye with a finger. As you push your eye
from side to side with your finger (thereby changing its position and
changing the feedback from position receptors in the eye muscles, if
such exist), objects in the world lose their position constancy and seem
to move in a direction opposite to that of the eye. The element that
is missing in this case is the normal innervation signal to the eye
muscles. Feedback there may be; but innervation is certainly missing,
and, in its absence, position constancy is lost (see Figure 3.5).

These two experiments have been taken as convincing proof that
eye position is specified by the efferent command signals to the eye.
Object position is thus supposedly specified by a combination of af-
ferent information (coming from a specific site on the retina) and the
information derived from the efferent signals controlling the position
of the eyes. Because of this, the theory is sometimes called the *efference-
copy theory* of position perception, which is taken to include both position constancy and perception of position change (movement).
Again, the theory is of considerable antiquity, hardly having been
challenged during its one-hundred-year sway. Despite its durability,
however, the efference-copy theory is certainly completely incorrect,
both in detail and in overall outline. Of the predictions one can derive
from the theory, almost none have been verified by experimental tests.
For example, on the basis of efference-copy theory, one would predict
that an observer with his eyes stationary staring at a stationary spot
of light in the dark should perceive the spot of light as being stationary.
If the light does not move and the observer's eyes do not move, surely
the observer should have no difficulty seeing the light as stationary.
This, in fact, does not happen. A stationary spot of light viewed in
darkness seems to move quite dramatically to a rather large extent.
This is the well-known *autokinetic effect.* An observer can be asked to
point to the light in darkness and follow its "movement" with his
finger. When the lights are switched on, the observer may be pointing
by as much as 40° in the wrong direction.

It was thought at one time that unnoticed eye movements were the

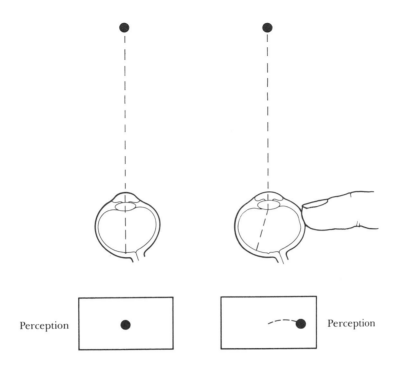

FIGURE 3.5   Passive movement of the eye results in loss of
position constancy.

cause of the autokinetic effect. The hypothesis was that the eyes moved
without the efferent signal being registered; thus, the resulting change
in the site of retinal stimulation was interpreted as resulting from
movement of the object. Note how this hypothesis weakens the efference-copy theory. If the system can miss movements of 40°, how
can the theory explain position perception and position constancy
under normal conditions, where accuracy is better than 1°? In any
event, the hypothesis has been directly disproved. Guilford and Dallenbach (1928) recorded eye movements during autokinetic movement and found that such movements effectively did not occur; eye
movements that did occur were uncorrelated with either the direction
or the amount of autokinetic movement. More recently, Gregory and
Zangwill (1963) have exploited the selective color vision of the center
of the retina to demonstrate that eye movement is not the cause of
the autokinetic effect. These researchers presented observers with a
spot of red light surrounded by an annulus of blue light. The observers

were instructed to fixate the red spot. The center of fixation, the fovea, is quite insensitive to blue light; as long as the observers continued to fixate, they could not see the blue annulus. If their eyes moved so that the spot and annulus would stimulate another part of the retina, the annulus became immediately visible. All observers reported autokinetic movement, yet did not report seeing the annulus— a neat proof that true eye movements are not the cause of the autokinetic effect.

To explain these results, Gregory speculated that there must be some random discharge of efference-copy signals without any corresponding efferent signal; the central correlator would be signaled to expect an eye movement, without an actual eye movement being produced. Since there is no eye movement, the site of retinal stimulation does not change; since the central correlator thinks an eye movement has taken place, the nonchange on the retina is interpreted as movement of the stimulus source. Again the explanation, designed to preserve the efference-copy theory, actually weakens the theory. If the system is so susceptible to random discharge, how can it attain the accuracy observed in normal life, where we never think the world has taken a 40° jump to one side or the other? If Gregory's explanation of the autokinetic effect were correct, we would be quite likely to suffer from autokinetic movement of our whole environment—something that never occurs.

The first prediction that we derived from efference-copy theory— that a stationary light viewed with stationary eyes should be seen as stationary—is thus not confirmed The autokinetic effect demonstrates that there are circumstances in which we perceive change of position when no actual change of position, no change in the site of retinal stimulation, and no eye movement occur. A different set of experiments leading to the same conclusion has shown that there are circumstances in which actual movement will not be perceived. In fact, there are circumstances in which an observer consistently misjudges which of two objects (one stationary, one moving) is actually changing its position. Figure 3.6 outlines some of the elegant experiments conducted by Duncker (1938) on induced movement. Suppose we have a luminous frame surrounding a luminous spot. The spot moves to the right. What does an observer see? He sees the spot moving to the right. So far, so good. Now suppose the frame moves to the left. What does the observer see? He sees the spot move to the right within the perceptually stationary frame! In other words, the actual motion of the frame is not detected, and the change in relative positions of spot

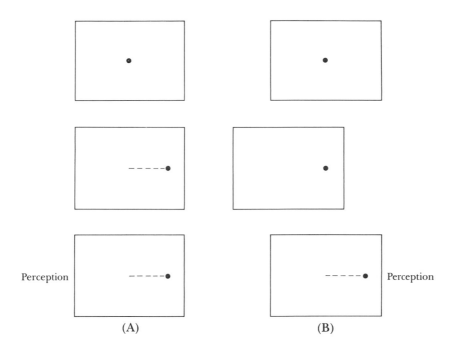

FIGURE 3.6   Duncker's (1938) experiments on induced movement.
(A) The spot moves to the right. (B) The frame moves to the left.

and frame is attributed to movement of the spot. The effect is quite
independent of whether spot or frame is fixated. If the stationary
spot is fixated, the observer thinks that the spot and his eye are moving.
If the moving frame is fixated, the observer thinks that the frame and
his eye are stationary. A number of complex variations of this experiment have been carried out without changing the basic conclusion;
that is, when a small object or its frame moves (regardless of which
one actually moves), the motion will be attributed to the small object.
In other words, there are circumstances in which perception of position and change of position are determined not by the site of retinal
stimulation and changes therein, but by relationships between stimuli
that can overcome or reverse the simple effects of retinal stimulation.

   Another classic effect casts doubt on efference-copy theory; this
effect pertains to the threshold for perception of change of position.
Change of position, like every other perceived event, has a threshold
value below which the change is too small to be perceived. Efference-
copy theory would lead us to believe that the determinant of the

threshold is the amount of change of position, its speed, the site of retinal stimulation, and nothing else. In fact, this is completely in error. The major determinant of the threshold for change of position is the presence or absence of another stationary object. Wallach (1968) has shown that the eye is one hundred times more sensitive to change of position when another stationary object is in the field than when a solitary object is in the field. Wallach has argued that the visual system can detect the change of position of one object relative to another—a phenomenon he calls *object-relative movement*. When the moving object is alone in the field, its change of position is a change relative to the viewing subject only; Wallach calls this situation *subject-relative movement*. Wallach argues that his results show that observers are much more sensitive to object-relative movement than to subject-relative movement. We shall subsequently argue against this position. For the moment, however, the point to be remembered is that these experiments, like the experiments of Duncker, show that the stimulus array is much more important in determining perception of position and change of position than are site of retinal stimulation and eye position at the moment of stimulation.

A more striking negation of the efference-copy theory is found in the work of Stoper (1967)—a negation that is all the more convincing since Stoper's experiments might have been tailored to demonstrate the validity of the theory. Stoper designed a situation to measure the accuracy of position constancy—the very phenomenon that efference-copy theory is supposed to explain. His situation was stripped down so that only those subsystems assumed by efference-copy theory (site of retinal stimulation and eye position) could be effective; all other sources of information were removed. At the same time, Stoper recognized that he must have a response measure that would be unaffected by the reduced conditions of viewing. A pointing response, as used in the autokinetic effect, could not be used since accurate pointing might require sight of the hand, which is not possible under conditions of reduced vision. (This objection does not apply to Duncker's or Wallach's experiments. However, with adults as with infants [see Chapter 2], one must be certain that the response used to index a perceptual process is as accurate as the perceptual process itself and is unaffected by variables controlling the perceptual process.) Stoper solved this problem in a very elegant way. His subjects were asked to track a spot of light slowly moving in a horizontal plane.

After the beginning of an excursion, a second spot of light was flashed on for 25 milliseconds. The second spot was flashed on again 250 milliseconds later. The position of the flashed spot could be varied

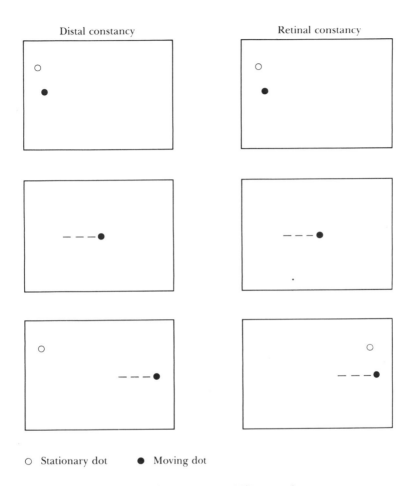

Distal constancy   Retinal constancy

○ Stationary dot   ● Moving dot

FIGURE 3.7   Stoper's (1967) experiment.

between its first and second appearance. At one extreme, it could reappear in exactly the same distal position; its position relative to the observer's head was thus unchanged, while its position relative to the moving spot was different. Its position on the retina, therefore, was also different since the eye had rotated in the interval between the two flashes as it followed the moving spot. We will refer to this extreme as *distal constancy*. At the other extreme, the flashed spot could appear in the same position relative to the moving spot, thus stimulating the same site on the retina on both of its appearances but changing its position relative to the observer's head. This extreme will be called *retinal constancy* (see Figure 3.7). Any position between distal constancy and retinal constancy could also be obtained. The subject was asked to say when the flashed spot appeared in the same position on both

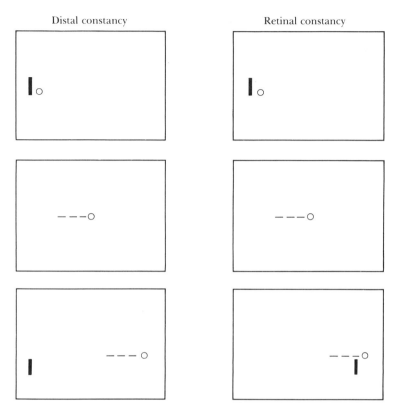

FIGURE 3.8   This is the same situation as that shown in Figure 3.7, except that a stationary bar of light is flashed instead of a dot of light.

occasions that it was presented. If the subjects had been able to obtain position constancy in this situation, they would have reported that the spot appeared in the same position only under the distal-constancy presentation condition. In fact, this is precisely what did not occur. Subjects reported that the spot appeared in the same position only in the retinal-constancy presentation condition. In other words, in this experimental situation, designed to fulfill all of the conditions required by efference-copy theory, position constancy simply is not obtained. Stoper carried out various other versions of this experiment (see Figure 3.8), all of which point to the same conclusion. Where the only information about position is provided by eye position and site of retinal stimulation, position constancy disappears. These results, taken together with the other data presented above, show conclusively

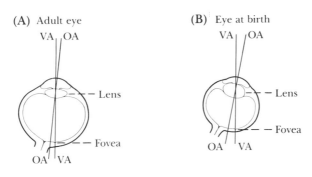

(A) Adult eye

(B) Eye at birth

OA = Optical axis   VA = Visual axis

FIGURE 3.9   Diagram of (A) the adult eye and (B) the eye at birth, seen from above.

that the efference-copy theory of position perception and position constancy cannot be correct. If the only information provided to the perceiver is that deemed necessary by efference-copy theory, then the whole system of position perception breaks down completely.

The evidence indicates the efference-copy theory as a whole is wrong, but we are not told specifically where it is wrong. Obviously, the perceptual system does not combine information about the site of stimulation with information about the efferent commands to the eye muscles. This could be a result of the visual system's inability to combine the information or a result of the unavailability of one or the other or both sources of information. From the results so far discussed, it would seem likely that the perceptual system has no information about eye movements. It seems possible, from Stoper's results, that there is some system of retinal labeling—some way of knowing which part of the retina is being stimulated. It is here that the special problems of the development of position perception can provide some useful leads on a possible basis for a theory. The problems found on examining position perception in adults are greatly compounded when we examine the infant eye. The infant eye is quite different from the adult eye, as Figure 3.9 shows. The infant eye has about the same optical power, but it is much shorter and it has a different radius of curvature. Most importantly, the fovea is in a different place relative to the optical axis of the eye. A beam of light passing through the center of the optical system of the infant eye will not strike the fovea, but rather a point 10° to 15° on the nasal side of the fovea (Mann, 1928). As the eye grows, the fovea rotates until it

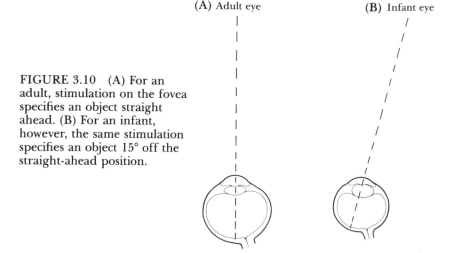

(A) Adult eye   **(B)** Infant eye

FIGURE 3.10 (A) For an adult, stimulation on the fovea specifies an object straight ahead. (B) For an infant, however, the same stimulation specifies an object 15° off the straight-ahead position.

reaches the adult position relative to the optical axis of the eye. Obviously, if simple efference-copy theory were correct, infants would have a wildly inaccurate system for position perception. For example, in the adult it is roughly true that, when the eyes are straight ahead and stimulation is on the fovea, the position of an object straight ahead of the observer is specified. In the case of the infant eye, this conjunction would specify the position of an object 15° off the straight-ahead position (see Figure 3.10). Obviously, if there were a built-in rule of this sort, infants would be unable to locate the position of objects relative to themselves with any accuracy at all (until the fovea had rotated to the adult position). As we shall see, this is not the case. Infants show accurate radial localization long before this time. What this means is that, even if eye position is signaled and registered, there can be no way of combining this information with retinal-site information to yield an invariant that could be correlated with any specific position relative to the observer. The same combination of retinal-site and eye-position information would mean different external positions in the course of development.

One obvious way out of this impasse is to posit some sort of calibration mechanism that can tune or correct the inaccuracies resulting from growth processes. Some researchers (Held, 1965; Kohler, 1964) have argued in favor of such a process on the basis of experiments with adults. In these experiments, the distal position specified by a retinal-site/eye-position combination is changed by an optical device,

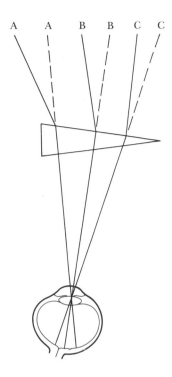

FIGURE 3.11 The distal position specified by the retinal-site/eye-position combination is changed by this wedge prism.

such as a wedge prism (see Figure 3.11). When adults utilize such devices, their radial localization is initially inaccurate to some extent but gradually becomes accurate again. There is a mountain of literature on these corrective processes, which argues for the relative importance of various mechanisms in the process of correction. Kohler and Held have explicitly asserted that similar corrective processes must be involved in the development of the perception of radial position in infants. I would disagree and argue instead that the mechanisms proposed are not even involved in the adaptation to prisms in adults! It is a curious fact that, although adaptation to prisms is usually described as a protracted process, 75 percent of total correction occurs instantaneously, as soon as the device is put on and before any of the proposed mechanisms could operate (Rock, 1966). A more convincing proof that distal position is *not* specified by a retinal-site/eye-position combination could hardly be devised!

Some clues to the true mechanism of position perception can be found among the data already reviewed. Stoper found that position constancy could be obtained in his experimental situation by adding a permanent stationary frame to the field. When this continuous stationary frame was added, the subjects' judgments of the "same" position approached the distal-constancy extreme. This recalls Wallach's finding that observers are much more sensitive to object-relative movement than to subject-relative movement. In Stoper's situation, object-relative position judgments were accurate, whereas subject-relative position judgments (those obtained with no stationary frame in the field) were of course totally inaccurate. The autokinetic effect also occurs under conditions where position can only be judged relative to the perceiving subject. Under these conditions, as we have seen, position perception becomes wildly inaccurate. One might wonder whether the autokinetic effect, like Stoper's illusion, is reduced by the addition of other points of light to the classic single point. This experiment has been tried, with negative results (Royce et al., 1962). As many as 60 dots will go into autokinetic motion together. Their position relative to one another does not change, but their position relative to the observer seems to change by large amounts.

The important point is that their position relative to the *observer* seems to change; their position relative to one another, specified in the pattern of light on the retina, does not change. In Stoper's situation, the illusion disappears as soon as the subject can make a position judgment that is relative to a visible stationary object. When position must be gauged with reference to the observer himself (an invisible, stationary object), position perception and position constancy disappear. The key word in this description of the reference anchor or observer is *invisible*. All of these experiments where position perception breaks down take place in darkness; the observer himself is not projected onto his own retina. In normal, everyday perception, where position is accurately localized, the observer is represented on his own retina; this occurs inevitably, without any mediating behavior of looking at hands or feet. As J. J. Gibson (1950) pointed out, the observer's nose occupies a large area of both retinas (see Figure 3.12). Under normal conditions of illumination, an observer asked to judge the position of an object relative to himself can see both the object and himself. By contrast, under conditions where position perception breaks down—conditions of darkness with luminous objects—the observer can only see the objects. We would not expect an observer to locate the position of an invisible object relative to himself. Likewise, we should not expect an observer to be able to locate the position of an object relative to himself when he is himself invisible.

We are arguing that the location of objects relative to the observer is possible only if the observer can see himself and the object to be

FIGURE 3.12   This drawing represents the visual field of the right eye: the nose, lip, and part of the cheek are visible on the left; the body of the viewer is at the bottom. (After *The Analysis of Sensations* by E. Mach. New York: Dover Publications reprint, 1959.)

located. We are saying that the retinal projection of the nose and orbit specify the observer's position to himself. If this information is available, position perception will be accurate. If it is not available, position perception will be inaccurate. In the standard autokinetic situation (a luminous spot in darkness), the observer cannot see himself, and his position perception is extremely inaccurate. In the converse case of a black spot viewed in homogeneous light by an observer who can see himself, the autokinetic effect vanishes; position perception remains highly accurate (Le Grand, 1967). Stoper's illusion occurs when the observer cannot see himself. That it does not occur when he can see himself is a matter of common observation, and some experimentation (Mack and Bachant, 1969).

Many of the problems associated with position perception simply disappear when it is admitted that the observer must see himself as well as the object and that the information for perception of change of position is a change in the relative position on the retina of observer and object. Consider the problem of position constancy. When the eye turns, every object is projected onto a different retinal site, *including*

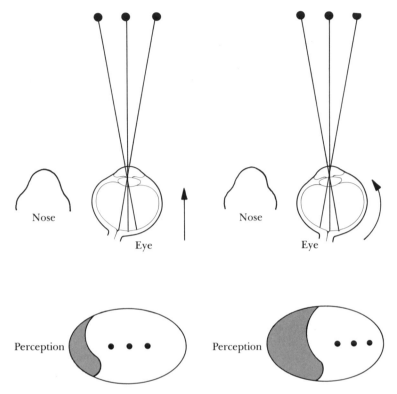

FIGURE 3.13   The relative positions of objects and the nose
remain the same when the eye is turned.

the projection of the observer; but there is no change in the relative
position of the retinal projections of objects and observer and therefore there is no information for change of position (see Figure 3.13).
Position constancy is therefore the only feasible outcome. Consider
the case where the observer turns his head (see Figure 3.14). There
is a change in the retinal projection of every object except the projection of the observer. If you recall the description of induced movement given in connection with Duncker's experiments, you will predict
that it is the observer who should be *seen* to move; indeed, this is what
occurs. The same principle can account for the phenomenon of induced movement of the self. If an observer is stationary in a moving
environment, the environment appears to stay still and the observer
perceives himself as moving (see Figure 3.15).

How would this system cope with perception of specific directions,
such as straight ahead? The direction "straight ahead of the observer's

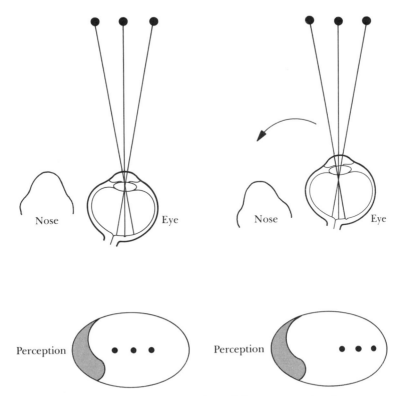

FIGURE 3.14 Only the projection of the nose retains the same retinal position when the head is turned.

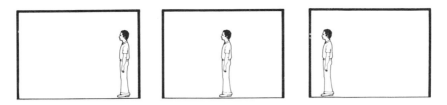

FIGURE 3.15 Although it is the room that is moving toward the observer, he perceives himself as moving forward.

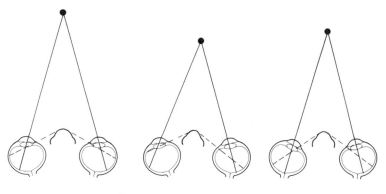

(A) Objects straight ahead

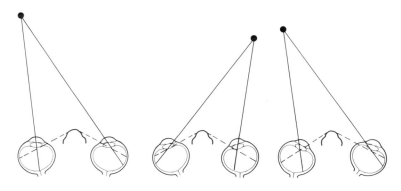

(B) Objects not straight ahead

FIGURE 3.16 (A) Regardless of the position of the eyes, the retinal projections of objects that are straight ahead are symmetrical with respect to the projection of the nose on the retina. (B) Retinal projections of objects that are not straight ahead are not symmetrical with respect to the projection of the nose on the retina.

head," as we have seen, has no specific retinal correlate. However the self, which is straight ahead, is continuously projected onto the retinas and could serve as an anchor point for that direction. As Figure 3.16 shows, all objects that are straight ahead are symmetrically projected onto the retinas with respect to the projection of the nose and regardless of eye position. All objects that are not straight ahead are asymmetrically projected with respect to the nose. The relative sym-

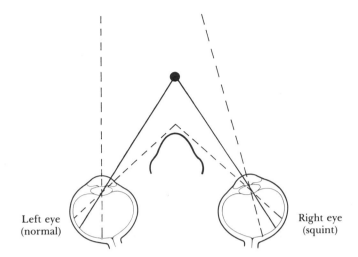

FIGURE 3.17   A case of squint. The foveas of the eyes
are permanently pointed at different places. The retinal
projections of an object fall on different parts of the
retinas of the two eyes, as do the projections from the
nose.

Left eye
(normal)

Right eye
(squint)

metry of the projection of an object could thus serve as the stimulus
to specify straight ahead.

This reformulation of the specification of direction (in terms of
projection onto the retina relative to the projection of the nose rather
than in terms of absolute site of retinal stimulation) solves certain
problems that are absolutely incomprehensible in terms of the traditional theory. The problem of instantaneous adaptation to prisms
is no problem as soon as one realizes that the retinal projection of the
self is displaced in the same way as other objects outside the body.
There is retinal displacement in absolute terms but not in relation to
the projection of the nose and orbit. The problem of squint can also
be handled by the proposed reformulation. In cases of squint, one
eye is permanently at an angle to the other (see Figure 3.17), which
means that the foveas of the two eyes are permanently pointed at
different places in the world. Despite this, the two eyes see the same
objects in the same directions—something quite impossible unless the
information specifying distal position is site of stimulation on the
retina relative to site of the retinal stimulation produced by the self
(Teuber, 1960).

The hypothesis proposed here can even account for the two most
beloved demonstrations of the proponents of efference-copy theory.

Consider the effects of passive movement of the eye. First, I defy anyone to produce a passive eye movement that is at all like an active eye movement in its visual effects. A normal eye movement is a rotation and produces no change in the relative projected positions of self and objects. As you can discover for yourself, passive eye movements do produce changes in the relative projected position of the self and other objects, which is the condition for perceived movement according to the hypothesis presented here. As for the results of obstructed movement, I cannot improve on the words of William James:

> I regret to say that I cannot myself make it succeed—I know not for what reason. But even where it does succeed it seems to me that the conditions are much too complicated for Professor Mach's theoretic conclusions to be safely drawn. The putty squeezed into the orbit and pressure of the eyeball against it must give rise to peripheral sensations strong enough, at any rate (if only of the right kind), to justify any amount of false perception of our eyeball's position, quite apart from the innervation feelings which Professor Mach supposes to co-exist. [James, 1890]

Subsequent replications have used chemical agents to paralyze the eye muscles. An attempt to move the eye then produces no eye movement, just as in Mach's situation. Some of those who have done such studies have repeated Professor Mach's observations; some, Professor James' counterobservation. A clue to the discrepancy lies in the cognitive judgments that some subjects make. "I have moved my eye. The object seems to be in the same place relative to my eye. Therefore, it must have moved." Inferences of this kind are not perceptual in any respect. They take far longer; they do not have the immediacy of perception. If subjects are warned to avoid inference, the paradoxical movement observed by Mach is not likely to be reported (Stevens et al., 1976).

Psychologists tend to think of the self as either a meaningless abstraction or a weighty problem deserving deep thought. The reduction of the self to the visual projection of the nose onto the retina is usually greeted with hilarity. Even J. J. Gibson (1950), who did more for the nose than any other psychologist did so with a kind of defensive flippancy. I would like to insert a few words in defense of the nose at this point. Among those species with chambered eyes, there is not one whose eyes do not pick up a projection of the nose or some other body part. Among those species that have evolved panoramic vision, the panorama is interrupted by a projection of the animal itself.

Among those predatory species with maximum frontality and maximum binocular overlap, there is always a projection of the self. This cannot be a biological accident. The projection of body parts onto the eye must be of functional importance to have been preserved in so many differently evolved forms. Indeed, the hypothesis about position perception presented here has the merit of making sense of what would otherwise be a continuing biological error (Walls, 1942) (see Figure 3.18).

The stimulus information described so far is of course not the only information that can specify the straight-ahead position. J. J. Gibson (1950) has described the stimulation consequent to the forward movement of an observer toward an object and the stimulation consequent to the movement of an object toward the observer. Consider an observer gazing at a textured wall like that shown in Figure 3.19. As the observer is moved toward the wall, the image projected on his retina will change systematically, as shown in the figure.

With forward movement, all of the spots are displaced save one— the one that is straight ahead of the observer. This locus of nonmotion, or center of expansion, defines a position straight ahead of the observer's body. The eyes or the head and eyes can turn to fixate some point that is not straight ahead, without affecting the specification of straight ahead as the center of the optical expansion pattern consequent on forward motion of or motion toward the observer. There are two important corollaries of this specification of straight ahead as the center of an expansion pattern. If an object approaches an observer (or vice versa) along some line that is at an angle to straight ahead (a so-called *miss path*, since it misses the observer), there is no center of expansion *within* the object. The absence of a focus of expansion thus serves to specify a miss path—a direction of approach other than straight ahead. Furthermore, the form of the displacement of the pattern specifies the angle of approach (see Figure 3.20). In a similar way, given movement toward a surface that is in the frontal-parallel plane, the rate of displacement of points will specify their angular separation from the position that is straight ahead of the observer (see Figure 3.19). The greater the angular separation, the greater is the rate of change.

Let us try to summarize the stimuli that could specify the radial position of objects. The cardinal radial direction, straight ahead, can be specified as (1) the locus of nonmotion during movement of the observer toward an object or during movement of an object toward

58

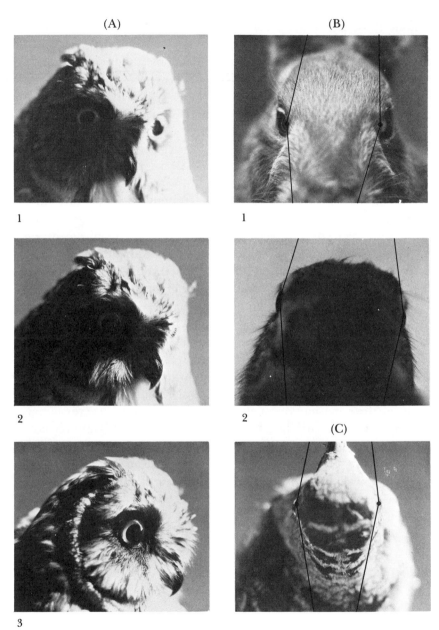

(A)   (B)

1   1

2   2

(C)

3

(D)

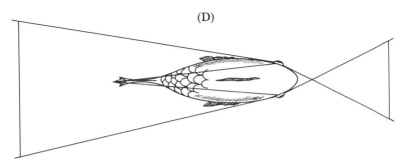

FIGURE 3.18   The visual field of various animals. (A) The owl has a visual angle of 110° with binocular overlap; its eyes point straight ahead. Yet the nasal tuft has developed to such an extent that it covers the central 30° of the owl's visual field. (B) The hare and (C) the woodcock, which are the prey of many other animals, have evolved an extremely wide visual field, amounting to some 200°. As a consequence of the wide visual angle, the hare can see its nose and its tail simultaneously, as can the woodcock. (D) The fish has a total visual field of 360°. A large part of the field is taken up by its own body and tail. (Photographs by Jennifer Wishart.)

the observer, or (2) the locus of projections onto the retinas that are symmetrical with respect to the projection of the self onto the retinas. Both of these specifying variables are invariant during growth. We might thus expect that very young infants would be sensitive to these variables. Radial position along any direction other than straight ahead can also be specified during movement of the observer or object by the locus of the center of the retinal expansion consequent to the movement. If the object is not straight ahead, the center of expansion is implicit, outside the object. The further away from the straight-ahead position, the greater will be the rate of minimal movement within the object. Although the utilization of this variable of stimulation would necessarily depend on complex internal circuitry, the variable is independent of growth and is valid for any size or shape of eye. We might thus expect very young infants to be able to detect the radial direction of a moving object or of a stationary object if they themselves were moving.

The stimuli that could specify stationary objects to a stationary observer pose quite different problems. Human adults can make such judgments, but the judgments must be made in terms of some kind of acquired retinal labels, since there is no stimulus variable available that would be invariant during growth (see Figures 3.9 and 3.10).

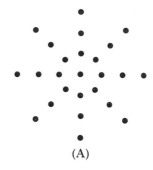

(A)

FIGURE 3.19 As the observer approaches the textured wall (A), the wall expands outward, as shown in (B). The superimposition of B on A (in C) shows how, although the center dot remains stationary, the other dots move outward, with those at the outside moving farthest. The locus of expansion is the center dot.

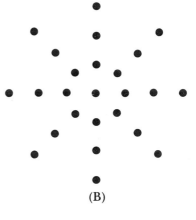

(B)

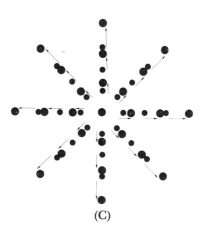

(C)

(A)

FIGURE 3.20 Here the observer
is approaching the textured wall
(A) on a miss path (B). There is
no locus of expansion within the
wall, and, when A is superimposed
on B (in C), we see that the form
of the displacement of the pattern
specifies the angle of approach.

(B)

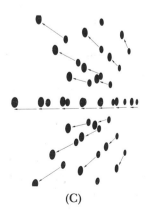

(C)

Similarly, monocular identification of direction, even including the straight-ahead direction, could only be accomplished via a set of acquired retinal labels. We would thus expect stationary infants presented with stationary objects to make poor identifications of directions other than straight ahead when functioning binocularly and to make poor identifications of any direction when functioning monocularly. The reason for such predictions is, simply, the presence or absence of a specifying variable that is invariant during growth. If there is no such invariant, it is unlikely that the organism would come equipped with enough information to function. That there is such a variable is, of course, no proof that infants are able to utilize it.

The actual amount of data available on the abilities of young infants to gauge radial direction is hardly overwhelming. However, there is enough evidence to confirm or negate some of the predictions described above. The information contained in optical expansion patterns is invariant during growth and so could be used by young infants without requiring readjustment during growth. It has been discovered that very young infants do in fact utilize this information. Bower et al. (1970a) found that very young infants display a coordinated, defensive response to an object approaching from a straight-ahead direction. Ball and Tronick (1971) extended this finding and showed that the response was specific to approach from straight ahead; approach along a miss path did not produce defensive behavior at all. It would thus appear that infants in the first week of life can identify the direction of movement of objects relative to themselves.

Whether infants can identify stationary directions is a much more difficult question. Again the problem is largely one of finding appropriate response measures. An obvious measure would seem to be accuracy of eye movements. The accuracy with which infants can move their eyes to fixate a target presented in various directions might seem to be an ideal measure of accuracy of perception. Above we predicted accurate perception of the straight-ahead direction and inaccurate perception of all other directions. If one could discover that infants can turn their eyes to look at a straight-ahead object more rapidly and with less undershoot or overshoot than they can turn to look at an off-straight-ahead direction, the data would lend support to the hypothesis advanced above. Unfortunately, while experiments of this sort have been done, the results are ambiguous for our purposes for the simple fact that young infants are quite unwilling to look at anything that is off the straight-ahead position (Tronick, 1971; Peiper, 1963). While this may indicate the sort of perceptual inability we are arguing for, it could also reflect lack of attention to peripheral areas. The required control condition would be to present an infant with an object that is, say, 15° to its right while it is looking straight ahead. One would then compare the speed and accuracy of the responses in this condition with responses to an object that is straight ahead while the infant's eyes are turned 15° to the right. To my knowledge, this has not been done systematically. The data of Tronick and Clanton (1971) could be interpreted as evidence that the accuracy of eye shifting does increase with age; however, it is not possible to say from their data whether the straight-ahead position has any priority. The same lack of data prevents us from coming to any conclusion about the differences between monocular and binocular looking.

The situation then is that we know infants can identify radial direction during movement. We do not know whether they can identify radial direction while they and the objects are stationary. However since the condition of stationary infant and stationary object is rare, and since infants can always move their heads slightly, there is no reason to believe that imprecise radial-position perception would impose a severe handicap on infants.

4
Distance Perception

The conventional supposition has been that it is the third dimension of space—the distance dimension—that poses the true problem of space perception. The following quote from Bishop Berkeley illustrates this view.

II. It is, I think, agreed by all, that *distance* of itself, and immediately, cannot be seen. For *distance* being a line directed end-wise to the eye, it projects only one point in the fund of the eye. Which point remains invariably the same, whether the distance be longer or shorter. [see Figure 4.1A]

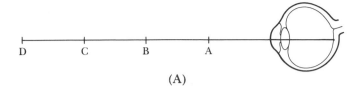

(A)

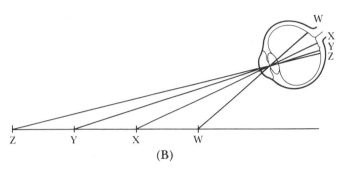

(B)

FIGURE 4.1 (A) The problem of distance perception according to Bishop Berkeley. (B) J. J. Gibson's alternative statement of the problem.

III. I find it also acknowledged, that the estimate we make of the distance of *objects* considerably remote, is rather an act of judgment grounded on *experience* than of *sense*. For example, when I perceive a great number of intermediate *objects* such as houses, fields, rivers, and the like, which I have experienced to take up a considerable space; I thence form a judgment or conclusion, that the *object* I see beyond them is at a great distance. Again, when an *object* appears faint and small, which, at a near distance, I have experienced to make a vigorous and large appearance; I instantly conclude it to be far off. And this, it is evident, is the result of *experience;* without which, from the faintness and littleness, I should not have inferred any thing concerning the distance of *objects.* [Berkeley, 1709]

Although this view is still encountered (Gregory, 1966) it should not have survived the clarifying analysis of J. J. Gibson (1950) (see Figure 4.1B). Gibson pointed out that there are many stimuli that specify distance. Once projected onto the two-dimensional retina, the stimuli are not themselves three-dimensional. However, variations within these stimuli specify variations in distance to a degree of accuracy limited only by the resolving power of the optical system of the eye. We thus see distance as directly as we see color.

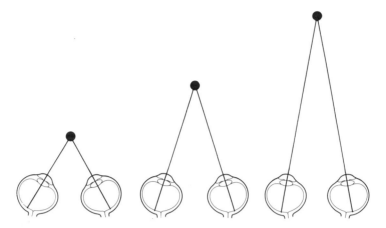

FIGURE 4.2   Convergence angle declines with distance.

There are a variety of stimuli that specify distance. One of them, *binocular parallax,* has long been supposed to be "primary" in some sense. Binocular parallax, as the name implies, is dependent on relations between the two eyes. There are two components to binocular parallax—the convergence angle for binocular fixation and binocular disparity. *Convergence angle* (see Figure 4.2) changes systematically with the distance of the object being looked at (declining with the distance of the object). *Binocular disparity* arises, by contrast, whenever we have a visual field containing a nonfixated object at a distance different from that of the fixated object. Because our two eyes are side by side, they each get a slightly different view of the world; this means that any object that is not being fixated will be projected onto noncorresponding points in the two eyes (see Figure 4.3).

Note that there are two different forms of disparity, crossed and uncrossed. *Crossed disparity* arises when there is an object nearer than the object to be fixated. *Uncrossed disparity* arises whenever there is an object farther away than the fixated object. The nearer an object is, the greater the crossed disparity that it produces; likewise, the farther away an object is, the greater the uncrossed disparity that it produces. The total range of binocular stimulation can thus specify relative position in depth with an accuracy restricted only by our sensitivity to convergence angle and binocular disparity. With this set of stimuli available, we are able to gauge the relative position in depth of objects down to a separation of 27 sec of arc, a truly amazing performance

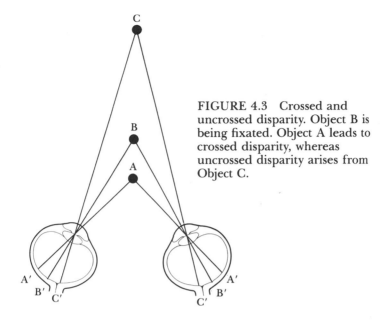

FIGURE 4.3 Crossed and uncrossed disparity. Object B is being fixated. Object A leads to crossed disparity, whereas uncrossed disparity arises from Object C.

(Graham et al., 1965). The problems with binocular parallax arise only when we begin to wonder whether it can specify *absolute* distance.

Under certain circumstances, these binocular stimuli could specify absolute as well as relative distance. Suppose we take an adult with an interocular distance of 6 cm. For this adult a convergence angle of 60° specifies an object 5.2 cm away; a convergence angle of 30° specifies an object 11.2 cm away, and so on. So far, so good; but consider this in a developmental perspective. An adult's eyes are about 6 cm apart, but an infant's eyes are only half that distance apart. The specification that holds true for an adult would not be true for an infant, and vice versa. Both convergence angle and disparity are a joint function of distance and *interocular* separation (see Figure 4.4). Since interocular separation changes continuously throughout development, there can be no possibility that binocular stimulation could specify absolute distance in any invariant way throughout development. If binocular stimulation does specify absolute distance at any point in development, it can only be as the result of a scaled matching or calibration process that imparts the requisite information to the binocular system.

These developmental considerations do not apply to the other major stimuli that specify distance—motion parallax and optical expansion pattern. *Motion parallax* is generated whenever an observer moves

(A) Adult eyes　　　　　　(B) Infant eyes

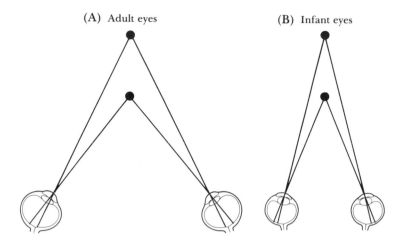

FIGURE 4.4　Convergence angle and disparity are greater for adult eyes (A) than for infant eyes (B) for objects the same distance away.

his head, as shown in Figure 4.5. If the observer's eyes are fixed on the horizon, the image of every object in the scene is displaced in the direction opposite to the movement of his head. The amount of displacement is a function of the distance of the objects; the greater the distance, the less the displacement (compare Box 2 to Box 1 in Figure 4.5). The situation is somewhat more complex if the fixation point is nearer than the horizon (see Figure 4.6). The same relation holds for objects nearer than the fixation point; however, objects farther away than the fixation point are displaced in the same direction as the head movement, and the amount of displacement increases with distance beyond the fixation point.

Motion parallax, the changes in retinal projection consequent to head movement, is obviously independent of growth. Changes in the size or location of the eyeball will not affect this stimulus system. However, one must again question whether motion parallax can specify absolute distance. Consider a lateral head movement of 20 cm with the eyes fixed on a point 3 m away. The projection of an object nearer than the fixation point, say 1 m away, will be displaced through an angle of 8°. Consider the same head movement with the position of fixation 2 m away; this time the projection of the object 1 m away will be displaced through an angle of 6°. Angular shift, therefore, could only be mapped into absolute distance if the distance of the fixation

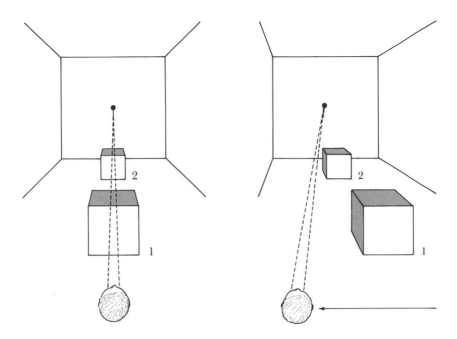

FIGURE 4.5 Motion parallax. If the head moves left and the eyes are kept fixed on the horizon, the nearer object appears to move farther and faster to the right than the more distant object does. (After "The Visual World of Infants" by T. G. R. Bower. Copyright © 1966 by Scientific American, Inc. All rights reserved.)

point were known beforehand, which would imply some means of gauging distance other than motion parallax.

The other classical stimulus for distance is *optical expansion*. Whenever we move toward an object (or whenever the object moves toward us), its retinal image expands (see Figure 4.7). The amount of expansion, under some circumstances, can tell us the distance of the object. Thus, if we move 1 m toward the object and its retinal image doubles, we know that the object was 2 m away when we began our movement and is now 1 m away at the end of our movement. If the retinal image size increases by only 25 percent after a forward movement of 1 m, we can deduce that the object was 4 m away to start with and is now 3 m away.

We can make such judgments only if we have some nonvisual way of calibrating our movements. Obviously, there is no requirement that

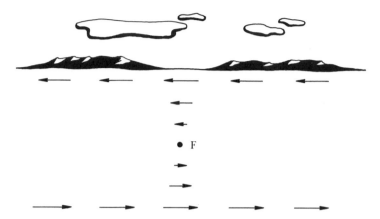

FIGURE 4.6   The effect of the distance of the fixation point on the amount of motion parallax. Objects nearer than the fixation point (F) move in the opposite direction when the observer looks to the left (as in Figure 4.5, when the fixation point is the horizon). Objects farther away than the fixation point are displaced in the same direction as the head movement. (After *The Perception of the Visual World* by James J. Gibson, Copyright © 1950, renewed 1978, Houghton Mifflin Company. Used by permission of the publishers.)

such calibration be in terms of meters and centimeters. An internal calibration in terms of paces or creeps would do just as well and probably better from a functional standpoint.

The situation is somewhat different in the case of an object moving toward a stationary observer. The information contained in this sort of optical event has been extensively analyzed (Hay, 1966; Lee, 1974). The amount of expansion consequent to object movement can specify the position of the object relative to its starting point—but in relative, not absolute, terms. That is, the information can specify that the moving object is now half as far away as it was. The information cannot specify in absolute terms how far away the object is or was. Optical expansion produced by a moving object can therefore specify *proportional* but not absolute changes in distance. It follows from this, however, as Lee (1974) has shown, that an organism is supplied with information that allows it to predict when a moving object will contact it, providing the organism can make certain extrapolations from the change in stimulation on the retina. This is all of the information conveyed by the optical expansion pattern. As can be seen, it does not

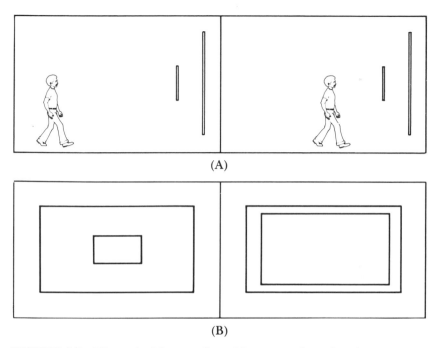

FIGURE 4.7 The retinal image of an object expands as the observer
moves toward it. This optical expansion pattern can indicate the distance of
the object to the observer. (A) Side view. (B) Observer's view.

convey any information about absolute distance to a stationary organism.

A large amount of additional information is available to organisms
that can specify the relative positions in depth of objects. Because
these systems of specification do not require movement and can be
picked up by a single eye, they are much used by representational
artists—hence the name commonly given them, "painter's cues." Some
of these are illustrated in Figure 4.8. J. J. Gibson (1950) has presented
the most complete and brilliantly lucid description of these stimulus
systems. Their utility is somewhat restricted in comparison to the
dynamic stimuli described above. Painter's cues can only indicate relative position, and even then they can only indicate with limited accuracy. There are many situations in which applying painter's cues
would lead the perceiver into error (see Figure 4.9). Brunswik (1956)
made a study of this for a number of painter's cues; the best of these
was relative height. He found that, in about 50 percent of the cases,

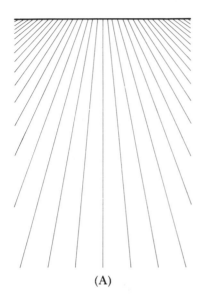

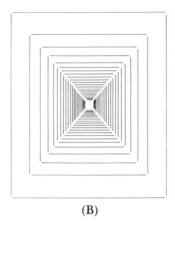

(B)

(A)

FIGURE 4.8 Painter's cues. These monocular cues do not require movement and can specify depth and distance to the observer. Other painter's cues (not illustrated) include interposition and relative height. (A) Linear perspective. Separation decreases with increasing distance. (B) Density gradient. Density increases with increasing distance. (After *The Perception of the Visual World* by James J. Gibson. Copyright © 1950, renewed 1978, Houghton Mifflin Company. Used by permission of the publishers.)

the "higher" of two objects was in fact farther away, as the cue indicated. However (excluding cases where the "higher" object was in fact at the same distance), the remaining proportion of cases where the "higher" object was in fact nearer was still very large—far too large for placing any great reliance on even this cue (see Figure 4.10).

Throughout the brief review of the problem of space perception given above, we have consistently returned to the problem of how organisms gauge absolute distance as opposed to relative distance. Absolute distance is the core problem in distance perception. As we have seen, there are many stimulus systems that specify relative position very reliably. They can tell us that one object is nearer to us or farther away from us than another with perfect reliability. But in many real-life situations, we need to know how far away an object is *from us;* the expression of *how far* must serve to control behavior taking place in the space occupied by ourselves and the object. Take the act of reaching and grasping an object. When this act is carried out by an adult, the hand goes to the object and grasps it. The hand does not overshoot or undershoot; it gets to where the object is. Furthermore the action need not be monitored by eye. We adults can look away or even close our eyes while we perform such acts. This means that the seen distance of the object has been translated into a set of motor commands that move the hand through the appropriate distance to the object. When speaking of the problem of absolute distance, it is this translation from sensory to motor that I am referring to. If an organism displays behavior that is appropriate to the distance of objects, if it can reach objects without overshoot or undershoot, then I would say the organism is responding to absolute distance. The term *absolute distance* serves as shorthand for "spatial variables translated into a form appropriate for the control of spatial motor movements."

This definition of absolute distance perception greatly restricts the range of experimental methods one can use to analyze the capacity. Obviously, the only acceptable indicators of this capacity are spatial behaviors—behaviors that are *necessarily* adjusted in space. I have given the example of reaching as a behavior whose successful occurrence indexes successful absolute distance perception. Reaching is a superb example of a spatial behavior. Another excellent example can be found in the classic experiment of Lashley and Russell (1934) on distance perception in rats. The subjects in this experiment were placed on a jumping stand at various distances from a target platform. The rats, who were visually naive, were forced to jump from the stand. The force of their jump to the platform was taken as an indicator of their absolute distance perception, which was extremely good.

It is difficult for a developmental psychologist not to drool with envy whenever he or she encounters experiments like that of Lashley and Russell. The young of nonhuman organisms have a much richer behavioral repertoire than do human infants. There is little point in testing jump responses of young infants, for young infants simply do not jump. Indeed, to the casual eye, human infants seem to do little except sleep and eat. As we shall see, the casual observer misses much, but the lack of responses does limit the range of experimentation possible with young infants. Even if one does find a usable behavior, the fact that the organism is a growing one limits the conclusions that can be drawn.

The motor system grows more than does any sense organ. If we test accuracy of perception within a growing perceptual system while using as an indicator accuracy of behavior within a growing motor

(A)

system, we are introducing two possible sources of error that cannot be separated. For example, it has been reported that young children—much less infants—will reach out for objects that are well beyond their reach. Does this indicate poor perception of object distance, poor awareness of arm length, or some combination of the two? This is not merely a methodological problem; it is also a severe theoretical prob-

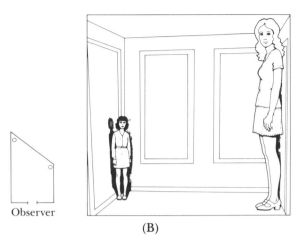

Observer

(B)

FIGURE 4.9   (A) "Waterfall" by M. C. Escher (1961). If we trace the
various parts of this construction, we are unable to discover any mistake in
it; yet it is an impossible whole. The two towers, for example, are the same
height, and yet the one on the right is a story lower than the one on the
left. (From the collection of C. V. S. Roosevelt, Washington, D.C.) (B) The
left portion of the farther wall recedes from the observer. The walls and
windows have been arranged to give the same retinal image as a normal
rectangular room, but the "smaller" figure is actually almost twice as far
away from the observer as the other. (After *The Ames Demonstrations in
Perception* by W. H. Ittleson. OUP, Princeton, N.J., 1952.)

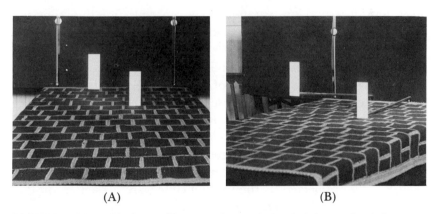

(A)   (B)

FIGURE 4.10   This figure illustrates how relative height can lead the
perceiver into error. In A, the block on the left looks farther away than the
one on the right. A glance at B (the same array seen from a different
angle) shows that this is not the case. (After *The Perception of the Visual
World* by James J. Gibson, Copyright © 1950, renewed 1978, Houghton
Mifflin Company. Used by permission of the publishers.)

lem. It has been argued that infants learn to see distance by watching their hands; since the motor system "knows" where the hand is, it can impart that information to the visual system and so calibrate it. It has likewise been argued that the eye educates the motor system—that infants watching their hands are learning how to interpret and control motor movements (Harris, 1965). Proponents of either position are assuming, erroneously, that either the visual system or the motor system can serve as a source of information that is invariant during growth. But neither of these systems can provide much invariant information during growth. The invariant information that the visual system can provide, as seen above, is not the sort of information that can control precise action. Action in space must be precisely oriented, not relatively oriented. The visual system can tell the infant that one object is half as far away as another, but we have not so far come across any stimulus that would say exactly how far away an object is. Without this information, accurate motor behavior is impossible. The theoretical problem of how one growing system is calibrated onto another growing system is very difficult and creates the greatest single methodological problem in the study of infancy.

These problems have led many investigators, including the present writer, to take refuge in discrimination methods that rely on simple, available, easily counted responses. An elegant example of the simplicity and utility of such methods is a study of shape perception reported by Day and McKenzie (1973). One group of infants was given ten 20-second presentations of a constant cube in a constant orientation. They duly habituated, looking less and less at the stimulus presentation on the repeated trials. Another group was shown the same cube, but in a different orientation on each presentation. They also habituated; indeed, their rate of habituation was indistinguishable from that of the first group. These infants clearly were able to recognize the cube as the same cube on each presentation even though its retinal shape changed greatly from one presentation to the next (see Figure 4.11). That the changes were not due simply to fatigue was shown by a third condition, in which shapes equivalent to the retinal images projected by the varying cube were presented; in this case there was no decline in looking time over trials.

This kind of method could be extended to test the fineness of discrimination, the range over which discriminations can be made, and so on. Obviously, these methods cannot be applied to the assessment of perception of absolute distance as it has been defined here, since that can only be indexed by spatially appropriate behavior. However, considering the growth-induced imprecision of these behaviors, one might conclude that relative-distance perception is the only capacity that could be studied anyway. Why not, then, utilize the simpler, more available discrimination methods? This would seem to be a plausible step. As we have indicated before, however, it is not a feasible step. The objections to discrimination methods that were outlined before in connection with the study of radial localization apply here as well. Discrimination methods cannot tell us the basis of discrimination when there are alternative bases for the discrimination. Distance in perception is specified by the set of stimuli described above (binocular parallax, motion parallax, optical expansion, and painter's cues); any one of them can specify the distances of objects to some degree of precision. Distance cannot be specified unless one or another of these stimulus variables is available. Suppose our organism could display differential responses to objects at different distances. Take another McKenzie and Day experiment as an example. If the proportion of time an infant spends looking at an object 90 cm away is constant but increases when the distance of the object is changed, can we conclude that the looking has increased because the infant has noticed the change in distance? This is a tempting inference but entirely unwarranted. The change of distance is specified at the infant's eye by changes in the variables specifying distance. The recovery of looking indicates that the infant has detected a change, but it does *not* tell us whether the infant detected a change of distance or a change in the variables specifying distance. How can we tell from the recovery of looking that the infant detects a change in distance rather than a change in convergence angle? A change in convergence angle might be detected as such without being translated into perceived change in distance. The same goes for all of the other stimulus variables specifying distance. Motion parallax changes might be seen as changes in movement across the retina. The approach of an object might be seen as expansion with no approach.

To some extent, human adults can "see" the variables that specify distance rather than distance itself, although they are not very good at it. Perhaps this is because it takes a long time to develop the ability to see these variables, or because the habit of perceiving in terms of distance overcomes the initial tendency to perceive the variables rather than what they specify. Both theories have been put forward. Infants are the only organisms who can decide between the theories. Unfortunately, the discrimination methods cannot make the decision; no simple discrimination experiment can tell us whether an organism is

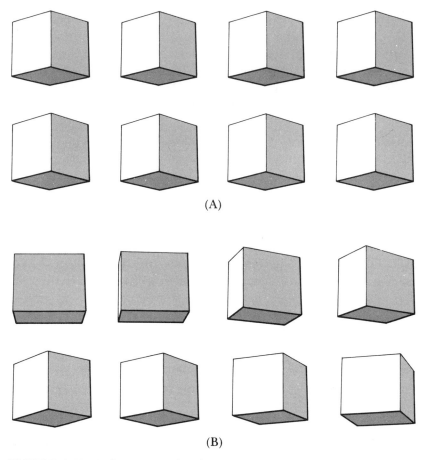

(A)

(B)

FIGURE 4.11 Infants recognize the constancy of a cube, even when its orientation is changed (from A to B). (C) Results of the experiment. (After *Human Development* by T. G. R. Bower. W. H. Freeman and Company. Copyright © 1979. Data from "Perceptual Shape Constancy in Early Infancy" by R. H. Day and B. E. McKenzie. *Perception*, **3,** 315–326, 1973.)

responding to distance as specified by some variable, or responding to the variable itself. The key word here is *simple*. It is theoretically possible to devise discrimination experiments that would index distance perception, although such experiments would be rather complex.

Suppose that we presented an infant with an event in space specified by only one of the possible variables that could specify such an event. For example, an infant could be presented with an object moving toward and away from it, the approach and withdrawal being specified

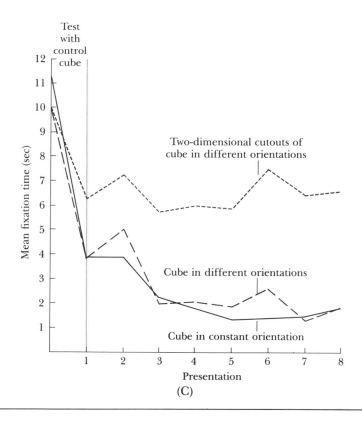

Test with control cube

Two-dimensional cutouts of cube in different orientations

Cube in different orientations

Cube in constant orientation

Presentation

(C)

by the optical expansion pattern. In time, we might suppose, attention to the event will decline. Suppose we then presented the same event, this time specified by binocular parallax changes only. Would the attention to the event continue to decline? If it did, we could conclude that the infant was responding to the spatial event and not to the variables that specify it. The spatial event is constant, and there is no reason to expect recovery of attention when the same event is presented, even though specified by different variables. If, on the other hand, the infant were responding to the variables, we would expect an upsurge in attention after the transition from one variable to the other. I have attempted experiments of this sort but have continually been defeated by methodological problems, such as selection of an attention measure, methods of ensuring smooth transition from one variable to the other, and selection of an appropriate event. Faced with problems of this sort, one feels that the natural response methods are a refuge. If an infant reaches out for an object intentionally, no matter how inaccurately, there can be no doubt that the infant sees the object in the third dimension.* This kind of simple certainty we just cannot get from discrimination experiments.

To sum up, there are three main problem areas that concern us when we study the perception of distance in infants. The first is: do infants perceive distance at all, or do they simply perceive the variables that specify distance? When presented with an approaching object, do they see the object approach (perception of distance), or do they simply see it expand (perception of the specifying variables)? The second problem area is: when and how do infants succeed in correlating perception and action to produce accurate behavior in space? Third, once these two are correlated, how does the organism adjust to growth within the components?

The first of these questions has provoked a great deal of theoretical argument but little research. As indicated, the problem really requires spatial behavior as an indicator measure, and the repertoire of the infant is not rich in spatial behavior. In the classic studies of Gibson and Walk (1960) on behavior on the visual cliff, crawling was used as an indicator behavior. The *visual cliff* is illustrated in Figure 4.12. The researchers found that infants who could crawl would not crawl over the deep side of the visual cliff under any circumstances, showing clearly that infants of crawling age do perceive distance. Unfortunately, infants who are old enough to be able to crawl have a long history of experience behind them and so can hardly tell us anything about the origins of space perception.

A number of researchers have thought that response to approaching objects might allow us to assess the perceptual abilities of younger infants. White (1963) did a very carefully controlled study of the development of one response to approaching objects—the blink. The infants in the experiment were laid on their backs. Immediately over the infant's face was an optical tunnel containing an object that could be dropped toward the infant from various heights (see Figure 4.13). A window of transparent plastic at the bottom of the tunnel prevented the object from actually hitting the infant. The window also prevented any air from being blown in the infant's face as the object dropped. This made sure that the response was a response to the visual event, not the air movement. The blink responses were picked up by elec-

---

*An attempt to demonstrate the role of intention in infant reaching has been made by Bower et al. (1970b).

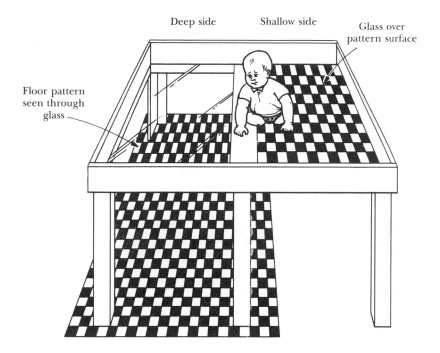

Deep side   Shallow side   Glass over pattern surface

Floor pattern seen through glass

FIGURE 4.12   The visual cliff. The infant crawled across a heavy sheet of glass toward the mother. Under the glass was a textured piece of checkered linoleum. For half the distance, it was about a meter below the surface of the glass. At the midpoint, the infant was faced with a visual cliff. (After "Basic Cognitive Processes in Children" by Jerome Kagan, 1963. The Society for Research in Child Development, Inc.)

trodes attached to the infant's temples and recorded on the moving paper tape of a polygraph. It was found that the first blink in response to the dropping object occurred around the age of 8 weeks. The blink at that time was specific to the dropping object; withdrawal of the object produced no blink response at all. Prior to 8 weeks of age, no blinking could be elicited.

It would thus appear from this study that distance perception can be demonstrated around the age of 8 weeks. But can we therefore conclude that it is absent prior to this time? Blinking is in the infant's behavioral repertoire and can be elicited by air movement alone well before 8 weeks. If we accept blinking as a fair indicator of distance perception, it seems that we must also accept the conclusion that distance perception is absent prior to 8 weeks in the conditions of this

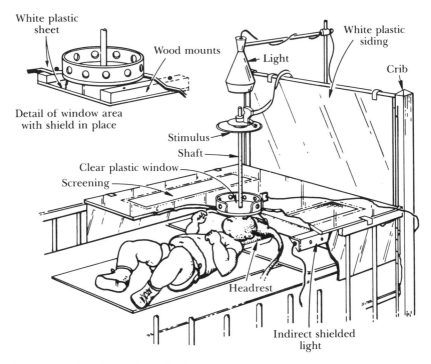

White plastic
sheet

Wood mounts

White plastic
siding

Light

Crib

Detail of window area
with shield in place

Stimulus

Shaft

Clear plastic window

Screening

Headrest

Indirect shielded
light

FIGURE 4.13   The blink-eliciting apparatus used by White. (After *Human Infants: Experience and Psychological Development* by B. L. White. Copyright © 1971. Reproduced by permission of Prentice-Hall, Inc., Englewood Cliffs, N.J.)

experiment. There are two qualifications that must be entered at this point. Can we accept blinking as a fair indicator of distance perception, and can we accept the conditions of this experiment as representative of the conditions under which perception normally occurs? Let us first consider blinking. In a functional context, does it make any sense for an organism to close its eyes as an object approaches its face? It would surely make more sense to take some kind of avoiding action, with eyes open on the object. It would also make more sense for experimenters to look for functional responses, rather than what appears to be a maladaptive response to the approach of an object. After all, there is no evidence that human adults close their eyes when an object approaches their faces, save as a desperate last resort. Why should infants? The second problem concerns the conditions of the experiment. The range of object movements used by White was very short. The longest drop was 30 cm. Since the object dropped under the force of gravity, the entire event was over, drop and stop, in a few milliseconds, very possibly too quickly for any response to be organized. Before the infant could respond to approach, the event would be over. If a response were simply triggered by the event, this would not matter, but there is no reason to believe that human behavior is triggered and will then continue in the absence of the stimulation that caused it.

One last point about the conditions of stimulation must be made. White used a transparent plastic shield to prevent displaced air from reaching the infant's face, thereby ensuring that the response was elicited by the visual stimulus alone. This might seem like a very necessary control measure; however, it makes the stimulation presented very unrepresentative of the stimuli that occur in the real world. Whenever an object approaches an observer outside a laboratory, it simultaneously produces a complex of visual changes and a gradient in time of air pressure against the skin. Either change alone is abnormal. It may be that both together are necessary to produce a response very early in infancy. Since this kind of compounding is quite probable, the presentation conditions should allow one to discover whether or not it is important. Vision plus air movement may be quite different from vision alone or air movement alone. We cannot assume from a vision-alone presentation that vision is not important; we must test for its role in conjunction with stimuli that normally covary with it.

Bower et al. (1970a) have carried out a study that attempted to meet these criteria. They presented infants with real object movements that produced air displacement as well as visual changes. The objects were moved in slowly, and all of the behavior produced by the infants was recorded, not just the behavior of their eyelids. The results, unfortunately, were exiguous until one further modification was introduced—that was to present the stimuli only when the infants were in an upright or semi-upright position. This modification was necessary since it appears that very young infants never become fully awake as long as they are lying on their backs (Prechtl, 1965). Since one can hardly expect coordinated behavior from an organism that is half-asleep, at least a semi-upright posture seemed necessary. Once the latter modification was introduced, an obvious defensive behavior was elicited from the infants, who were in their second week of life. This is illustrated in Figure 4.14. The defensive behavior had three clear components: (1) eye widening, (2) head retraction, and (3) interposition of hands between face and object. Blinking was not observed.

0 msec

480 msec

200 msec

840 msec

280 msec

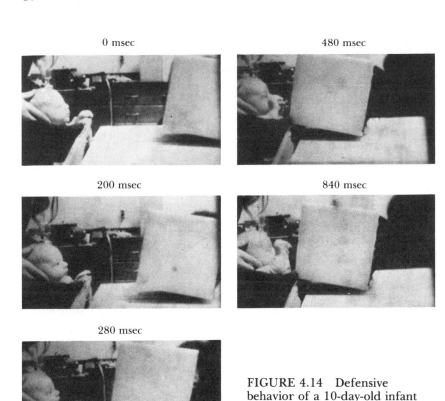

FIGURE 4.14 Defensive behavior of a 10-day-old infant elicited by an approaching object.

The behavior was clearly functional. It would have produced the best possible defense against the object, had the object been allowed to strike the infant. The response of course was a response to real object movement with associated air displacement.

The next stage of the experiment was to discover the response to air displacement alone and to the visual changes alone. Air displacement produced a marked response that was totally different from the response produced by the approaching object. The air movement alone produced very rapid eye closure followed by slight rotary head movements; there was no head retraction and no hand raising. Air displacement alone cannot, therefore, be responsible for the defensive movements elicited by an approaching object. The next thing that should have been studied was the response to visual stimulation alone, but unfortunately this was not done. Instead of testing response to

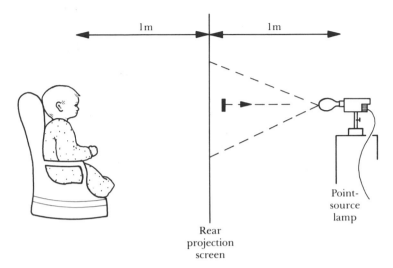

FIGURE 4.15 Shadow caster. As the object is moved farther and farther away from the screen and toward the point-source lamp, the shadow of the object increases in size. As there are no distance cues from binocular or motion parallax, the optical expansion pattern is the only distance-specifying variable present.

the whole complex of visual changes, the investigators studied response to one component of the visual changes—the optical expansion pattern—using the device shown in Figure 4.15. This device excluded changes in binocular parallax and changes in motion parallax. The only specifying variable presented was the optical expansion pattern. Infants in the second week of life did show defensive behavior when presented with an approaching object defined solely by an optical expansion pattern. However, the intensity of the response was less than that elicited in the natural situation. Since the other variables were not presented, we cannot say whether the diminished intensity of response was due to lack of visual stimuli or to lack of air movement.

Ball and Tronick (1971) repeated the experiment, adding the variable of relative movement within the moving object by rotating the object as it approached. They found that the addition of this visual variable did not increase the intensity of response. This might seem to argue that the air displacement is required for a total response; however, until the experiment is repeated using the full battery of visual variables, the question must remain open. It seems safe to conclude nonetheless that the defensive behavior elicited from 1-week-old infants by an approaching object is primarily elicited by visual stimulation, although possibly supported by air-displacement stimulation.

Bower et al. (1970a) performed two further modifications in a series of experiments. One modification was carried out to ensure that the infants were in fact responding to changes in the distance of the object. It could be argued that the infants were responding not to the approach of an object, but rather to its apparent expansion. It is not clear why an organism would defend itself against an expanding object; however, the argument can be made. To control against this complication, the experimenters presented the infants with a pair of objects, first one then the other. One object was small (a foam-rubber cube with 20-cm sides) and approached to 8 cm from the infants; the other object was large (a 50-cm cube) and approached only to 20 cm from the infants. At a 20-cm distance, the large object projected an image onto the infants' retinas that was identical in size to the image projected by the small object only 8 cm away. The geometry of the situation is shown in Figure 4.16. If the infants were responding simply to magnification of the retinal image seen as such, they should not have differentiated between the two presentations, which would be seen as equally threatening. If, on the other hand, they were responding to change in distance, we would expect a much greater response to the small, near object, since it comes closer and is that much more dangerous. There was indeed full-scale response to the small, near object and no response at all to the large, distant object. This indicates that it was in fact perceived change in distance that was being responded to.

The last variation of this presentation was varying the speed of the approaching object. It was found that as object speed increased, probability of response declined. At the highest speed used, the event still took 2.7 seconds, so the decline in response was not due to lack of time to complete a response. Instead, it seems likely that the information specifying the event was presented too fast for the infant visual system to register it. Object movement above a rate of 32° per second cannot be seen as movement by adults (Graham et al., 1965). It seems quite likely that the infant visual system has a much lower cutoff point.

This set of experiments would thus seem to indicate that 1-week-old infants do perceive distance and change of distance as specified by, at least, the optical expansion pattern. Since the ability is present at 1 week, it seems likely that it is an unlearned ability. However, we cannot be certain. In the first edition of this book (Bower, 1974), I

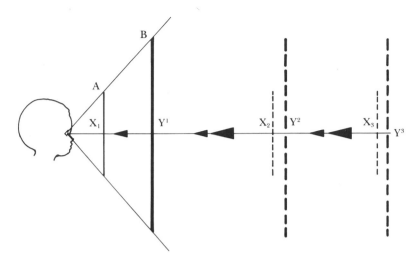

FIGURE 4.16 Different-sized objects approaching to the points where they project the same size of retinal image for the infant. Object A is a 20-cm cube and approaches to a point 8 cm (X_1) from the infant. Object B is a 50-cm cube and approaches to a point 20 cm (Y_1) from the infant. At these points, the large and small objects project retinal images that are identical in size, since angle of convergence is the same in both cases.

argued that a learning theory explanation was implausible. How many times, I argued, has a 1-week-old infant been struck in the face by an approaching object. A flood of letters convinced me to the contrary. During breast feeding the infant of an inexperienced mother is quite likely to be struck in the face; indeed, overenthusiastic application of the breast can result in a response very like that elicited by an approaching object (see Figure 4.17) (Gunther, 1961). It is possible that the response to an approaching object is learned on the basis of experience with the breast. Such an argument, however, would not explain the behavior of bottle-fed babies, nor could it account for some consensual data to be described below. On the whole, I would prefer to conclude that these experiments do demonstrate a built-in capacity for perception of the third dimension.

A demonstration that infants perceive the third dimension allows us to make a strong interpretation of the results of discrimination experiments. Since infants perceive distance in one situation, it would seem overly cautious to deny that they can perceive it in other situations. It seems most likely that distance is the basis for the discriminations demonstrated, for example, in experiments by Bower (1965a)

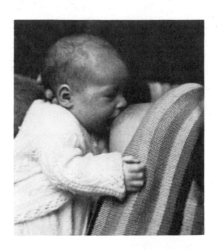

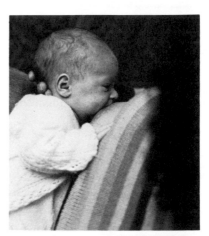

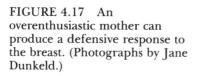

FIGURE 4.17 An overenthusiastic mother can produce a defensive response to the breast. (Photographs by Jane Dunkeld.)

(see Figure 4.18). Bower's experiments would imply that motion parallax is important in early visual perception and that painter's cues are simply not registered as stimuli. Very young infants, then, perceive distance and differences in distance.

How soon do they become able to perceive distance in ways precise enough to control precise action? A number of investigators have studied the development of reaching. The results seem to indicate that this behavior (subject to growth within the perceptual control system and the effector system) does not become precise until quite late in infancy. The classic study is that of Cruikshank (1941). Her experiment is shown schematically in Figure 4.19. In essence she presented infants with two objects of different size at two distances and counted the number of arm extensions that occurred toward the objects. She found that the infants, 5 to 6 months of age, would extend their arms toward the faraway object, even though the object was well out of reach. Since the infants tried to reach the object, either their perception of object distance, their perception of their own arm length, or both must have been in error.

Cruikshank (1941) and Brunswik (1956), her main interpreter, had no doubt that it was space perception that was defective. Indeed, neither of these researchers mentioned the possibility that faulty arm perception might be responsible—a surprising omission since the growth problems of the arm are much greater than those of the eye. Before getting into the nasty problem of trying to separate out the relative contributions of arm perception and object perception to the erroneous behavior of the infants, it might be well to ascertain that the behavior was indeed as erroneous as it initially seemed to be. The observed arm extensions might not indicate anything erroneous at all. The infant might extend its arm for a number of reasons other than to grasp an object lying within its field of view. How can we be sure that the extensions observed in this kind of experiment are really attempts to grasp the object? How in fact can we be sure that arm extensions in any kind of experiment are really attempts to reach and grasp an object that happens to be in the visual field at the time? An adult who points at the moon is not reaching for it. Pointing and reaching both involve arm extension; one must therefore be certain that the *intent* of an extension is reaching, and not pointing or some other activity. The point is that different functional behaviors use the same behavioral components. It is risky to infer one particular functional behavior from the occurrence of a behavioral component that is used in a variety of situations.

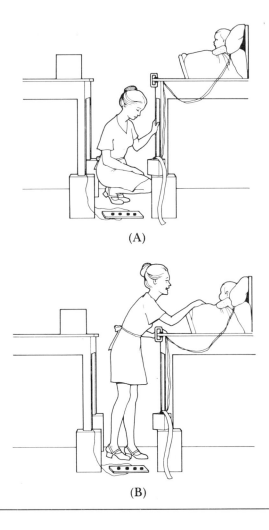

(A)

(B)

How can we be sure that the infants in Cruikshank's experiments were really trying to reach the distant object? One way is to look for other behavior components that are characteristic of reaching. In the normal reaching of infants of the age studied by Cruikshank, one can observe finger adjustments prior to contact with the object and hand closure simultaneous with arrival at the object. One could thus inspect the behavior of the infants for the presence of these other components that occur in the course of reaching for objects that are attainable. If they do not occur, one could not conclude that the infants were trying to reach the object. On balance, it would seem more reasonable to conclude that the arm extension indexed some other behavior. One could also observe the behavior of the infants after the arm extension.

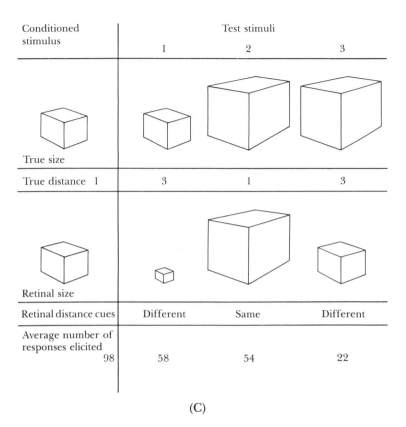

Conditioned stimulus	Test stimuli		
	1	2	3

True size

True distance 1	3	1	3

Retinal size

Retinal distance cues	Different	Same	Different
Average number of responses elicited 98	58	54	22

(C)

FIGURE 4.18   Bower investigated size constancy by using cubes of different sizes placed at different distances from the infants. The conditioned stimulus was a 30-cm cube at 1 meter, and the test stimuli were 30- or 90-cm cubes at a distance of 1 or 3 meters away. (A) The experimental setup. The experimental procedure began with conditioning, and the response was reinforced by a "peekaboo" (B). The conditioned response, head turning, closed a microswitch that operated a recorder. After training, a screen was placed between the infant and the stimulus area each time the stimulus object was changed. (After photographs by Sol Mednick.) (C) This figure shows how the test stimuli were related to the conditioned stimulus in various respects and the results obtained. From these results, it would seem reasonable to conclude that distance perception contributes to the discriminations shown. (After "The Visual World of Infants" by T. G. R. Bower. Copyright © 1966 by Scientific American, Inc. All rights reserved.)

(A) Small object within reach

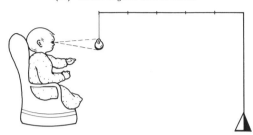

(B) Large object well out of reach

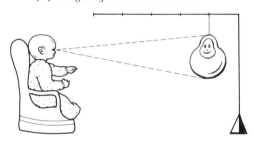

(C) Small object well out of reach

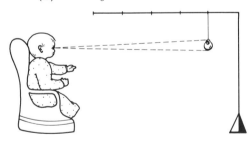

FIGURE 4.19 Cruikshank's (1941) study of the development of reaching. In A and B, the stimulus object subtends the same visual angle. In B, although the object is much larger, it is set at a distance proportionately farther away so that it projects the same size of retinal image for the infant. (An object four times as large would be put four times farther away.) Situations A and B elicited much the same number of reaching attempts. Situation C, with the small object at the farther position, elicited somewhat fewer reaches.

If the infants were trying to reach the distant object, the arm extension would necessarily fail. One might then expect to see some signs of disappointment or upset at the failure. Lack of upset, along with lack of grasping components, would seem to indicate that the behavior is not reaching. Unfortunately, these measures were not taken in Cruikshank's study, nor do they seem to have been taken in any follow-up study. However, informal observations by a number of individuals would suggest that the arm extensions toward out-of-reach objects by 5-month-old infants are not true reaching. These arm extensions are not accompanied by hand shaping; their termination with no grasping does not produce upset; the infants tend to keep their arms extended toward the object; and the attempts are usually accompanied by "pleading" vocalizations. One could interpret these arm movements as indicator gestures intended to affect the behavior of nearby adults, rather than as attempts to obtain the object without help. This interpretation could be tested quite easily. If correct, the behavior should disappear in the absence of adults, and appear again whenever attentive adults are around. If the infant can reach the object, the behaviors associated with the arm extensions should be quite different. Samples of the two behaviors are shown in Figure 4.20.

If this interpretation is correct, the Cruikshank experiment does not show that 5-month-old infants lack precise perceptual–motor maps. In addition, other investigators have found that reaching within reaching range is accurate around this age (White et al., 1964; Alt et al., 1973). Thus, we can tentatively conclude that perceptual–motor mapping is complete by this age. This does not tell us how the map has been constructed, of course, but simply that we should study infants younger than 5 months if we wish to get a handle on the process of construction.

Bower (1972) studied reaching in infants in the second week of life. He presented infants with two objects—one just out of reach, the other twice as far away. The near object elicited twice as many arm extensions as the distant object, indicating some discrimination of distance. However, there was no difference between the behaviors elicited by the two objects, except frequency. In line with the discussion above, we apparently must conclude that the infants were trying to reach the distant object, which indicates that at this young age there is as yet no precise perceptual–motor mapping. The interim period between 2 weeks and 5 months is bare of data. We simply do not know when the behavior becomes precise, since the relevant experiments have simply not been done.

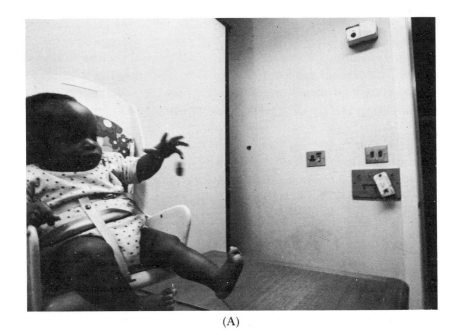

(A)

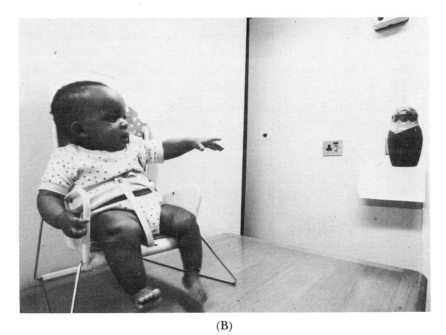

(B)

FIGURE 4.20   (A) An infant reaching for an object within reach. (B) An infant "reaching" for an object well out of reach. (Photographs by Jennifer Wishart.)

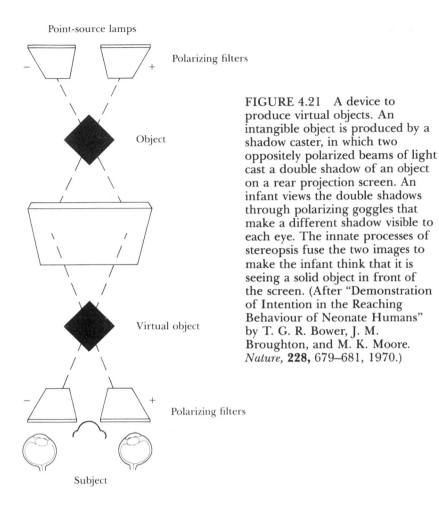

Point-source lamps

Polarizing filters

Object

Virtual object

Polarizing filters

Subject

FIGURE 4.21 A device to produce virtual objects. An intangible object is produced by a shadow caster, in which two oppositely polarized beams of light cast a double shadow of an object on a rear projection screen. An infant views the double shadows through polarizing goggles that make a different shadow visible to each eye. The innate processes of stereopsis fuse the two images to make the infant think that it is seeing a solid object in front of the screen. (After "Demonstration of Intention in the Reaching Behaviour of Neonate Humans" by T. G. R. Bower, J. M. Broughton, and M. K. Moore. *Nature,* **228,** 679–681, 1970.)

Some points are to be made in connection with this experiment. First of all, the infants did reach out for the objects. Since neither infants nor objects were moving, so that there was therefore no possibility of optical expansion information, some or all of the other space-specifying variables were being responded to and were specifying position in depth. The most likely variables would be motion parallax and binocular parallax. Bower et al. (1970b) did an experiment in which only binocular parallax was available to the infants. The experimental setup is shown in Figure 4.21. All of the infants in the study (all in their second week of life) reached out for the intangible, binocularly created object. This demonstrates that, by this age, binocular parallax specifies objects in depth. To be sure, it does not specify with perfect accuracy, but at least extension in depth is specified. There are thus at least two variables that specify position in depth to very young infants—binocular parallax and optical expansion pattern.

A second feature of the binocular experiment may suggest a way in which absolute distance perception could be attained. All of the infants were surprised and upset when their hands reached the location of the intangible object and failed, of course, to make contact with it. The upset was much greater than the upset observed in the Bower (1972) experiment, where the infants failed to contact the object because the object was out of reach. Also, whereas the rate of reaching dropped off in the out-of-reach case, it stayed high in the binocular-object case. This might be taken as an indication that the infants know why they failed in the out-of-reach case; they know that their hands had not reached the position where the object was. In the binocular object case, the infants know that their hands had reached the object location; therefore, they could not comprehend their error. If infants are able to detect the conjunction of hand and object, they can obviously detect errors and, therefore, possibly correct them. This sort of error correction could produce perfectly accurate behavior *with no calibration of the perceptual system or the motor system.* Each of these systems could remain "erroneous" without detracting from the accuracy of performance at all, provided an error-detecting and error-correcting mechanism is built in, as these two experiments would suggest.

An hypothesis very similar to this has been advanced by Held, who has performed a number of ingenious experiments designed to demonstrate its validity (Held and Hein, 1963; Held and Bauer, 1967). If a correcting mechanism is truly operative in infants, then the problem of absolute space perception is no problem at all. The mechanisms sensitive to binocular parallax, motion parallax, and the optical expansion pattern can specify the relative positions of objects very precisely in very young infants. The processes of adjustment would ensure that accurate relative position perception could be converted into accurate spatial behavior, provided the effector in use (the hand, say) could be seen in the same visual field as the object it was directed against. Held has performed numerous experiments to show that sight of the effector organs is necessary for accurate spatial behavior (absolute space perception) in cats and monkeys.* Although the experiments Held has performed would not be possible with human infants, there is no reason to doubt that similar results would be obtained if the experiments were performed. The factor that makes a correcting mechanism necessary is growth, and humans grow more than either cats or monkeys; thus they have an even greater need of a calibration mechanism to allow them to discount the changes caused by growth.

A mechanism of this sort could also be used to adjust perception of radial position. A stationary infant, uncertain of the precise position off the straight ahead of an object, could nonetheless get its hand to the object if it could use sight of hand and object together as an error-correcting signal. There is evidence that infants can and do make such adjustments. However, the process is developmentally complex, as we shall see in Chapter 6.

Recently, von Hofsten (1976) has proposed that none of the above is necessary, that there is indeed a built-in link between eye and hand, in particular between eye growth and arm growth, so that a given convergence angle determines a given arm extension invariantly during growth (see Figure 4.22). He has found that infants wearing converging or diverging prisms, which alter the convergence angle required to fixate an object at a given distance, make errors in reaching, errors that they do not correct. Other researchers found adjustment in similar situations (Field, 1976; see also pp. 89–93); however, their studies were not as well controlled as von Hofsten's. The picture is even more complicated in the case of adjustment to prisms producing errors in perception of radial direction, where ability to correct seems to change with age (Dunkeld and Bower, 1981). We will postpone discussion of this developmentally complex matter until Chapter 6.

So far, the discussion in this chapter has focused on visual perception of distance. This focus is traditional; few investigators have ever looked at any other way of perceiving distance. Despite this, there are other ways of detecting distance. For many species, audition is the prime distance receptor system. Auditory information can specify distance in two ways. The first and less important way depends on the increasing decline in the energy (and hence perceived loudness)

---

*Walk (1969) has reported results suggesting that sight of the hand is not necessary for perception of absolute distance in the context of reaching in monkeys—at least if one considers only initial reaches. This raises the possibility that the process of adjustment to growth is initially genetically preprogramed. However, this seems unlikely for most postnatal growth, since this is subject to environmental vicissitudes.

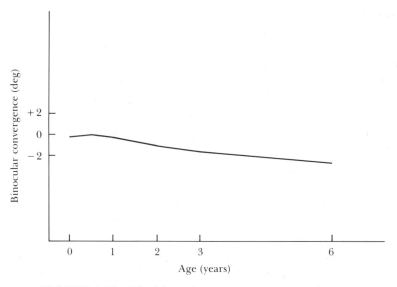

FIGURE 4.22   The binocular convergence at arm's
length for different age groups. (After "Binocular
Convergence as a Determinant of Reaching Behaviour in
Infancy" by C. von Hofsten. *Perception*, **6,** 139–144, 1976.)

of a sound wave at a point as that point increases its distance from
the sound source. It is thus possible, if we know the loudness of a
sound source at a given distance, that we could compute how far away
it was at any time from changes in perceived loudness. If we ourselves
could move, we could use the change in loudness consequent on movement to work out distance just as we can with visual input (see Figure
4.7). However, neither the dynamic nor the static use of perceived
loudness as an indicator of distance is likely to be frequently possible,
since there are few objects in the world that constantly emit an un-
changing volume of sound. The only study I know of that looked at
adult ability to make sense of this kind of information found that
utilization was rather poor, perhaps reflecting its infrequent utility
(Brunswik, 1956).

   A far more important source of information about object position
is echo location. Many organisms depend entirely on an echo-location
system to detect objects. Bats are a good example (Griffin, 1960). It
is known too that some blind adults can use echoes to detect objects
(Supa, et al., 1944; Cotzin and Dallenbach, 1950). The psychophysics
of echo location are quite simple. A sound is emitted by the perceiving
organism; the sound radiates out and is reflected back by any object

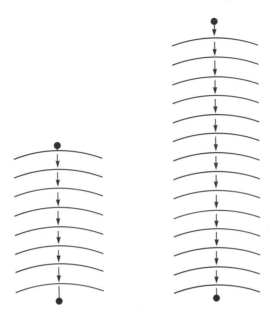

FIGURE 4.23   The farther away an object is, the longer it will take for an echo to return from it.

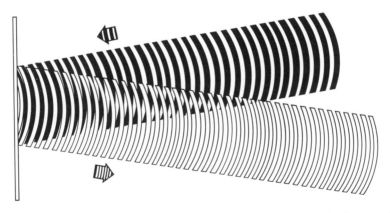

FIGURE 4.24   Interference patterns can be created between echoes and emissions, giving another source of information about distance.

it hits. Distance can be specified by the time interval between emission of the sound and return of the echo (see Figure 4.23). If the emissions are frequent and the distance is short, interference patterns may be available to signal distance (see Figure 4.24). Distance is not the only information that can be specified in an echo. The size of the reflecting

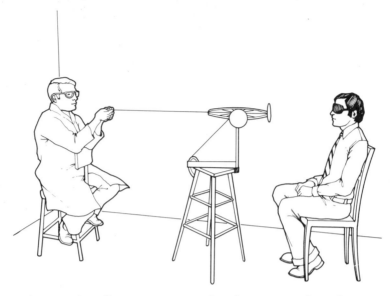

FIGURE 4.25   The apparatus used to demonstrate that echo can specify size as well as distance. The standard and comparison disks were mounted on a wheel that could be silently rotated by the experimenter. The disks were made of ¼-inch fir plywood and painted with sand-textured paint to give a hard, diffuse reflecting surface. Later experiments by Rice and Feinstein (1965) showed that objects with area ratios as low as 1.07/1 could be discriminated by blind subjects. (After "Sonar System of the Blind" by W. N. Kellogg. *Science,* **137,** 399–404, 1962. Copyright © 1962 by the American Association for the Advancement of Science.)

object can also be specified; the larger the object, the greater the echo; magnitude of echo, along with distance information, can clearly specify size. Radial direction will also be specified, as in normal auditory localization.

Adults can certainly make use of this kind of information (see Figure 4.25). Can infants? There are some data indicating that some blind infants do elaborate a system of echo location. One study observed this kind of behavior in a 16-week-old infant who had been blind from birth (Bower, 1979a). This infant produced a very large number of sharp clicking noises with his lips and tongue, noises never made by sighted babies of this age. When a large ball was dangled in front of him, completely silently, he turned to "look" at it; and when it was silently moved to a new position, after a vocalization interval of clicks, he again turned toward it. Similar behavior was also observed in a 13-

month-old blind infant. Since both were blind, the inference that they were using the information in the echoes is tempting.

While fascinating, these data leave open a number of issues. Why, for example, is it that only two of the twenty or so blind infants I have worked with ever developed an echo-location system? Of what use would the system be in normal development? The answers to these two questions may be interlinked. Let us begin with the latter, the utility question. We can define the utility of any echo-location system with reference to the frequency of its emitted sound component. The higher the frequency of the emitted sound, the smaller is the object that will produce an echo; with low frequencies like those of the voice many objects will be too small to be detected. The system will thus only be useful in detecting the most gross features of the environment, features useful for mobility to be sure, but not useful to an immobile infant. This lack of utility may contribute to the lack of development, our first question, although general environmental features could also be involved; most home furnishings would simply absorb rather than reflect any sounds designed to produce echoes while the high level of ambient noise from household appliances, hi-fi equipment, and the like would obviously further reduce the possibilities of echo location, simply by swamping the echoes.

An attempt to find a way around these problems led me to use a very sophisticated echo-location device, the sonic guide (see Figure 4.26). This device, designed by Professor Leslie Kay and developed and manufactured in spectacle form by Wormwald Vigilant, was modified for me for use with infants by Telesensory Systems Inc. of Palo Alto, California. The guide is an ultrasonic echo-location system that continuously irradiates the environment with ultra-sound and converts reflections from objects into audible sound. Ultrasound was chosen because the size of an object that will produce an echo is inversely proportional to the frequency of the sound source. Ultrasound will thus generate echoes from smaller objects than will audible sound. The conversion from ultrasound to audible sound codes the echo in three ways. The pitch of the audible signal is arranged to indicate the distance of the object from which the echo came—high pitch means distant objects; low pitch, near ones. The amplitude of the signal codes for the size of the irradiated object (loud = large, soft = small), and texture of the object is represented by the clarity of the signal. In addition, the audible signal is stereophonic so direction to the object is perceived by the difference in time of arrival of a signal at the two ears.

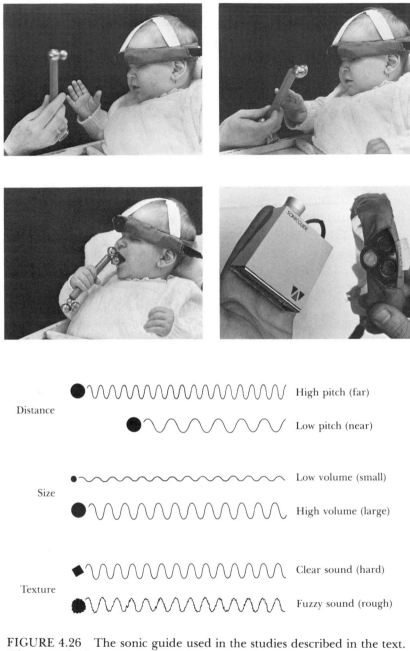

FIGURE 4.26   The sonic guide used in the studies described in the text. (Photographs from *New Scientist,* February 3, 1977.)

I must emphasize that this device is an entirely man-made system. Human beings have no evolutionary history of using information like this. In terms of the specific sensory decoding structures that could have been built in to the human organism in the course of evolution, no child using this device would be thought to have any possible evolutionary head start. Any utilization would have to be based on slow, gradual learning, an option we have reason to be pessimistic about (see above). The results in the first session were thus rather astonishing.

The subject was a 16-week-old infant, born prematurely and suffering from bilateral retrolental fibroplasia. At the time of initial testing, there was no sign of visual function at all. At the age of 16 months, the scar tissue in one eye peeled back to reveal a peripheral crescent of intact retina in one eye. I think it unlikely that this sliver of retina was involved in the early testing, buried as it was under a layer of scar tissue. The infant was in generally good shape. His sensorimotor development was better than that of the average blind infant. He would, for example, reach for noise-making objects, albeit inaccurately.

In the first session, a silent object was introduced and moved slowly to and from the infant's face, close enough to tap him on the nose. On the fourth presentation, we noticed convergence movements of the eyes. These were not well controlled but the eyes were converging as the object approached and diverging as the object receded. On the seventh presentation, he interposed his hands between his face and the object. This behavior was repeated several times. He was then presented with objects moving to the right and left; he tracked them with head and eyes and swiped at the objects. The smallest object presented was a 1-cm cube dangling on the end of a wire, which the infant succeeded in hitting four times.

His mother stood the infant on her knee at arm's length and chatted to him, telling him what a clever boy he was. The infant was facing her and wearing the sonic guide. He slowly turned his head to remove her from the sound field, then slowly turned back to bring her in again. This behavior was repeated several times to the accompaniment of immense smiles from the infant. All three observers had the impression that he was playing a kind of peekaboo with his mother, and deriving immense pleasure from it. This infant's subsequent development has been described elsewhere (Bower, 1977a; Bower, 1979a).

The early facility shown by this infant is not unique. I have examined eight other infants, all of whom showed a rapid ability to pick up the spatial information provided by the guide (see, e.g., Bower, 1979a).

Such results, while heartening to the applied developmental psychologist, pose an immense theoretical puzzle. How is it that the infants pick up the information so quickly? Is it very rapid learning? Is contact with an object the reinforcement that allows the infant to decode the information presented at its ears? This is an unlikely explanation, given all that we have said about perceptual learning in the young infant. One study attempted to rule out this explanation by presenting approaching objects to sighted infants in the dark. The infants were wearing guides so that, from the point of view of information available, they were in the same state as a blind infant suddenly provided with a guide. Since there was no therapeutic need to make sure that these infants could decode the sonic information, the object was presented without contact, without any possible reinforcement. Despite this, some of the infants showed full-scale avoidance responses, as rapidly as any blind infant (Aitken, 1981). There is thus no way in which learning could be involved.

If learning is not involved, can we assume an innate ability to respond to sonic guide information? If we do, we must reconsider the meaning of the word *innate*. Under some circumstances, a perfectly rational case can be made for saying that any given sensory or perceptual capacity is innate. The circumstances are that the information required is invariant during growth and that it has been invariant during all of the millenia of evolution. Only if the latter is true can we begin to imagine how organisms would evolve structures to pick up the information in question. It is this latter requirement that the sonic guide signally fails to meet. The sonic guide is an entirely man-made artifact. The information it provides is not in the least "natural," not at all like the information that is used by organisms who have evolved a natural echo-location system. How then is it possible for a sonic guide to be used so rapidly? We can get a beginning of an answer, I feel, if we reconsider the information that is used in early perceptual development. Thus far, we have emphasized the specific, sensory nature of the information available to the infant. We have treated the optical expansion pattern as just that, a change in the pattern of stimulation on the retina. However, it can be viewed in a different way, simply as a change over time (Lee and Lishman, 1977). The interesting point about that (see Figure 4.27) is that the resultant curve is not modality-specific, and could, in theory at least, be presented through any modality. What happens as an object approaches a sonic guide? There are two changes, a change in the magnitude of the signal and a change in pitch, both of which bear more than a passing

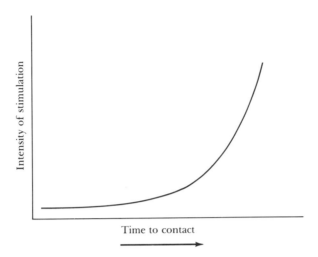

FIGURE 4.27   The approach of an object can be represented as a change in stimulation over time.

resemblance to the curve shown in Figure 4.27. The sonic guide does not provide the same information as a natural source, if we look at information at the level of sensory specifics. If, however, we look at information as a more abstract property of input, then we can see that the sonic guide, man-made as it is, provides the same information as do natural sources.

The above would imply that evolution has operated to produce in the newborn neural structures that are sensitive to the higher-order properties of stimulation—properties or variables that are not specific to a single sensory modality. Following Michotte et al. (1964), we can refer to these as *amodal variables;* if following J. J. Gibson (1950), we would refer to them as *higher-order variables*. It is clear that there is an amodal or higher-order variable that can specify approach of an object. We could argue that there is an amodal variable that specifies straight ahead. As we have seen, for olfaction, audition, and vision (Chapters 2 and 3), straight ahead is signaled by symmetry of stimulation at two receptor sites. Similarly, we could argue that not-straight-ahead is signaled by an amodal variable, asymmetry of stimulation.

Is there any advantage to this shift of emphasis? One clear advantage is that it gives us a way of accounting for the seeming success of the sonic guide with young infants. It also carries exciting implications for therapy with other sensorily handicapped infants: audition is as much or more susceptible to amodal analysis than is vision (Scott, 1979; personal communication, 1980). From a theoretical point of view, the most satisfactory aspect of the amodal response hypothesis is that it simplifies the long-term problem of accounting for innate abilities. It is quite clear that the complement of genes inherited by human beings does not carry enough information within it to account for the complexity of the human nervous system; indeed, there is not enough information to account even for the complexity of a single perceptual system. The DNA present in the nucleus of the fertilized egg may at most code a few million proteins. There is little variation between mouse, chimpanzee, and man. If we recall that the visual system of man has more than 9 million synaptic connections, we can see how unlikely it is that each of these connections is formed by a specific, individual protein match. The most important data on this point, for me anyway, are those reviewed by Changeux and Danchin (1976); working with populations of genetically identical organisms, investigators have found marked differences in the neural organization of the sensory areas. Since these organisms were genetically identical, they offer a direct disproof of any straightforward protein match theory; clearly, environmental influences, as yet undescribed, are modulating the processes of gene expression.

However, the genes could cope with amodal structures of the type postulated here. A single symmetry–asymmetry detector, receiving inputs from all modalities, would require less genetic information than would multiple detectors. There is some evidence that there are units in the nervous system that respond to amodal input (Fishman and Michael, 1973; Murata et al., 1965). The existence of such structures allows us to reconcile the level of ability demonstrable in the newborn with the considerable amount of brain growth that occurs after birth. That growth could be responsible for fleshing out the rather skeletal view of the world that is conveyed by amodal variables.

The analysis offered here has important implications for the problem of intersensory coordination. We discuss that problem in Chapter 5.

5

Object Perception

Thus far, we have been discussing objects only as things in space. We have considered how the infant comes to locate objects in space, but we have not considered how the infant comes to see objects as objects. This is not a meaningless question. There is a profound problem to be worked out in relation to why we see *things* rather than the spaces between them. Illustrations like those shown in Figure 5.1 indicate the nature of the problem. As we look at those figures, we see segments

(A)

(B)

FIGURE 5.1 Figures such as these alternate
spontaneousely. (A) "Sun and Moon" by M. C.
Escher (1961). In this figure we sometimes see the
white birds as birds, whereas at other times they
become spaces between the gray birds. They
alternate between being object and background.
(From the collection of C. V. S. Roosevelt,
Washington, D.C.) (B) Similarly, this figure
alternates between being a white cross on a black
background and a black cross on a white
background.

of them now as things and now as spaces between things. Why is it that in our normal environment we do not make such errors? How do we predict as well as we do that things are things and the empty spaces between them are in fact empty?

The Gestalt psychologists worked out a set of rules that human adults seem to use to define objects in an array. There were many such rules (well over 100 in one count) formulated in the heyday of Gestalt psychology (Helson, 1933), but most of these are of no great importance. Three major rules include many of the others as special cases. They are called common fate, good continuation, and proximity. The rule of *common fate* states that, in any array, those contours that move together along a common path of movement will be seen as the external edges of a single moving object (see Figure 5.2A). Common fate is a rule that can be applied not only to an array that contains moving objects but also to a stationary array seen by an organism that is moving itself (see Figure 5.2B). This rule is of no use to a stationary observer looking at a stationary array. The rules of good continuation and proximity, by contrast, are specific to a stationary array and a stationary observer. *Good continuation* states that the contours within a visual array, which can be described by the same equation in a coordinate system, will be seen as contours of a single object. In fact, the rule requires that some more complex factors be taken into account. As Figure 5.3 shows, location in the third dimension is a necessary prerequisite to applying the rule of good continuation. The same constraint does not apply to the rule of *proximity*, which states that, in any array containing more than two contours, the contours that are closer than average will be seen as contours of a single unit. Some examples of this are shown in Figure 5.4.

These rules are extremely effective in predicting which units adults will see in an array. They are psychophysical rules that predict what will be seen from the characteristics of the stimulation at the eye. One might expect that the rules would be valid and useful in predicting the true units in an array. Brunswik (1956) tested the utility of these laws in an ingenious experiment. He took a large number of photographs of everyday objects in normal surroundings and then measured the separations between contours. He used the rule of proximity to predict where the objects actually were in the photographs. The rule was useful, but not *very* useful since its application led to a number of errors (see Figure 5.5). A similar analysis carried out for good continuation turned out to be slightly more useful. Common fate has not been analyzed in this way. It seems unlikely that it could ever lead

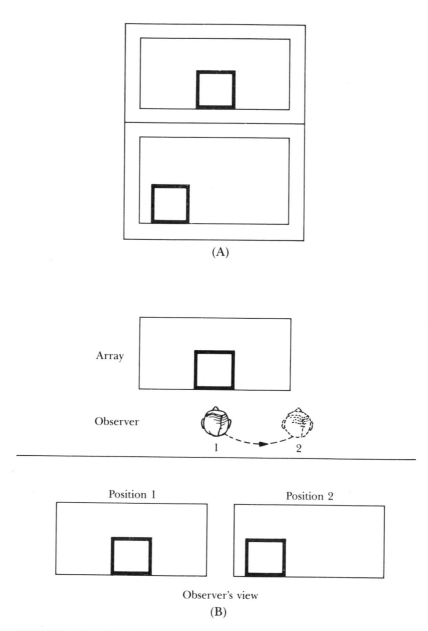

FIGURE 5.2   The rule of common fate. (A) When the thick lines move together along a common path of movement to their new position, they will be seen as the external edges of a single object that has moved to the left. (B) When the observer moves, his view of the contours changes. As the observer moves to the right, the contours move to the left. The rule of common fate holds in this situation also, and the contours are seen as a single object.

FIGURE 5.3   This figure is not seen as a triangle by adults unless a pencil or similar object is placed in front of the gaps. The pencil occludes information that the triangle is not complete, allowing good continuation to operate.

This is seen as four vertical columns.

This is seen as four horizontal rows.

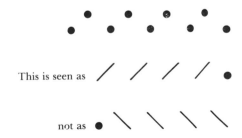

a   b   c   d   e   f
● ●   ● ●   ● ●

This is seen as three pairs, ab, cd, and ef; bc and de are never seen as pairs.

This is seen as

not as ●

FIGURE 5.4   The rule of proximity.

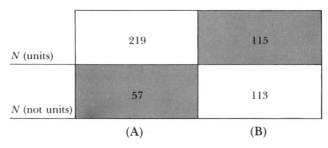

FIGURE 5.5 The shaded boxes indicate the number of times application of the rule of proximity led to incorrect predictions in Brunswik's (1956) experiment. (A) Contours closer than average. (B) Contours farther apart than average.

to errors, except in very special cases. Although its utility has not been analyzed, it seems likely that it is the most useful of the three rules.

The Gestalt psychologists argued vigorously that these three rules could not be learned—that they must be built into the structure of the infant's nervous system. Their reasons for this were complex and relied heavily on inferences from physics and physiology. They did not rely on direct observation of infants. Despite this, their arguments were almost universally accepted (Hebb, 1949). The only person who offered an alternative explanation was Brunswik (1956), who argued that these rules could be learned by trial and error in infancy.

Recently, a few experiments have been carried out to discover whether infants perceive units and whether the rules they use are in accord with the Gestalt rules. The evidence that infants do segregate their environment into units is clear. A large number of studies on the eye-fixation behavior of infants has shown that infants will fix on the external contours of objects in their visual field. If the objects are moved, the infants will track them. If, after moving together, the contours of an object break up (see Figure 5.6) and begin to move independently, very young infants will display massive surprise. This indicates that the common motion (common fate) had specified for them a single unit (Bower, 1965b). There have also been attempts to find out whether proximity and good continuation operate at a similarly early age. A surprise paradigm was used to study the effectiveness of these rules with infants. The infants were presented with an array like that shown in Figure 5.7. Adults seeing such an array tend to see it as two units—*ab* and *c*. After some time, one of the dots, either *a* or *c*, was made to move while the other two stayed stationary.

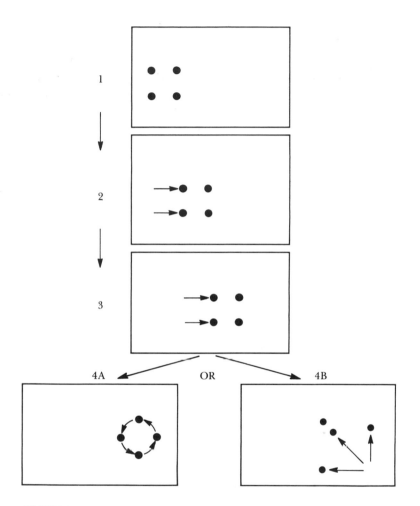

FIGURE 5.6 Event 4A is *consonant* with the information given in frames 1 to 3. The dots still move on a common path. Event 4B *contradicts* the information given before, since the dots now move independently after having moved together. When 3-week-old infants are shown the first sequence and then one of the other two events, the infants shown the *contradictory* event are more surprised than those shown the *consonant* event.

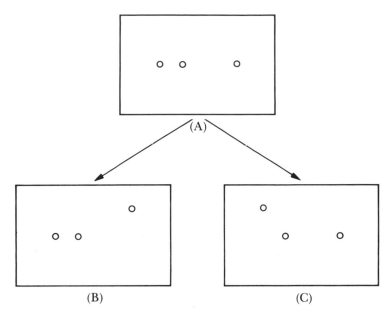

FIGURE 5.7   Application of the rule of proximity to picture A makes picture C surprising, whereas picture B is not surprising. Infants do not see things in this way until near the end of the first year.

It was argued that if the infants see *a* and *b* as a unit, the movement of *a* should surprise the infants more than the movement of *c*, since it results in the breakup of unit *ab*. Surprise was measured by cessation of sucking. It was argued that the more surprising event should lead to a longer cessation of sucking. To the experimenter's own surprise, there was no effect of proximity until very nearly 1 year of age (Bower, 1965b). These results thus do not at all support the Gestaltist claims, but rather are in accord with Brunswik's interpretation.

A somewhat different experimental method was used to assess the validity of the rule of good continuation (Bower, 1967a). Infants of around 6 weeks of age were presented with a display consisting of a black wire triangle with a bar over it, like that shown in Figure 5.8A. They were trained to emit a conditioned response in the presence of this display. After a brief training period, the infants were shown one of the four stimuli shown in Figure 5.8B. These figures were selected as possible ways of seeing the display they were originally trained with. If the infants perceived in accord with the rule of good continuation, they would perceive the training display, as adults do, as a triangle

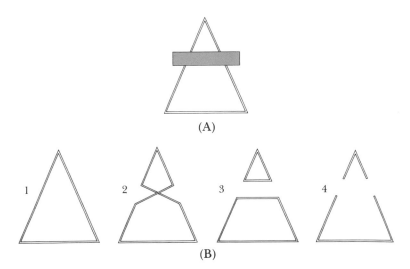

(A)

(B)

FIGURE 5.8   The completion experiment was conducted with these
objects. (A) The conditioned stimulus was a triangle with a bar attached to
it, thus interrupting its shape. (B) Of the test stimuli, 3 and 4 are more like
the conditioned stimulus than 1 and 2 are. Actually, infants seem to
complete objects as adults do, as shown by the fact that 1 was the most
effective stimulus. (After "The Visual World of Infants" by T. G. R. Bower.
Copyright © 1966 by Scientific American, Inc. All rights reserved.)

with a bar over it. If they do not perceive in accord with the rule of
good continuation, then they might think there was nothing where
the bar had been. In this case, they might have seen the training
display in any of the other three ways shown in Figure 5.8B. The
number of responses elicited by each display was tallied. The more
responses a display elicited, then the more that figure resembled the
training display. The results unambiguously favored the complete
triangle, indicating that the infants had seen the training figure as a
triangle with a bar over it. This shows that even 6-week-old infants
can use the rule of good continuation.

It thus seems that the Gestalt rules are not all innate; at least one
of them, proximity, develops very slowly, while common fate has been
shown to be effective at very early ages. It seems quite likely that a
mechanism for using the more valid common-fate information could
be built in, while the less useful rules for stationary displays could be
learned later on. An alternative possibility, to which we shall return,
is that the infants *could* respond to the rules for stationary displays
but do not, attending exclusively to the dynamic-movement infor-

mation. As we shall see later, there is more support for such an hypothesis than might at first appear.

Perhaps at this point the reader is beginning to feel restive about the experiments mentioned thus far. The experiments used to assess object perception were discrimination experiments. But surely *object* means something more than a discriminable unit in the visual field. To an adult, an object is not merely a discriminable unit akin to the discernible units in a drawing or photograph. An object is something solid and tangible; it can be grasped; it has a definite size; it can be hard or soft; and, if dropped, it will make a particular sort of noise. None of these properties is described by the Gestalt rules. Whereas the Gestalt rules may suffice to account for perception of units, there is nothing in them to account for the perception of the other, more distinctive properties of objects.

The Gestalt rules apply very well to marks on paper. They do not, however, tell us how we differentiate marks on paper from objects in the world—surely an important capacity. Tangibility, graspability, hardness, acoustic qualities, and specific size are all properties that differentiate real objects from representations. They sum up the quality that Michotte (1962) called "phenomenal reality." None of these properties is purely visual. Adults can predict the hardness of an object by eye, but hardness is a property that is more usually associated with the sense of touch, as are graspability and even size, as will be shown later in this chapter. Similarly, on the basis of visual information, adults can predict the sort of noise an object will make if dropped or struck; but noise is a property associated with the sense of hearing. The complex of object properties that define phenomenal reality is thus an intermodal complex involving several senses. Information is fed in through one sense—vision—specifying the information that would be fed in through other senses if they were utilized in the situation. When reality is detected by eye, it involves a prediction about information that is *potentially* available to other senses.

How does the eye predict properties such as hardness or tangibility? The psychophysics of visual tangibility have been worked out; Katz (1911) found that subjects will see surfaces of objects—tangible, contactable areas—whenever there is texture or microstructure within the area. If there is no texture or no variations in brightness within an area, the area is seen as empty and penetrable—the sort of area one could reach through or walk through without meeting any resistance (see Figure 5.9). If a texture or microstructure remains the same as long as the observer remains stationary, but changes when the observer

FIGURE 5.9 Film color. The white area has neither texture nor variations in brightness; it is seen as empty and penetrable.

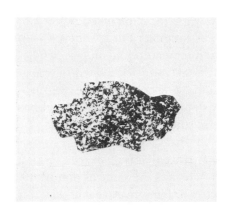

FIGURE 5.10 Surface color. Unlike the white area in Figure 5.9, this area seems hard and unyielding.

changes position, the area will tend to be seen as hard or unyielding (see Figure 5.10). If, by contrast, the texture and highlighting change spontaneously, while the observer is stationary, it will tend to be seen as liquid or foggy, yielding on contact, but different from the nothingness of an empty, untextured area. This is known as volume color and can be seen by looking, for example, at a puff of smoke. It is quite easy to produce and control perception of tangibility in adults. Although the information is presented visually, adult subjects perceive the situation so as to predict the intermodal consequences of the stimulus source.

Tangibility is not the most important of the properties listed above. Far more important for perception of the reality of an object is the dimension of graspability. Michotte showed adults pictures of objects

FIGURE 5.11 Adults can predict
with a good degree of accuracy
where the rear boundary of an object
is and what shape it will have, even if
the object is as unfamiliar as the one
shown here. (After "The Experienced
Continuations" by M. Johansen. *Acta
Psychologica,* **13,** 1–26, 1957.)

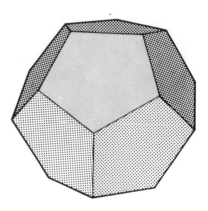

and asked them either to grasp the object or to insert another small
object within the pictured object. All of his subjects, according to his
own report, looked at him as if he were mad. A pictured object can
be seen, and indeed usually is seen, as tangible; but it is never seen
as graspable. What variables determine perception of graspability
then? Other phenomenal properties such as size are related to graspability but do not determine it. The most relevant correlate of graspability would seem to be three-dimensionality. A graspable object has
a top and a bottom, a left and a right, and a front and a back. The
critical dimension is obviously the front–back dimension.

A real, graspable object has a front surface that is all its own, unlike
the front surface of a pictured object, which is the same as that of the
paper, canvas, or whatever the object is drawn on. A real object also
has a perceptually distinct, if invisible, rear boundary that is just as
important as the front boundary in the context of action. When grasping an object, we curl our hands round *behind* the object, to contact
the rear boundary of the object. It is a matter of common observation
that adults can do this accurately; adults can predict where the rear
boundary of an object is and also what shape it will have (Michotte,
1962; Johansen, 1957) (see Figure 5.11).

What stimulus variables allow us to do this? Since it is a matter of
tridimensionality, we can draw on the information discussed in the
last chapter. Specification of a front surface standing free of adjacent
surfaces can be accomplished by motion parallax and binocular parallax. As we saw in the previous chapter, these variables can specify
with very high accuracy the relative position of planes in depth, which
is all that is needed to specify the separation of the front surface of
an object. The back surface is more difficult. In the case of some

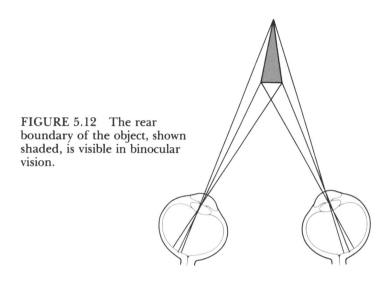

FIGURE 5.12   The rear boundary of the object, shown shaded, is visible in binocular vision.

objects, the location of the rear boundary of an object may be visible to binocular vision (see Figure 5.12) or to a single eye that is moved to pick up motion parallax. However, there are cases in which neither of these variables is present and yet subjects still distinctly perceive the invisible side of an object.

Michotte had a nice example of this with perception of a sphere. Subjects presented with a whole sphere report seeing a sphere. If the invisible side of the sphere is progressively sliced away (see Figure 5.13A), there comes a point where subjects report seeing a section of a sphere. According to Michotte, that point comes when the top-bottom/right-left boundary of the sphere cuts the surface of the sphere so that the subject can see that the surface does not continue on the same three-dimensional path (see Figure 5.13B). In the absence of this information, subjects apparently assume that the surface of an object will continue on the same path. Michotte explicitly links this kind of rule with the rule of good continuation. Subjects seem to operate the rule in three dimensions as well as in two dimensions. From the available information, it would seem that parallax information plus a rule of good continuation could account for perception of the rear boundary of objects, and thus for perception of graspability.

An intimate connection exists between perception of tangibility and perception of graspability. Presence of parallax variables at the edges of a bounded contour does not ensure perception of graspability, if

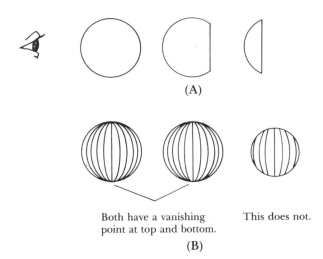

(A)

Both have a vanishing   This does not.
point at top and bottom.

(B)

FIGURE 5.13   If an observer is presented with a
sphere that is progressively cut away from behind,
as shown, there comes a point at which the subject
can *see* that it is not a sphere and that its rear
surface is not the same as its front surface. (A) Side
view. (B) Observer's view.

the information specifying tangibility within the contour is not simultaneously present. This can be demonstrated by using a binocular
shadow caster to project a shadow of an object (see Figure 5.14). If
one cuts a hole in the center of a screen and projects the shadow of
the screen binocularly onto another screen, the subject will only be
able to see two disks of light, one going to each eye. The edges of
these disks are binocularly disparate; this does not result in perception
of a disk in depth, however, but rather perception of a hole in a black
surface—something that no adult will try to grasp. If texture is put
in the hole, by contrast, it immediately takes on the appearance of a
textured *object*. Thus, parallax and texture variations are both required
for perception of an *object*.

Texture and parallax variables are visual stimuli that specify the
tactual properties of an object. At first sight, size might seem to be a
purely visual variable, giving no apparent intermodal predictions.
There certainly is a purely visual sense in which we can judge the size
of an object relative to other objects. However, size in the context of
an action is judged relative to the size of our own bodies or body parts.
The size of an object functionally means its size relative to our hands
or mouths. Adult subjects are able to make judgments of the size of

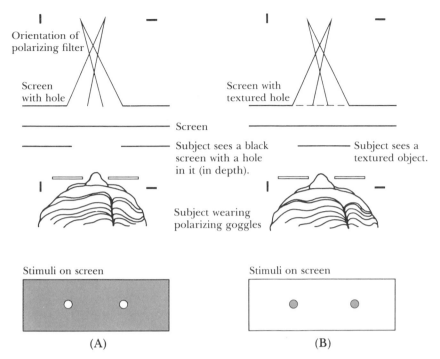

FIGURE 5.14   If one sets up a binocular shadow caster (see Figure 4.21) and projects two luminous disks onto a screen (one going to one eye, the other going to the other), a subject will see a black screen with a hole in it, in depth (A). If texture is put in the hole, the subject will see a textured object (B).

an object relative to their hands without having to look at hand and object simultaneously. Visual information is thus once again used to predict tactual information.

It has classically been argued that these intermodal predictions are learned. The sense of sight and the sense of touch are different senses, so the argument goes, and the only way one sense can come to predict the information potentially available to another sense is by associative learning. Chance tactile contact simultaneous with visual input will teach the developing child what visual inputs specify what tactual inputs—touch teaches vision. This argument was derived from discussion between adults. There was no inspection of infants or developing children involved in the theorizing. Recently, the theory has come under attack because it apparently fails to predict the results of experiments done on adults (Rock and Harris, 1967). It has been found that when vision and touch are put into conflict, vision invariably dominates. Thus, if an adult subject looks through a minifying lens that makes an object look smaller and simultaneously grasps the object, he feels the object to be the same size as he sees it to be. The subject grasps the object through a cloth, so that he has no clues to the size of the object from the sight of his minified hand. He is not aware of any conflict between vision and touch, and vision seems to dominate (see Figure 5.15). If touch were the teacher of vision, presumably the reverse would happen and the object seen would "grow" as soon as it was grasped. Rock and Harris report a number of other ingenious studies all pointing to the conclusion that, in adults, vision dominates touch and is, if anything, the teacher of touch.

The available studies on infants also contradict the idea that touch teaches vision. We have already described some studies that point in this direction. In the last chapter, we saw how visual information could specify the approach of an object so as to elicit a defensive reaction from very young infants (Bower et al., 1970a). The defensive reaction would imply that the infants expected a tactile input and were taking measures to protect themselves against it. The defensive reaction occurred, you will remember, when the input was purely visual, a shadow on a screen. On the other hand, when the input was purely tactual (a blast of air) and could have specified the approach of an object, no defensive reaction occurred at all. This result certainly is not in accord with traditional ideas. It suggests that vision can pick up hardness quite directly from the beginning.

In line with what was said in Chapter 4, we can argue that it is unlikely that an infant less than 2 weeks old could have been exposed to many situations where he learned to fear an approaching object and expect it to have tactile qualities. The only conclusion is that in humans there is a primitive unity of the senses, with visual variables specifying tactile consequences; further, this primitive unity is built into the structure of the human nervous system.

In an effort to test this hypothesis further, the original virtual-object experiment (a visible object that is empty air to the sense of touch) was repeated with a group of newborn infants (Bower et al., 1970b). It was not easy to do this, since the infants had to wear the polarizing goggles without fussing. Newborn infants do not reach for objects in the same way that older infants do; newborn infants will, however, reach out and grasp objects if they are supported so that their hands and arms are free to move to the objects in front of them.

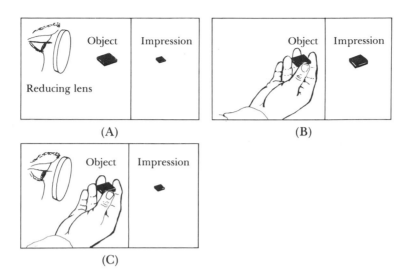

FIGURE 5.15 Vision dominates touch. A subject's impressions in various experiments involving the reducing lens are indicated. In some cases (A), the subject merely saw an object through the lens. In some (B), the subject only felt the object. And in others (C), the subject simultaneously saw the object and felt it, although he could not see his hand. (After "Vision and Touch" by I. Rock and C. S. Harris, Copyright © 1967 by Scientific American, Inc. All rights reserved.)

It was found that all the newborn infants touched and grasped real objects without any sign of being disturbed. They also grasped at empty air without upset when no visible object was present. The virtual object, however, produced a howl as soon as the infants' hands went to the location of the intangible object. Here too, then, we have evidence of a primitive unity of the senses. (Tactile input was absent in a situation where it was expected.) This unity is unlikely to have been learned, given the early age and the history of the infants studied.

These results do not support the notion that visual information can come to specify tactual properties only after a long period of apprenticeship. The youngest infant in these experiments was only 4 days old. Once again, in a Western culture at least, it is most improbable that infants of this age have experienced the tactual consequences of an approaching object. If they have, there is no particular reason why they should associate the tactual consequences with the visual input rather than with the concurrent air movement. Such arguments cannot *prove* that the coordination is not learned; one-trial learning is, after all, possible. But the subsequent history of the development of visual–tactual coordination would seem to argue against a learning-theory explanation.

Consider the virtual-object experiment (see Figure 4.21). The young infants showed some considerable degree of upset when their hands arrived at the location of the seen object but contacted nothing. This upset must reflect the violation of an expectancy that seen objects will be tangible. If the expectancy were learned through chance contacts with objects, one would assume that its strength would increase as the infants grow older and have more contacts with objects. This apparently does not happen, however.

If one studies the reactions of older infants to the virtual object, it is hard to see any change in behavior up to the age of approximately 6 months (Bower et al., 1970c). There is the same degree of upset and continued persistent attempts to grasp the ungraspable object. However, around 6 months of age the quality of the upset and the behavior change. The infants are still startled by the virtual object; however, their grasping behavior is quite different. Younger infants close their hands on the virtual object and, indeed, usually end up with their hands clenched at the object locus. Older infants stop the grasp action with their hands still open. One may also observe in older infants a variety of behaviors such as prolonged hand regard, rubbing the hands together, and banging the hand on a surface—all interspersed with further single attempts to grasp the virtual object. One could say that the infants were trying to verify that their hands were really working and had not suffered a loss of sensitivity. If one persists in observing the infant in this situation, one can usually then observe a range of exploratory *visual* behaviors. For example, the infant may sway its head from side to side through an extreme arc, thereby picking up the maximum amount of motion parallax. The motion parallax thus generated is the opposite of normal motion parallax (see Figure 5.16) and is highly abnormal visually. The infant will usually then stop reaching for the virtual object. If presented with new objects in that situation, infants will not reach out until they have tested the parallax properties of the objects; then they will only reach for those objects that have normal parallax properties.

Apparently, older infants faced with this abnormal situation first of all check out their hands and then check out the visual properties of the object. If the object is visually abnormal, they stop trying to reach for it. All of this is in marked contrast to the responses of younger

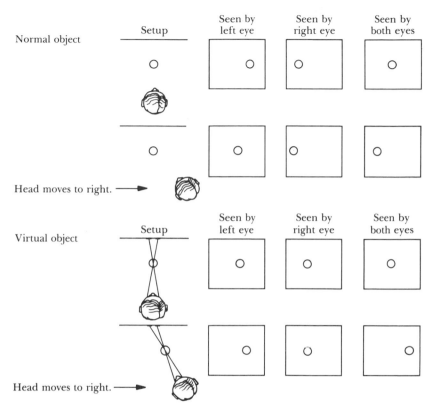

FIGURE 5.16 The motion parallax obtained with a binocular virtual object is extremely peculiar. The direction of shift consequent to a head movement is the opposite of that normally seen.

infants, who persist in their attempts to grasp the object; they are upset but seemingly unable to localize their upset. The older infants know something is wrong with the visual–tactual coordination and systematically check the tactual and then the visual halves of it. The responses of older infants are differentiated; they seem to be aware of vision and touch as separate modalities, unlike the younger infants, who apparently have a holistic, unanalyzed awareness of the situation. The younger infants have at their disposal all of the behaviors used by the older infants. They can show hand regard and they can generate motion parallax, but they do not do so in this situation. One must conclude that they have not yet differentiated the visible qualities of an object from its tangible qualities.

If one pursues development further yet, one can clearly observe the establishment of vision as the dominant sense. Infants between 4 and 5 months old will try to grasp a seen object and will continue to grasp an object that they cannot see. This indicates that both visual input and tactual input can specify the presence of an object to be grasped. Around 6 months of age, this is no longer true, however. An infant will drop an object that he is grasping if he can no longer see it. One only has to cover the infant's hand with a cloth for him to drop a grasped object. Indeed, if one places a tiny object in the palm of an infant's hand and the infant closes his hand over it, he will drop the object as soon as it is out of sight! It thus seems that one consequence of the differentiation of vision from touch is that touch loses its ability to specify the presence of an object and regains this ability only after a prolonged period. The process of recovery from differentiation is discussed more fully in the next chapter.

Thus far, we have pointed out that a real object or a virtual object with all of the visual attributes of a real object will be seen as real (graspable) by infants—even very young infants. Some further analysis of this has been undertaken and can be reviewed here. Adults clearly distinguish between objects and representations of objects. Infants do too (Fantz, 1961) and will only attempt to grasp an object that is defined by parallax variables. A representation of an object, a photograph or a drawing, will not be grasped at all. Infants will look at it but will make no attempt to grasp it. Thus, parallax variables are necessary for perception of graspability in infants. They are necessary but not sufficient. If infants are presented with a luminous disk in depth with no texture or microstructure, like adults, they will make no attempt to grasp the disk (Bower et al., 1970c). Furthermore, if infants are presented with an object that lacks a boundary of its own— whether top, bottom, front, or back—they will not attempt to grasp the object until they are 9 or 10 months of age (Piaget, 1937). One can make an object seemingly "disappear" by placing it in such a way that one of its boundaries becomes invisible (see Figure 5.17).

For infants, then, it seems that an object is a volume with its own bounds, defined by parallax and texture variables. The object thus defined is *seen* to be tangible; developmentally, visual tangibility precedes tactual tangibility, whereas undifferentiated visual–tactual concordance precedes both.

Thus far, we have discussed the ways in which the visual and tactual modalities can specify objects. We have not considered *audition* as a

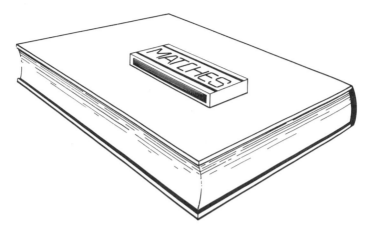

FIGURE 5.17   Until the age of 9 or 10 months, an infant will
not reach out to pick up the matchbox from the book. If the
infant is reaching for the box before it is placed on the book,
he will withdraw his hand and commonly grasp the book
instead, making no attempt to remove the box. It would seem
that the infant is unable to dissociate the two objects,
especially if the support (in this case, the book) is not much
larger than the object it is supporting.

modality that can specify the nature of objects. In the previous chapter,
we mentioned some experiments indicating that sounds can specify
objects to very young infants. Wertheimer (1961) showed that a newborn infant would *look at* a sound source, indicating that the infant
expected to see something. Similarly, infants will reach out to touch
a sound source presented in darkness, indicating that they expect to
grasp the thing specified by auditory stimulation (Wishart et al., 1978).
Aronson and Rosenbloom (1971) have been able to demonstrate an
even more complex degree of auditory–visual coordination. Their
apparatus is shown in Figure 5.18. The mother sits facing the infant,
who can see her through the soundproof screen. The infant can hear
the mother only through the loudspeakers. When the loudspeakers
are equally loud, the voice is heard as coming from its seen location.
If the volumes of the speakers are made unequal, the location of the
voice shifts toward the louder speaker and away from the seen location
of the mouth. This latter condition was very disturbing to a 3-week-
old infant, indicating that by the age of 3 weeks an infant expects a
voice to proceed from a mouth. The infant could tell when the voice

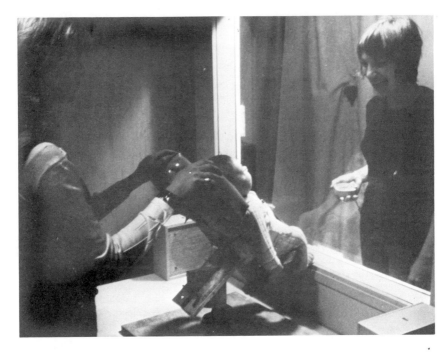

FIGURE 5.18   The mother-voice apparatus. (Photograph by Eric
Aronson.)

(a sound source) came from a different location than its mouth (a
visible source).* (See also Lyons-Ruth [1977] and Carpenter [1975].)

The question remains: Are these auditory–visual and auditory–tactual
responses built in or acquired? In the case of the coordination studied
by Wertheimer (1961), there is no question that acquisition was possible since the infant was newborn. This does not hold for the other
results, however, since the infants were older. Nevertheless, the pattern of development does not fit an acquisition hypothesis—but rather
a differentiation hypothesis.

Similar differentiation effects were found in the case of
auditory–manual coordination (Wishart et al., 1978). Infants up to 5
months of age were quite willing and able to reach out and grasp an
audible object presented in darkness. Older infants are increasingly

---

*This experiment has been criticized with the argument that the infants are trying
to orient in two directions at the same time. It is this conflict, rather than the dissociation,
that produces distress. This is a very important issue that should be resolved; as yet,
the necessary experiments have not been done.

less likely to do this; by the age of 7 months, the behavior simply cannot be elicited at all. The behavior does come back, of course, but it is not until the age of nearly 1 year that infants are as good again at reaching as they were at 5 months.

It is clear that these results suggest a novel approach to the problem of intersensory coordination (see Figure 5.19). Intersensory coordination has often been seen as the end point of learning processes by which input from one sense is associated with input from another sense (see, e.g., Piaget, 1936). On this view, the precocious unity of the senses described above would be impossible, as would the developmental pattern associated with it. While this associationist view has been sanctified by some authors (e.g., Dodwell et al., 1976) as the normal or traditional view, that is by no means the case. A more ancient tradition (dating at least from John the Scot in 1485) would propose that intersensory differentiation is the end product, with coordination the starting point. In more recent times, this view has been associated with Werner (1947) and E. J. Gibson (1969). The theories of Werner, Gibson, and myself are frequently seen as indistinguishable (Gratch and Breitmeyer, 1978). In fact, Werner's theory is quite different from Gibson's, of which my own is a direct descendant. Werner proposed that early perceptual experience is *synesthesic*. For example, a visual input produces visual experience, auditory experience, and tactual experience; an auditory input produces the same kind of synesthesic complex of hearing, seeing, and feeling. With development, according to Werner, response becomes specific to the nature of the input presented, so that, for example, an auditory input will elicit only an auditory experience. My own view, which, as I said, is a development of Gibson's, would argue that early perceptual experience is amodal rather than synesthesic. The infant that turns its eyes in the direction of a sound source does not do so because it has a visual and an auditory experience, but because it has neither; the early experience is of the form "Something is happening on my right/left," an experience that elicits total orientation of all receptors—eyes, ears, nose, and hands. Thus, looking at a sound source is equally likely in light and dark in the young infant (see, e.g., Mendelson, 1975; Bower, 1979b). With development the "something" in the proposition above is refined to "I hear a sound on my right/left," an experience that would not naturally elicit multimodal exploration.

I hope it is clear from all of the foregoing that one or another differentiation theory offers the only hope of a valid account of the development of intersensory coordination. Classic empiricism would

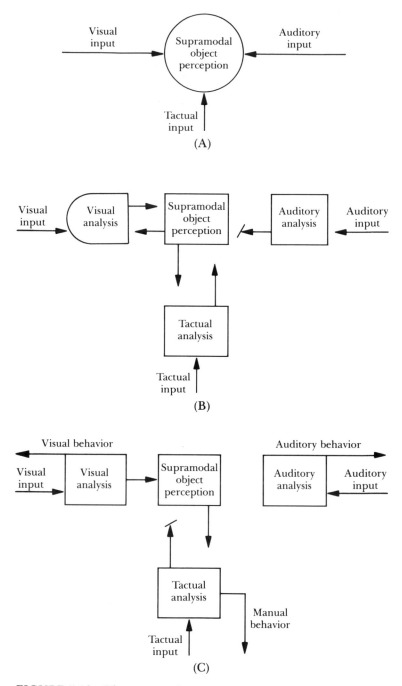

FIGURE 5.19   Three stages in sensory differentiation. (A) From birth to 4½ months. (B) From 4½ months to 6½ months. (C) From 6½ months on.

maintain that the senses are
associated together. Not only th
but also the pattern of change that h
a view. Reaching for noise-making obj
age (Wishart et al., 1978). Looking at soun
wise seems to decrease, if we compare the res
Haith (1976) with those of Wishart et al. (1978).
less clear. The data on auditory–visual and auditor
dination thus support a differentiation theory, as do
visual–manual coordination. In a differentiation theory, a se
does not exist as such in the perceptual world of the young i
A visible object is simply an event in a place, to be explored mu
modally or amodally. Thus, visually presented objects should elicit
compulsive manual exploration in young infants but not in older ones.
This does seem to be the case (Bower et al., 1970c; Schaffer and Parry,
1969, 1970). Some of the best evidence in favor of a differentiation
theory comes from studies of blind infants. What could an empiricist
make of data indicating that a blind infant will "look" at sound sources,
"look" at its hand, reach for noise-making objects, and then suddenly
stop all of these behaviors (Freedman, 1964; Urwin, 1973)?

Recently, several experiments have been published that purport to
contradict a differentiation theory of the development of intersensory
coordination. Those I am familiar with show the technical and conceptual difficulties involved in this area. Thus, Yonas and Pick (1975),
reviewing the work of Lasky (1973), present it as an embarrassment
to differentiation theory. Lasky found that the reaching of young
infants was less disturbed if they could not see their hands during
reaching than were older infants. This hardly seems to embarrass
differentiation theory. On a differentiation theory account, seen and
felt objects do not exist separately, nor therefore can the seen hand
be differentiated from the felt hand. With development, differentiation will occur and the infant will rely on the seen hand to reach a
seen object. Older infants, who have made the differentiation, will
thus be more disturbed than younger ones. Older infants will have
the problem of getting a proprioceptively-defined hand to a visually-
defined position, a problem that cannot arise with younger infants,
who have yet to differentiate the visual from the proprioceptive.

Field (1977) likewise believes that he has found data to embarrass
the differentiation theory. Some of his data seem to me to positively
support a differentiation theory. Thus, differentiation theory asserts
that older infants should be less likely than younger infants to grasp

initially separate but, with learning, are
initial state of the infant's awareness
as been described contradict such
cts in darkness declines with
d sources in darkness like-
lts of Mendelson and
The case in light is
-manual coor-
the data on
n object
fant.
i-

absence
he does
verging"
and a di-
ent in his
situation.
d's finding
tion. How-
se. Reaching
rising events
t experiment
that its hand
ne in a variety
object, so that
object." One can
nfant can adjust
se opportunities
Field's study. His

for be.. g
lack of results is the.. a differentiation
theory.

Dodwell et al., (1976) have also presented a pro-empiricist argument. Their study embodies a number of methodological and technical flaws (Bower et al., 1979). Perhaps its most serious weakness is that it relies on lack of behavior. It is, alas, only too easy to fail to elicit behavior from newborn infants. In general, in infant research, studies that demonstrate some behavior should carry more weight than studies that fail to demonstrate any behavior whatsoever.

Thus, all of these studies intended to contradict differentiation theory either support it or are irrelevant to it. While the issues involved are not simple, I trust this digression has made them a little clearer.

The choice then remains between a synesthesic theory and an amodal theory. The data most often cited in support of an amodal theory are the data that most embarrass it. I refer to the data on early imitation. It is quite clear that infants in the newborn phase can imitate a variety of gestures, including facial gestures (Dunkeld, 1978; Maratos, 1973; Meltzoff and Moore, 1977). Since the youngest subject in such experiments was, I believe, 17 minutes old, learning is clearly irrelevant. The fascinating point here is that the imitation is quite specific: when the model's mouth opens, the infant's mouth opens; when the model's eyes widen, the infant's eyes widen, and so on. This would seem to indicate a highly specific mapping between vision and the proprioceptive senses. Interestingly, however, the authors of the best study of imitation, Meltzoff and Moore (1977) interpret this as evidence of amodal coordination that is not sensorily specific. Their reasons for this are complex; I confess that I do not fully comprehend them. Nonetheless, it would appear that some of the data on early imitation point away from early sensory specificity toward an amodal perception of the world. Consider, for example, an earlier study published by Gardner and Gardner (1970). They found that there was a possibility of confusion in early imitation between formally similar behaviors, such as mouth opening and hand opening, or tongue protrusion and finger protrusion. These confusions suggested that the infant was picking up from a mouth-opening model, not the specific information (a mouth is opening), but the more abstract information (something is opening). Nonetheless, the overall pattern of data on early imitation supports the hypothesis that the early pickup of information by the young infant is a great deal more detailed than we would expect if the infant could respond only to amodal variables.

On balance I still incline to the amodal hypothesis, partly because it offers a better account of "the innate," partly because it seems to offer a better account of the changes in intersensory coordination that actually occur. The changes are more like those we would expect if development were the addition of detail to a skeletal beginning. Thus, the changes in response to the virtual object outlined above could be seen as the consequence of sufficient visual development for the visual abnormalities of the display to be recognized. They do not necessarily reflect the loss of the original coordination, as Werner, I think, would have to maintain. Imitation, too, does not seem to suffer a necessary decline. If one pools the data of all of the investigators who have looked at imitation (Maratos, 1973; Meltzoff and Moore, 1977; Dunkeld, 1978), it would appear that there is no steady decline from the repertoire of the newborn. The strongest evidence in favor of the Wernerian hypothesis of inevitable decline comes from studies of congenitally blind infants. However, there may be other reasons for this decline. The pattern of change in the blind again cannot possibly be seen as supporting an empiricist hypothesis. The choice remains between one or another of the differentiation hypotheses. At present we cannot say decisively which is the more valid.

One intermodal dimension we have not yet discussed in a developmental context is *object size*. Size poses a double problem to psychologists. The seen size of objects depends on the size of the image projected on the retina. Image size varies with the distance of an object from the eye (see Figure 5.20); despite this, adults at least see objects as maintaining a constant size at any distance. However, image size also varies with eye size, which changes during development (see Figure 5.21). Nevertheless, infants as well as adults can successfully adjust their hands to grasp objects at various distances. It is this motor adjustment of hand to object that poses the theoretical problem. In the act of grasping, it is not necessary for an adult to match up his hand separation to the size of an object he is attempting to grasp. He can reach out, open and close his hand on an object without waiting for visual feedback of any sort, which implies that the seen size of an object can be matched to finger–thumb separation. Visual information can be matched to manual information. Even very young infants are capable of this sort of matching (see Figure 5.22); despite this, it seems a priori very unlikely that this degree of organization could be built into the structure of the human brain.

In addition to the developmental problems posed by the growth of the eye, there are massive developmental problems posed by the growth of the hand (see Figure 5.23), which has a growth curve quite different from that of the eye. Held (1965) has argued that the matching of visual and proprioceptive extents is done visually. The infant looks at its hand in the visual field; it can thus see its hand and the object simultaneously. By watching its finger–thumb separation, the infant comes to calibrate its seen extent with its felt extent, so that, in time, when presented with a seen object, the infant can match its finger–thumb separation to the extent of the object, without having to look at both simultaneously. This theory is highly plausible, and Held has been able to back it up with a number of highly ingenious animal experiments (Held, 1965). It is certainly true that, in the context of reaching for objects, neonate humans will look at their hands in a way that is rarely observed in older infants (see Figure 5.24). It may well be that, in this kind of situation, infants are calibrating a seen extent with a felt extent. It may be that this kind of behavior is necessary for the accurate grasping behavior that is seen in very young infants. It would take an heroic effort, after the fashion of Wertheimer's study of auditory localization, to prove the point, and that effort has not so far been made. Although Held's theory seems very plausible, it might be worthwhile to make an effort to put this issue in a position beyond doubt.

The problem of size constancy is less complicated than that of size perception itself. It is generally agreed that any organism that has distance perception should be capable of size constancy. As we have

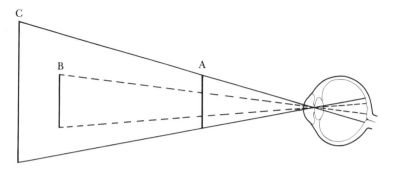

FIGURE 5.20   Size constancy. An adult will see that Object A is the same size as B and smaller than C, even though the retinal image of A is the same size as that of C and larger than that of B.

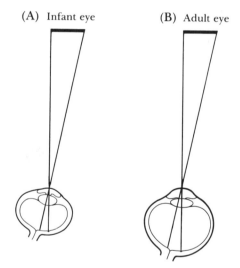

(A) Infant eye   (B) Adult eye

FIGURE 5.21   The infant eye (A) is much shallower than the adult eye (B), so that objects of the same size will project a larger retinal image to the adult eye than to the infant eye.

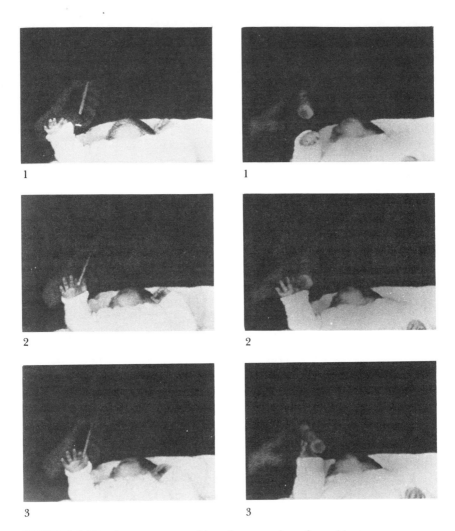

FIGURE 5.22   A neonate matching the seen size of an object to finger–thumb separation. (After "Object Perception in Infants" by T. G. R. Bower. *Perception,* **1,** 15–30, 1972.)

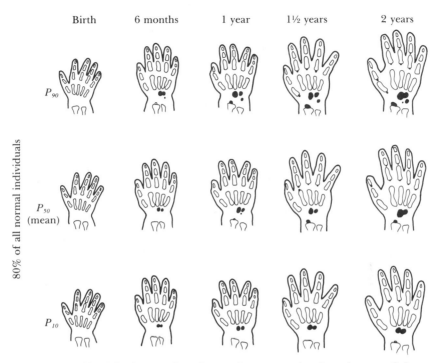

FIGURE 5.23   The human hand at various ages, showing change of size and change of components. P = percentile. (From Documenta Geigy Scientific Tables, K. Diem and C. Lentner, Eds. CIBA–Geigy, 1940.)

seen, young infants do perceive distance and they do seem to be able to use distance information to attain size constancy (Bower, 1966a; Bower et al., 1970a). It is usually assumed that size constancy can be attained by combining retinal image size information with distance information to yield a true size for any object. Something like this must indeed go on. However, it has also been assumed that at an early stage of development infants might be *aware* of retinal image size, distance, and then true size and that it is only with practice that they can go directly to true size without the other variables entering consciousness. This does not seem to be the case. Infants are apparently quite unaware of retinal image variables and, indeed, of distance variables in situations where they show an ability to appreciate "true" size.

In an experiment on shape constancy (a special form of size constancy), it was found that infants could identify a shape even after it had been rotated into the third dimension, altering its projected retinal image as well as its orientation (the relative distance of its edges) (see

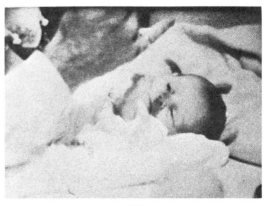

(A)

FIGURE 5.24 Hand regard
in a 12-day-old infant. This
neonate, when given a finger
to reach for, looks at her
hand when it comes into the
visual field (A). She looks at
the finger as she raises her
hand to it (B), but the reach
stops as she catches sight of
her own hand again (C).
(After "Object Perception in
Infants" by T. G. R. Bower.
Perception, **1,** 15–30, 1972.)

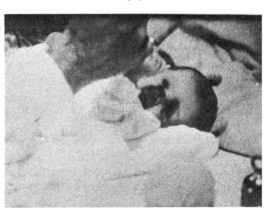

(B)

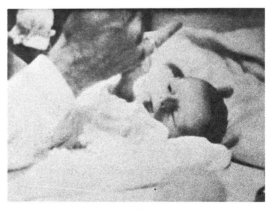

(C)

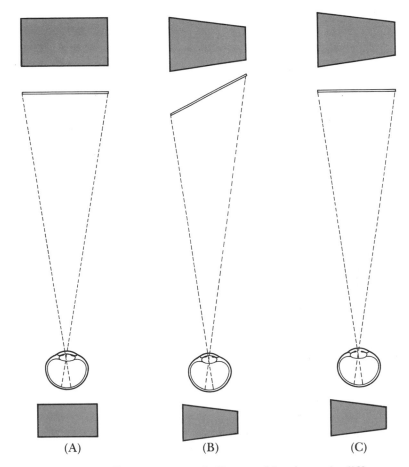

FIGURE 5.25 Shape constancy is illustrated by shapes in different orientations. (A) A rectangle presented in the parallel plane projects a rectangular image on the retina and is seen as a rectangle. (B) Presented at a slant, it projects a trapezoidal image, yet is usually seen as a rectangle. (C) A trapezoid in the parallel plane projects the same shape. (After "The Visual World of Infants" by T. G. R. Bower. Copyright © 1966 by Scientific American, Inc. All rights reserved.)

Figure 5.25). Despite being quite able to identify true shape, the infants were unable to discriminate or identify on the basis of retinal image shape or orientation alone. They were quite unable to respond differentially to a square in its fronto-parallel plane and to a square that had been rotated 45° away from the fronto-parallel plane. These two presentations were very different in retinal image shape and orientation. The only thing they had in common was their true shape,

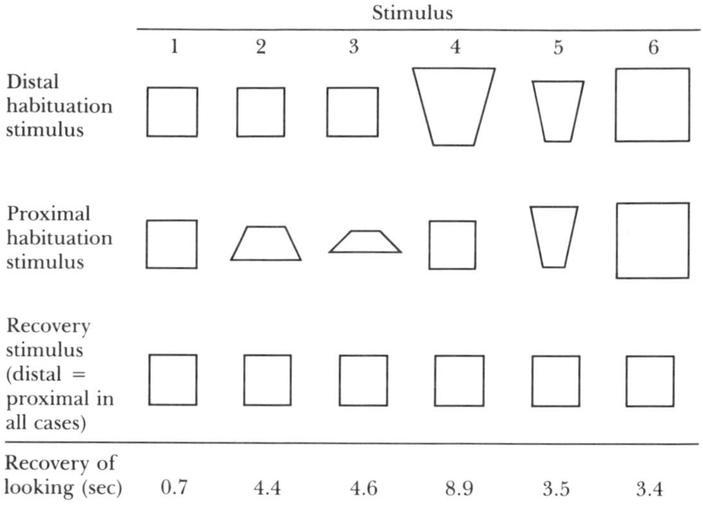

	Stimulus					
	1	2	3	4	5	6
Distal habituation stimulus						
Proximal habituation stimulus						
Recovery stimulus (distal = proximal in all cases)						
Recovery of looking (sec)	0.7	4.4	4.6	8.9	3.5	3.4

FIGURE 5.26   The stimuli and results of the Caron et al. (1978) experiment.

and the infants' responses to the shape were so forceful that the other variables were simply ignored. Similar results have been reported by Day and McKenzie (1973) and Caron et al. (1978). Using six different stimulus presentations, Caron and coworkers presented a constant form in a constant orientation to 12-week-old infants and, like Day and McKenzie, produced habituation. They then changed the shape of the habituation stimulus, its orientation, or both (see Figure 5.26). The last change was arranged so as to minimize the projective difference between habituation and test presentation. Indeed, in terms of retinal image, there was no difference at all between the two. Despite this, it was the dual change that produced the greatest recovery of attention.

Such studies seem to indicate that inability to handle all of the information presented in an array is a characteristic of young infants. It has been found, for example, that infants around 6 weeks of age are as likely to smile at two dots as at a real face with two eyes, implying that all of the other information in a real face is not registered by the baby (Ahrens, 1954). Gradually over the next three months, the overall contour of a face—the presence of a mouth, eyebrows, and so forth—becomes important. However, up to the age of 3 months and even beyond that age, a single feature, such as eyes or face contour, can be

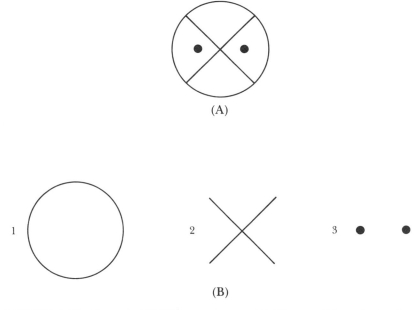

FIGURE 5.27   Bower's (1966b) experiment. (A) The conditioned stimulus was an abstract display. (B) Each of the test stimuli was a component of the original conditioned stimulus.

just as effective as the whole face; it is not until 5 or 6 months of age that a whole face is essential for smiling. At that age, a mutilated face elicits withdrawal, showing that the whole of the information in a face is being picked up and absent features are being detected (Ahrens, 1954).*

It might be thought that the human face, a particularly significant stimulus for infants, is a peculiar case. However, Bower (1966b) found similar results with an abstract display, as shown in Figure 5.27. Infants who were trained to respond to the whole pattern would respond to *any* of its components presented in isolation, showing that they had detected that component. However, the fact that the components were aggregated in the CS (conditioned stimulus) was not detected until the age of 16 weeks; not until that age or later did the whole pattern become essential for response.

These results suggest that young infants simply cannot take in at one moment all of the information they can take in over time. If given

---

*But see studies above on imitation and studies on smiling (Chapter 8).

a complex object to look at, they are likely to be aware of only one of the dimensions that distinguish the object. Salapatek (1969) has found that infants under 10 weeks of age will attend to the external detail of a pattern and will not look at internal detail; as long as the internal detail remains internal, it is functionally invisible.

Studies of the information-handling limitations of the young infant have abounded since the first edition of this book was published. Theories have proliferated too (e.g., Cohen, 1976, 1977). Unfortunately, the intervening years have also seen a number of studies indicating that the newborn may not be as limited as we thought. The response to the face, as outlined above, is a paradigm of the development of information-processing capacity. The infant begins with response to very simple features, gradually elaborating the list of features until all of the information in a face is registered. Recent studies indicate that this paradigmatic developmental pattern either does not happen at all or happens very rapidly indeed. We have already referred to data on imitation. For the present context, this implies that a newborn can indeed discern most of the features of a face—eyes, mouth, and tongue—plus what they are doing, a significant advance over the 6-week-old's attention to eyes only, the implication of the smiling studies. Yet more impressive data have been put forward by Carpenter (1975). Carpenter was able to show that a 2-week-old infant was capable of remarkably refined discrimination between its mother and a female stranger. In her experiments she used a viewing box like that shown in Figure 5.28. The window was big enough that the entire face of a human adult could be presented in it. In one study the infant was presented with six different stimuli.

1. The mother's face presented silently.
2. A female stranger's face.
3. The mother's face talking to the infant.
4. The female stranger's face talking to the infant.
5. The mother's face "talking" to the infant but with the stranger's voice presented.
6. The female stranger's face "talking" to the infant but with the mother's voice presented.

The infant looked longest at its mother talking to it with her own voice. The next most attractive stimulus for the infant to look at was its mother's face presented in silence. Both of these stimuli were sig-

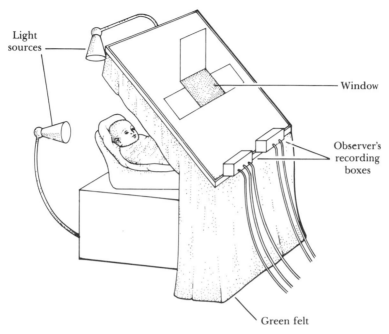

Light
sources

Window

Observer's
recording
boxes

Green felt

FIGURE 5.28   The viewing box used in Carpenter's (1975)
experiment. (After *Human Development* by T. G. R. Bower. W. H.
Freeman and Company. Copyright © 1979.)

nificantly more attractive than the stranger's face presented with the
stranger's voice. Thus, even by 2 weeks of age there is identification
of the mother and preference for her. Perhaps the most interesting
result came from the two mismatch conditions: the mother's face with
the stranger's voice and the mother's voice with the stranger's face.
The infant found both of these presentations aversive, as shown by
the way it tried as hard as possible not to look at the faces in this
condition, sneaking occasional furtive glances at the face and occasionally bursting into tears. This mixture of the familiar and the unfamiliar seemed to elicit, if not outright fear, at least something that
was well on the way to it.

A clear implication of this study is that infants can recognize a face
and a voice—simultaneously. Voice recognition has been demonstrated by a number of other investigators (Mills and Melhinsh, 1974;
André-Thomas and Dargassies, 1952). How much information is required to recognize a given face? How much information is required
to recognize a given voice? How much information is required to

recognize face and voice simultaneously? My first reaction to these data was to quibble. I think most proponents of an information-processing approach would display a similar response. Strictly speaking, none of the studies has demonstrated recognition; they have demonstrated discrimination between the familiar and the unfamiliar. Discrimination between two familiar faces or two familiar voices would have been more impressive evidence of recognition. (The execution of such an experiment has so far defeated me.) However, even without such an experiment, we must ask how a face or voice could become familiar if its own distinctive features were not detected. Even if the infant were responding to some higher-order variable defining "faceness," as it seems the infant can by 10 minutes of age (Jirari, 1970), the more specific variables defining a familiar face would have to be registered to permit discrimination of the familiar from the unfamiliar. We have the same difficulty with the face that we have with shape. In both cases, the infant must register more information than is obvious in the responses elicited.

The only solution to this dilemma would be to assume that the infant can detect more information than it uses. It is clear that we can set up situations in which infants will demonstrate less information-handling capacity than in the studies described above. Such situations typically involve such stimuli as crosses, circles, red triangles, green triangles, blue squares, yellow dumbbells, and yellow diamonds (see, e.g., Bower, 1966b; Cornell and Strauss, 1973; Cohen and Gelber, 1975; Fagan, 1977). It is not unlikely that such stimuli have less intrinsic interest for infants than faces and voices and so are less likely to engage the full range of the infants' attention.

Is interest the sole determinant of use or are other factors involved? At this point we are verging on the study of cognition, an area of research in itself, to which Chapter 7 is devoted. We will postpone discussion until then.

Meantime, can we offer any outline picture of perception and its development in the young infant? The set of abilities we refer to as "perception" is certainly not innate. Some aspects of perception may be. Perception of growth-invariant variables may well be innate, particularly if these variables are by their nature amodal. Development after this beginning will consist of a rapid calibration and specification of the information provided. Some of the determinants of these processes have been discussed in the preceding pages. The consequences of these processes will be a change in the way the infant uses the information presented. The obvious case is that of the sensorily handicapped infant. All infants, as we have seen, respond to asymmetric stimulation by orientation of all receptors to the source of the asymmetry. Around 4 months or so, the blind infant stops turning its eyes to the source of an asymmetry (Freedman, 1964). The infant has learned that this action is pointless. The sighted infant, presented with an asymmetry in darkness, behaves in the same way; it has learned that the action is pointless in the absence of light. In a sense, then, the newborn begins life perceiving the world; with development, the infant can sense it. The shift from perceiving to sensing is an important aspect of development that is only now receiving the attention it deserves (see, e.g., Bullinger, 1976). It is a change that can have deleterious consequences. I can perhaps best illustrate this with reference to one of the blind infants I have worked with (Bower, 1979a). This infant was 13 months old when first introduced to the sonic guide. Her initial response to the guide was extremely negative. After two lengthy sessions, however, there were some signs of use, and reaching became fairly easy to elicit when an object came within the field of the guide. The infant's standard response, however, was to take the object to her ear, at which point, of course, the sound disappeared. For her, sound appeared to be a property of objects rather than a medium for locating objects. A change like this could be a change in the use of information. It does, however, appear to be a change in use that determines future possibilities of use, to an alarming extent. For years, there have been devices available to the blind that present information about the spatial position of objects as sound messages. These devices have not been popular with blind adults, and only about 5 percent of the blind population can use even the best of them. Teachers of the blind believe only the most intelligent blind children can learn to translate the sounds given by such machines into useful information about the world. If, however, the hypothesis about intersensory coordination advanced above is correct, then, provided the information is given early enough in development, the infant should simply latch on to the information provided, with no special learning required at all. It would thus appear that only the young infant is open to all of the possibilities of its environment. Beyond that glad, innocent morning, what has been learned will determine what can be learned.

6

Motor Development

Motor behavior presents a much more satisfactory area of study than does perception. In the study of perception, one is always forced to make inferences from indicator behaviors. In the study of motor behavior, the subject of study is at least clearly visible, even though the mechanisms controlling it are not. Perhaps because of this, there have been many studies of the development of motor behaviors during infancy. Most texts include a schedule of development like that shown

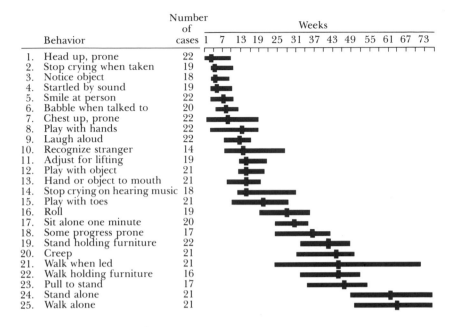

Behavior	Number of cases	Weeks
1. Head up, prone	22	
2. Stop crying when taken	19	
3. Notice object	18	
4. Startled by sound	19	
5. Smile at person	22	
6. Babble when talked to	20	
7. Chest up, prone	22	
8. Play with hands	22	
9. Laugh aloud	22	
10. Recognize stranger	14	
11. Adjust for lifting	19	
12. Play with object	21	
13. Hand or object to mouth	21	
14. Stop crying on hearing music	18	
15. Play with toes	21	
16. Roll	19	
17. Sit alone one minute	20	
18. Some progress prone	17	
19. Stand holding furniture	22	
20. Creep	21	
21. Walk when led	21	
22. Walk holding furniture	16	
23. Pull to stand	17	
24. Stand alone	21	
25. Walk alone	21	

FIGURE 6.1 A schedule of motor development. (After *The First Two Years.* Vol. 1: *Postural and Locomotor Development* by M. M. Shirley. © 1931, 1959 University of Minnesota.)

in Figure 6.1. Investigators have been concerned both with the details of development and with the general principles that a particular behavior can elucidate. Studies of motor behaviors have contributed much to our understanding of the process of maturation, the role of learning in constructing behavior, and the nature of nonspecific environmental effects in the growth of specific motor skills.

Despite the general importance of learning theory in psychology, there have been few attempts to account for motor development in terms of learning theory. This must be partly due to the fact that whereas learning theories can account for changes in the frequency of a behavior or for the establishment of a sequence of behaviors, learning theory has nothing to say about the genesis of *new* behaviors. The behaviors that appear in development are or seem to be new behaviors, so that learning theory is not really applicable.

A number of ingenious studies have been carried out to support the general hypothesis that motor behavior develops as a result of maturational processes—simple growth of nerve circuits, apparently unfolding inevitably and requiring no specific intervention. One of the simplest ways of testing this hypothesis is to compare the behavior of premature infants with that of full-term or post-term infants. The normal infant is born 40 weeks after conception; thus, when its chronological age is zero, its conceptual age is 40 weeks. Premature infants may survive when born at a conceptual age of 28 weeks. Thus, when a premature infant has a chronological age of zero, its conceptual age may be only 28 weeks. At the other extreme, some infants remain in the womb as long as 4 weeks past term; thus, when a post-term infant has a chronological age of zero, its conceptual age may be 44 weeks. Now, if behavior development is determined entirely by experience outside the womb, then chronological age should be our best predictor of the onset of any particular behavior. Further, we should find no differences between premature, term, and post-term infants of the same chronological age. On the other hand, if behavior simply "grows" from conception onward and is unaffected by events in the environment, then conceptual age should be our best predictor of the onset of a particular behavior, and we should find no differences between premature, term, and post-term babies of the same conceptual age. The logic of such studies is very clear. It allows us to decide between two extreme theories of the development of motor behavior.

Smiling is one behavior that has been studied in this way (see, e.g., Dittrichova, 1969). Normal infants will smile in response to a visual stimulus such as that described in Chapter 5 at a chronological age of 6 weeks, at which time their conceptual age is 46 weeks. The question is: will premature and post-term infants also smile at a chronological age of 6 weeks, or will their response begin at a conceptual age of 46 weeks, regardless of chronological age? The results for smiling are quite unambiguous. Infants smile at a conceptual age of 46 weeks, regardless of their chronological age. The extra time outside the womb does not accelerate the development of the premature infants, nor does the extra time inside the womb retard development of post-term infants. Is it therefore fair to conclude that smiling is primarily determined by processes of maturation? The answer must be negative. The environmental differences of premature, term, and post-term infants do not affect the conceptual age at which smiling begins. It is possible, however, that stimulation from the environment is critical, but only after a conceptual age of 44 weeks has been reached. Thus, the study could indicate that a given level of maturation is required before environmental events could have any effect. Further research is needed to show that no environmental event is critical for the development of the behavior, however (see Chapter 8).

FIGURE 6.2   An infant secured to a cradle
board.

Investigators have also used intercultural differences in rearing
patterns to assess the effects of environment on behavior development. Different cultures treat infants in different ways. If these differences produce no differences in the onset of behavior, it is argued
that the behavior is the result of maturation rather than the result of
environmentally induced processes. A classic example of this kind of
study is Dennis's (1940) investigation of the development of walking
in the Hopi Indian culture. Some groups of traditionally minded Hopi
Indians still bind their infants to cradle boards during the early
months of life (see Figure 6.2). An infant tied to a cradle board cannot
raise its body, roll over, or move its hands. Infants on the cradle board
are unwrapped only once or twice a day to have their clothes changed.

Even feeding and nursing are carried out on the cradle board. These traditionally reared infants were compared with other Hopi infants whose parents, affected by European practices, did not restrict their infants at all. The results, perhaps surprisingly, indicated no difference at all between the two groups of infants. Both groups walked unaided around the age of 15 months. The seemingly severe restrictions on the traditionally reared infants did not slow down their development in comparison to the unrestricted infants. This finding would therefore tend to support the argument for the primacy of maturation over experience in producing behavior. However, this conclusion is not incontrovertible. Use of the cradle board stops when infants are about 9 months old, and infants do not start to walk until about the age of 15 months. Between 9 months and 15 months there are lots of opportunities for practice and function to affect the development of this motor capacity. Had the Hopi babies stayed on the cradle board until they were 15 months old, the maturationist case would have been stronger. As it is, all we can conclude from this study is that the restriction of movement imposed by a cradle board does not slow development significantly, provided this restriction is limited to the first 9 months of life. The effects of restriction beyond that age are completely unknown.

One other argument that could be made against experiments like these is that, even though the number of infants in each experiment was quite large, there was still no control over the individual rates of maturation. The age of onset of any behavior is variable in any population of infants. Some infants simply develop faster than others. Whenever we compare two groups of infants, it is possible that one group contains a greater number of fast developers than does the other group. There are various ways of controlling against this—the simplest being the use of large numbers of infants. The most satisfactory guard is to used matched pairs of genetically identical infants, so that the genetically determined rate of development will be the same. Identical twins satisfy this requirement, since it is argued that differences between identical twins can only result from environmental differences. Similarly, if different environments fail to produce differences in behavior between identical twins, then the behavior in question must be genetically or maturationally determined.

Quite a number of studies have been carried out on this somewhat suspect logical base. One of the most interesting, certainly from a practical point of view, is McGraw's (1940) study of toilet training. McGraw introduced one twin to toilet training at a rather young age.

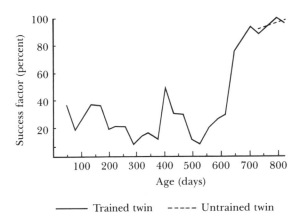

FIGURE 6.3   Success rates of response to toilet training in a trained and an untrained twin. (After "Neural Maturation as Exemplified in Achievement of Bladder Control" by M. B. McGraw, *Journal of Pediatrics,* **16,** 580–590, 1940.)

When the behavior had reached a very high level of success, the other twin was introduced to toilet training. The level of success of the previously untrained twin was no different from that of the trained twin (see Figure 6.3). In other words, 23 months of toilet training had produced no higher level of proficiency than did no training at all—a fascinating result that is completely contrary to the folklore on the subject.

Gesell and Thompson (1929) found similar results in their study of the development of two motor skills in a pair of identical twins. One of the skills studied was stair climbing. The trained twin (T) was introduced to stair climbing at the age of 46 weeks and was given daily practice in climbing until the age of 52 weeks; at this time she had been climbing the stairs alone for two weeks and could get from bottom to top in 26 seconds. The other twin, the control (C), was introduced to climbing at 53 weeks of age. At this point, without practice, she could climb the stairs alone in 46 seconds. After only two weeks of practice, the control twin could climb the stairs in 10 seconds. In other words, the study showed that climbing ability developed without benefit of practice and that speed of climbing was only min-imally affected by practice. The same twins were used in a subsequent study of cube stacking. After six weeks of training, T did no better in terms of speed or numbers stacked than did C, who had no practice whatsoever. The training experience produced no acceleration of development at all. The conclusion of both studies is that maturation is what produces development of new behaviors; at best, practice merely serves to produce a fine tuning of behaviors already established by maturation; at worst, practice has no effect at all.

Any straightforward interpretation of these studies leads to problems. None of the studies mentioned thus far has provided precise definitions of the behavior, its antecedents, the practice, or the environment. The studies show that certain selective manipulations of an infant's environment do not accelerate or retard the appearance of certain behaviors in some form. There are no criteria as yet for assuming that the manipulations involved are likely to be relevant to the behavior under study. When twin T in Gesell's study was undergoing practice in stair climbing, she was simply moved up and down the stairs for the first four weeks: she was quite passive, and her limbs were moved for her. The question is: why on earth should we assume that passive limb movements are in any sense an antecedent to active stair climbing? In fact, this seems to be rather unlikely. It seems much more likely that active crawling on a flat floor would be the antecedent of stair-climbing behavior, but crawling of that sort was not observed or controlled in Gesell's study. The point is that we do not know whether or not crawling on a flat surface is the true antecedent of climbing; and, unless we do know, we are in no position to talk about the effects of special experience on the development of climbing. If the special experience is not applied to the relevant behavior, then it is hardly surprising that it produces no effects.

The problem of defining the antecedents of a behavior is a considerable one. Indeed, the magnitude of the problem sets behavioral embryology apart from any other branch of embryology. In embryology, one can stain a cell in such a way that all of the descendants of the cell show traces of the stain. It is thus relatively easy to identify the antecedents of any organ as far back as one wishes. In the case of a mosaic egg, one can destroy a cell or set of cells; the normal descendants of the destroyed cell will be missing in the experimental animal, again allowing one to infer the antecedents of the structures in question (see Figure 6.4). Obviously, one cannot stain behaviors, nor can one destroy them. This makes it difficult to say with certainty that any particular behavior is the ancestor or antecedent of any subsequent behavior. If a behavior appears de novo in full-fledged fashion, it is difficult to argue that it was formed by any other process than the maturation of independent circuits within the brain. However,

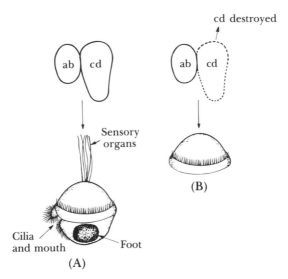

cd destroyed

ab   cd

ab   cd

Sensory organs

(B)

Cilia and mouth   Foot

(A)

FIGURE 6.4   In the study of structural development, it is possible to trace the ancestry of body parts by destroying cells at an early stage of development and then observing what part of the developed organism is missing. (A) A normal trochophore larva. (B) If the cd cell is destroyed at the two-cell stage, one obtains the partial organism shown, indicating that all of the missing parts develop from the destroyed cd cell, and all of the existing parts develop from the ab cell.

even when a late-appearing behavior is very much like an earlier behavior, one cannot say for sure that the earlier behavior is the causal ancestor of the later one. Temporal succession simply does not imply a causal relation.

The development of walking exemplifies one such problem. Newborn infants will "walk" after a fashion if supported (see Figure 6.5). This behavior normally disappears, and true walking begins many months later. Is the early walking an ancestor of later walking? The two behaviors are separated by many months; yet they are commonly referred to as primary walking and secondary walking. It is argued that primary walking disappears because of an active inhibition that is necessary for secondary walking to appear. Such theorizing is purely speculative, however, since it is quite possible that the two behaviors are independent of each other. We could ask what evidence would convince us that the two behaviors are connected. If the earlier behavior is an ancestor of the later behavior, surely environmental modifications that affect the first would also affect the later; this could be compared to introducing a stain into a primordial cell that can later

154

FIGURE 6.5　A neonate walking. (After
*The Neuromuscular Maturation of the Human
Infant* by M. B. McGraw. New York:
Columbia University Press, 1943.)

be discovered in its descendants. An experiment of this sort was done
by André-Thomas and St. A. Dargassies (1952). They exercised the
primary walking of a group of infants on a daily basis, rather than
ingoring the behavior as is commonly done.* When it came to secondary walking, this group of infants was greatly accelerated. Since
the early training produced effects on the later behavior, the study
demonstrated that primary walking is indeed the ancestor of secondary walking. If the early training had produced no effects, we would
have been forced to conclude that the two behaviors were unrelated.
If one accepts this criterion for the connection between earlier and
later behaviors, then one must assume that studies where early practice
has no effect on later behavior are in fact showing that the practiced
behavior is unrelated to the criterion behavior—a conclusion quite
different from the desired one (see also Zelazo et al., 1972).

If there are severe problems in connecting an early behavior with
a later behavior, then there are far more difficult problems involved
in establishing the relation between an environmental event and some
subsequent behavior. The studies cited thus far have all tried to prove

---

*The duration of primary walking was much longer in these infants than in normal
infants, which rules out the inhibition hypothesis mentioned above.

that *no* environmental event is involved in the development of a particular behavior. But it would seem to me that this kind of experimental conclusion simply cannot be sustained—except under severely abnormal conditions. Just how abnormal these conditions must be is shown by one study that can claim to show some development as the result of pure maturation with no possibility of the influence of environmental events.

Wolff (1969) studied an infant with congenital arrhinencephaly (failure of separation of the hemispheres of the brain) along with other neural disorders. A consequence of this condition was that the infant experienced continuous random seizures—a condition that, in adults, prevents the registration of external events. If this infant were similarly disturbed by the seizures, then she too would have had no awareness or registration of the events in her environment. Despite this, some development did occur. The infant developed the ability to raise her head when in a prone position, to support herself on her elbows, and to make coordinated "creep" movements. This is no great catalog of development, and yet it apparently occurred with no external support at all.

Studies of infants with less severe sensory handicaps have provided models for the ways in which environmental events seem to interact with maturational processes in generating behavior. The study of vocal behavior in deaf infants is a case in point. Normal infants begin to babble around the age of 5 months. This initial phase of babbling continues for about one month, with the infants producing a wide variety of sounds. Indeed, some investigators have claimed that infants produce all possible sounds of all possible human languages. Deaf infants also go through this babbling phase, even though they have never heard a spoken word. They continue babbling as long as normal infants do, despite the fact that they cannot hear themselves babble. This evidence would seem to show conclusively that audition is not necessary for the establishment of this phase of babbling and that auditory feedback is not necessary for its maintenance. After the first phase of babbling is over, toward the end of the first year, normal infants begin to change their babbling; it turns gradually into the spoken language of the child's environment. This second phase does not occur in deaf infants. It would seem then that the second phase of babbling, which leads to proper speech, does require auditory input for its initiation and maintenance. Evidence also shows that maintaining speech depends on auditory input for some time after this; the utterances of children who become deaf during childhood regress in extreme cases to the level of congenitally deaf children. The later the deafness occurs, the less likely this is, however. Eventually, around the age of 6 years, deafness has no effect on the vocal behavior of children. At this point, the behavior has become independent of auditory support. Further evidence is provided by studies on the speech of children who were born deaf and provided with hearing aids at some point during development. The earlier the hearing aid is furnished, the more rapid is the acquisition of language. If it is postponed long enough, language may never be acquired (Lenneberg, 1967).

Data like these force one to reconsider the relationship between environmental events and development. Learning-theory approaches argue that development will not occur without specific environmental intervention; if the specific environmental event does not occur, development does not occur, and *neither does anything else.* The organism simply stays stationary until the event comes along. The maturational theorists—Gesell, McGraw, and Dennis—argue that development proceeds successfully in the absence of any particular environmental event. They emphasize the attainment of successful behavior through maturational processes. We must agree that the learning theorists are wrong in asserting that behavior will remain stationary in the absence of environmental stimulation. Behavior, as we have seen, will change regardless; but the change need not be successful. In the absence of relevant input from the environment, behavior may take a completely aberrant direction, and that direction may become so firmly established that no environmental intervention will suffice to redirect the behavior to its proper course.

Waddington (1957) proposed a model of development that encompasses the features of interaction between the organism and environment that have so far been mentioned. Suppose we imagine a landscape like that shown in Figure 6.6. The ball rolling down the valley on the right represents the path of development of vocal behavior. The hillock represents the environmental intervention—the effect of hearing spoken language. It serves to tip the path of development down the route leading to language. If the hillock were not present, the ball would continue down the path leading to nonlinguistic vocal behavior. The later the hillock is introduced, the more difficult it is to redirect development. The path of normal development is at a higher level than the other path; so that, if linguistic support is removed, the ball will roll back to the nonlinguistic behavioral path, at least initially. This *epigenetic landscape* is a convenient model for many aspects of development, particularly organogenesis. It serves to de-

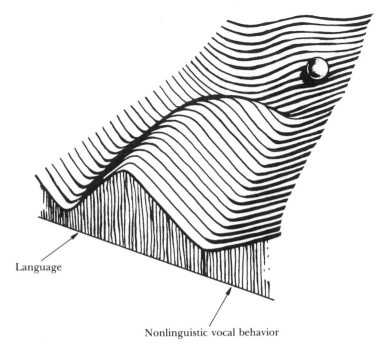

Language

Nonlinguistic vocal behavior

FIGURE 6.6   Part of an epigenetic landscape. (After *The Strategy of the Genes* by C. H. Waddington. London: Allen and Unwin, 1957.)

scribe some aspects of behavioral development as well, as we have seen. It must be emphasized that the epigenetic landscape is primarily a *model* of development. It is not intended to serve as a theory that makes predictions; it is rather an after-the-fact, descriptive model.

Piaget (1954) has presented an account of the development of some motor behaviors that is primarily descriptive but still does justice to the complexities of behavior development, while introducing concepts that could be predictive. In Piaget's model, the initial creation of behaviors is still accomplished through maturational processes. What happens thereafter is determined by interaction with the environment; the interaction itself is determined by two fundamental processes—assimilation and accommodation. *Assimilation* is the process that determines the range of things or events to which the behavior will be applied. In more conventional terminology, we might say that an object elicits a behavior; for example, a seen object might elicit reaching. In Piaget's terminology, the seen object is assimilated to the behavior of reaching. Piaget argues that, if a behavior is given nothing to assimilate, it will simply die away. As we have seen, language development fits such a description. *Accommodation* is the process whereby behavior is adjusted to the requirements of the object or event assimilated to it. In the case of reaching and grasping, the behavior must be adjusted to the size, weight, and shape of the object. In Piaget's theory, development is accomplished by the interaction of assimilation and accommodation which continues until a state of equilibrium is reached. The processes leading to equilibrium are called *equilibration*. Equilibrium is reached when a behavior assimilates only those objects to which it can accommodate. In the case of reaching and grasping, the infant will only attempt to grasp those objects whose size and weight are within the infant's capacities when equilibration is over. Larger or heavier objects are excluded, as are objects that are too fragile or insubstantial.

In the preceding chapter, we talked about hand adjustments made prior to contacting objects. These are examples of the processes Piaget is talking about. Infants will only reach for objects that they can grasp. That is, assimilation is restricted to objects that are within the range of accommodation. The hand adjustments—accommodation—are anticipatory, and they result is successful assimilation. Assimilation and accommodation are thus in equilibrium.

There are some subtleties in this statement of equilibrium and equilibration. A behavior is only in equilibrium if the infant can anticipate its consequences. In order to inhibit grasping, for example, the infant must know that an object is too heavy *before* trying to grasp it; the infant must know how heavy an object is *before* he or she can grasp it without dropping or crushing it. Thus, equilibrium requires anticipation. In addition, since the theory provides no mechanism for the establishment of the anticipation of consequences, some anticipation must be built in and must develop along with the behavior. Perhaps this characteristic more than any other sets Piaget's theory apart from the other theories into which it could be translated.

One other feature of the equilibration model of development must be mentioned. Equilibration may terminate when equilibrium is reached with a specific set of environmental inputs; it may then start anew when the set is enlarged to include new objects or events. In the case of reaching and grasping, one can imagine an infant in perfect equilibrium with a single object. As long as that one object is presented, behavior will remain equilibrated, and *there will be no further development of that behavior.* When a new object is presented (an object beyond the accommodatory range of the behavior), the behavior will assimilate it, compelling a new process of equilibration and, with it, development. Eventually, such specific adjustments must cease, and accommodation must become predictive over the entire range of assimilation, including all objects that could be met as well as those that already have been met. In other words, a very special kind of *generalization* is required. In behavior theory, generalization refers to the process whereby different objects come to elicit the same response. What is required for equilibration is a process whereby objects that differ along some particular dimension will elicit appropriate, differentially graded responses. Thus, in grasping, the heavier an object is, the greater is the force that must be applied to grasp it securely.

Piaget would insist that these rules exist in some form within the nervous system of the child, interposed between perceptual input and the responses to it. Although these rules are formed in the course of equilibration, Piaget (1967) argued very forcefully that all behaviors, from the very beginning, occur under the control of rules, however crude or general they may be. For Piaget, behavior is never the result of simple stimuli eliciting simple responses in a one-to-one fashion; behavior is always a matter of the assimilation of objects, graded in some fashion, to a class of behaviors, graded appropriately, through a mediating rule that links input to output.

Piaget is relatively open on the precise processes that go on during equilibration. One problem that he preserved his options on is whether development is best described as a process of *differentiation* or *integration,* or indeed whether development may be a succession of waves of differentiation followed by waves of integration. Some theorists (Gesell and Amatruda, 1941) have argued that development is differentiation; in development, behavior becomes more selective and more precise, and its components became segregated from one another. An example of the studies supporting this view is shown in Figure 6.7. Other researchers have argued that behavior begins as a set of segmental responses and that these are organized together during development. Although Piaget's theory tends to reflect the differentiation view, he did not commit himself on this point. He appears to argue that both processes may be necessary at some stages in development.

Reaching and grasping comprise a convenient behavior for the analysis of these various models. It is a behavior of tremendous importance in human life. Our whole tool-using society depends on the refined manual skills that humans share with no other primate. This superior skill is largely due to the human's superior skeletal equipment

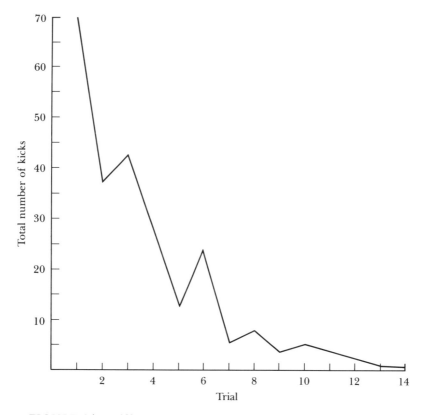

FIGURE 6.7 Differentiation as illustrated in the development of grasping. The curve shows the decrease in diffuse (kicking) activity involved in attempts to grasp a rattle held before the infant. (After *Child Psychology* by M. W. Curti. Philadelphia: Longmans Green, 1930.)

(see Figure 6.8). The question is: Does the ability to use this superior skeletal equipment grow with it, or is interaction with the environment necessary for the formation of the skills that capitalize on this endowment?

Like walking, reaching begins well before birth. All of the components for reaching and grasping can be elicited in fetuses at a conceptual age of 14 to 16 weeks. As mentioned previously, visually initiated reaching can be elicited in newborn human infants. In average infants, this precocious behavior vanishes, and reaching reappears somewhere between 4 and 5 months of age. Humphrey (1969) has argued that this, as in walking, is the takeover of reaching by cortical centers; the inhibitory connections grow in first, so that the

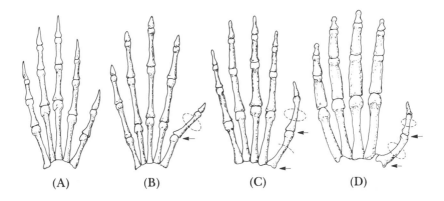

(A)   (B)   (C)   (D)

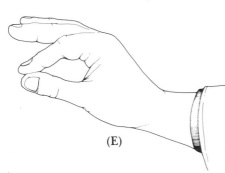

(E)

FIGURE 6.8   The superior skeletal equipment of the human allows perfect opposability of the thumb. While convergent fingers and an opposable thumb are present in many primates (A–D), only the human (E) has perfected thumb and index finger opposition.

behavior *necessarily* disappears during the period when inhibitory connections are the only ones that have been formed. The behavior will reappear as soon as excitatory connections are formed. Humphrey is quite explicit in pointing out that it is the same behaviors that reappear. The corticalization enhances coordination between behaviors, but the behaviors remain the same. Humphrey is quite emphatic that the observed sequences are caused by maturation—by the growth of circuits within the nervous system.

White (1963; White et al., 1964; White and Held, 1966) has reported research that shares some affinities with Humphrey's interpretations, even though the work seems diametrically opposed. White has emphasized the role of environmental factors in the development of reaching. He sees environmental influences as coordinating forces, generating integration between disparate behaviors. White's model is explicitly Piagetian, although it is also different from Piaget's. White sees mature reaching and grasping as the result of the integration of diverse sets of initial coordinations, including touch–grasp, eye–object, eye–hand, and eye–arm.

According to White, the development of reaching takes the following path. In the beginning, infants have a primitive visual–attentional behavior that involves them in looking at and following seen objects. This behavior is limited in range initially. Infants also have a touch–grasp behavior that leads them to grasp objects that touch their hands. In White's view, these behaviors are initially isolated from one another. However, as visual attention improves and as the infant latches on to moving objects or attends to nearer or farther objects, the infant catches sight of its hand—an interesting object in its own right. This generates a new behavior—eye–hand coordination—which is evidenced by the fact that infants spend a good deal of their time looking at their hands. Soon after this occurs, the hand is brought to an object in a fast swipe, with no opening of the hand prior to contact. The next step in the development occurs when the infant looks back and forth from an object to its hand, while holding the hand in the visual field. At this point, according to White, the infant is putting together eye–hand and eye–object behaviors.

Another behavior that emerges at this point is mutual hand clasping, with visual attention to the hands. This results in awareness that the seen hand is also the grasping hand. After this point, the various behaviors become coordinated, and one can see the hand go out and grasp an object. With practice, this crude grasp becomes what White calls a top-level reach; it is anticipatory, with the hand opening before contacting the object and with initiation of the act from outside the visual field.

White's model of development represents a considerable advance over Humphrey's model, in that clear patterns of behavior are presumed to change and to coordinate with one another to yield new behaviors. Humphrey and other maturationists have left reaching a relatively unanalyzed behavior. Clearly, White has an environmentalist position. His theory postulates several essential environmental occurrences in the development of visually guided reaching.

First, the infant must catch sight of its hand. The sight of the hand then generates eye–hand coordination, without which no further development would be possible. It follows that any procedure that speeds eye–hand coordination should also speed the development of mature reaching. Anything that retards it should necessarily retard the development of mature reaching. After eye–hand coordination is attained, the infant must still integrate arm movements with hand movements. White argues that, when targets for swiping are touched, grasping is produced; in time, the object–eye–hand–touch–grasp sequence will be short-circuited to produce direct reachings with grasping anticipated. Thus, in White's model, once swiping is established, presenting further objects for the infant to swipe at should accelerate the development of mature reaching and grasping. However, as Piaget cogently points out, withdrawal of objects at this stage will not retard the development of reaching and grasping for long; as soon as the infant can bring both hands into the visual field, one hand may serve as a target for reaching and grasping by the other. One hand can serve as a surrogate object, ensuring that the mature behavior will not be indefinitely retarded in the absence of objects.

Nevertheless, if White is correct about the growth of mature reaching and grasping, the presentation of objects immediately after the establishment of swiping should accelerate the development of mature reaching and grasping—particularly in comparison with the infant who must utilize its own hand as an object. White's theory therefore can be reduced to a sequence of behaviors that must be invariant, along with a list of environmental events that trigger the steps from one behavior to another. The hypothetical sequence is;

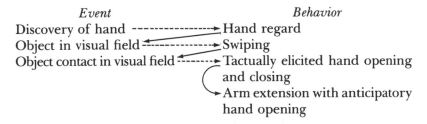

Event	*Behavior*
Discovery of hand	Hand regard
Object in visual field	Swiping
Object contact in visual field	Tactually elicited hand opening and closing
	Arm extension with anticipatory hand opening

White constructed his theory upon observations of development in 34 infants. The infants were in an institution that provided a somewhat odd environment. The infants lay in a supine position on mattresses that, hollowed out with use, served to restrict their movements. The visual surroundings were a homogeneous white, with few contours. The environment thus contained few of the features that we would deem normal. To test his theory, White modified the environment of two other groups of infants. Two different modifications were introduced. One group—the massively enriched group—had a very elaborate multicolored stabile hung above their cribs from age 37 days to

124 days. Multicolored sheets and crib sides were also substituted for the standard white ones. The intention was that these changes would heighten visual interest and increase viewing of hand movements, since infants tend to swipe at visible objects nearby. With the other group—the slightly enriched group— there was only one modification to the standard institutional situation from age 37 days to age 68 days. Two pacifiers that stood out visually against a red and white polka-dot disk were attached to the sides of the cribs, in a position designed to elicit maximum attention, 6 to 7 inches away from the infants' eyes. At 68 days, until 124 days of age, this second group of infants was given the stabile used in the massively enriched situation.

If White's theory is correct, what changes would one expect from these modifications? The first significant environmental effect is discovery of the hands. White has argued that the more things there are for the infant to look at, the less likely the infant is to notice its hands. We should thus expect hand regard to be delayed and, with it, swiping. However, once swiping begins, there will always be an object for the hand to contact that should nurture tactually elicited grasping; this would then speed the conversion to anticipatory grasping.

By trying to produce two effects working in opposite directions, White has elegantly solved the problem of how to ensure that an accelerated group of infants are not simply fast developers. If both effects occur in opposite directions, there could be no argument that White had simply hit on a group of faster developers. Unfortunately, though both effects did occur, they occurred in a way that destroyed the theory used to predict them. Hand regard was delayed in the massive-enrichment group. In fact, it was delayed until after the onset of swiping; hand regard did not begin until the hand was seen in contact with an object. This clearly contradicts the theory, since it was claimed that hand regard is a necessary precursor of swiping. Similarly, top-level reaching with anticipatory grasping was accelerated in both groups. It was accelerated so much that it appeared *before* tactually elicited grasping. This also clearly contradicts the theory since it asserts that top-level reaching grows out of tactually elicited grasping. Thus, while White has clearly demonstrated environmental effects, his results also destroyed his theory of development.

How should one interpret these results? One argument is that White's control group did not show normal development, but rather the disintegration of a behavior given nothing to assimilate. In this view, the components that White thought led to mature reaching and grasping would have appeared individually as the integrated behavior fell apart. Further, the group that was given objects to assimilate would not show the same disintegration. This is a plausible argument, since we know that matured behaviors will disintegrate through lack of use (see above). However, this account does not explain the occurrence of behaviors (such as tactually elicited grasping) that did appear in *all* groups, albeit in no consistent order with anticipatory grasping. If the control group displayed this behavior as a result of the degeneration of anticipatory grasping, why then did the group with objects to assimilate and therefore no reason for degeneration show the same behavior? Certainly, no maturational theory could give a coherent account of why this occurred after the attainment of anticipatory grasping—supposedly the end point of development.

It is possible that the behaviors are quite unrelated. However, before multiplying the behaviors to be explained, we would do well to reexamine the whole sequence of development. White began his study when his subjects were 4 weeks of age and ended it when they were about 5 months old—at which point he assumed that reaching had attained an adult form. There were two errors in this selection of a segment for study: the segment began too late and ended too early.

As we have noted in earlier chapters, reaching can be elicited in the immediate postnatal period. Also, the reaching of the average 5-month-old has some way to go before it becomes the same as that of an adult. If one begins at the beginning of postnatal life, one can observe behavior that looks like reaching and grasping. Newborn humans will reach out and grasp objects under certain specific conditions. The infants must be wide-awake if the behavior is to occur—a state not always easily obtained. They must also be in a specific posture that allows them free use of their arms and free head movement. This too is a condition not always readily obtained. The newborn infant tends to use its head and arms as supports while lying or reclining (see Figure 6.9). Obviously, if arms are being used as supports, they cannot move freely. Conditions where the head and arms are free to move occur naturally while the infant is being held or carried. Some infant carriers seem ideal for this purpose (see Figure 6.10). In laboratory situations, a certain amount of propping is required to ensure free movement. When these conditions are met, newborn infants will reach out and grasp visually presented objects. Their reaching has a hit rate of about 40 percent, more than half of their misses landing within a handbreadth of the target object. Reaching is primarily one-handed

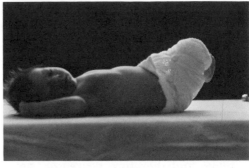

(A)

FIGURE 6.9 A neonate
lying unsupported on a
tabletop. Note the support
role of the head and arms
(A). If the infant moves its
arms, it is unable to
maintain posture (B), save
by propping itself on its arm
(C). This precludes any
attempt to reach.
(Photographs by Jennifer
Wishart.)

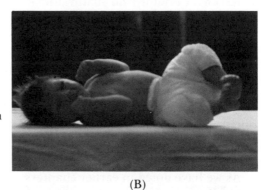

(B)

(C)

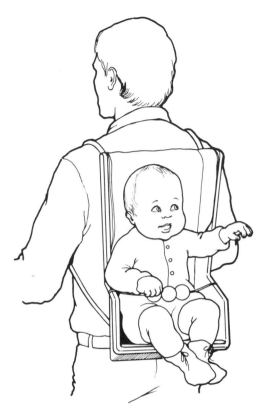

FIGURE 6.10 Infant carriers such as the
one shown allow the infant free arm and
head movement, which is essential if
precocious reaching is to occur.

(see Figure 6.11). Two-handed reaches are only observed when an
object is in the midline position. Some of the reaches clearly anticipate
grasping. The hand opens before contact and closes on contact, but
too quickly for the contact to have released the hand closure. The
infant does anticipate the tactile consequences of reaching since it
seems to expect tactile input when its hand reaches the place where
the object is seen to be. Virtual objects produce considerable upset,
as we have previously discussed. Also, reaching at this stage is at least
partly accommodated to the size and distance of objects.

As Butterworth (1978) has recently pointed out, attempting to demonstrate that neonates do not reach may soon become a minor cottage
industry. To date, two independent groups of investigators, using

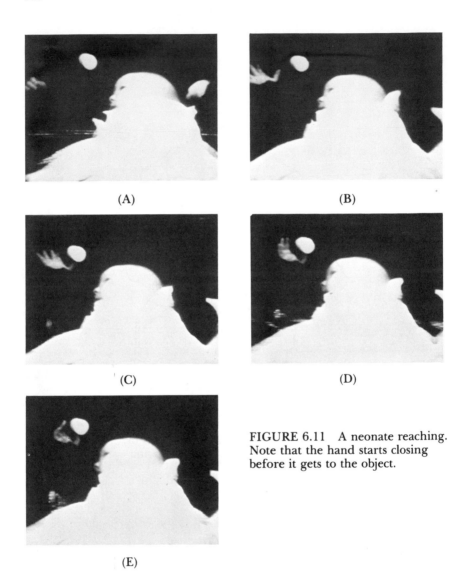

(A)

(B)

(C)

(D)

(E)

FIGURE 6.11 A neonate reaching. Note that the hand starts closing before it gets to the object.

different techniques, have proposed that neonates do reach (Bower, et al., 1970b; Trevarthen, 1974; Trevarthen et al., 1975). Butterworth seems to have observed the behavior as well, although with difficulty.

> In my own laboratory, we allow two hours to obtain a five minute video recording of one infant reaching. Most of the time is spent ensuring that the baby is in the optimal condition to display the behaviour, if he (or she) is going to. We have the mother feed and change the baby at the lab and generally ensure that the infant is wide awake. Having taken these precautions, there is little doubt that infants in the first few weeks of life can reach toward and sometimes grasp objects on which they fixate visually. . . . [Butterworth, 1978]

Two independent groups of observers have proposed that newborns do not reach (Dodwell et al., 1976; Ruff and Halton, 1978). The former study used Trevarthen's techniques, without seeming to be aware of their origin or the precautions necessary for their successful use (Bower et al., 1979). The other study was similar to the original study by Bower, Broughton, and Moore (1970b).

Before describing either the original or the replication study, I would like to outline some of the problems that faced Broughton, Moore, and myself in devising the original study. It appeared to us that neonates did reach. (The history of the dawning awareness is detailed in Bower, 1977b.) We also knew that neonates made lots of arm movements that were not reaches, by any stretch of the imagination. Could we demonstrate that the movements that looked to us like reaching movements were reaching movements, and not simply random arm activity? It seemed to us that the most basic characteristic of reaching, as opposed to random arm activity, is directionality: If the arm activity is reaching, then there should be a correlation between object position and the pattern of destinations. Accordingly, we serially presented infants with an object in five positions—in the midline, 30° to the left or right, and 60° to the left or right—and looked at the distribution of arm-movement destinations in each case. The arm-movement sample was restricted to those that could have touched the object had they been accurate (i.e., those movements in depth that reached out to the arc of object positions). The results were clear enough that statistical analysis was hardly necessary. Had statistical analysis been used, it would have been moderately complicated. On a strict assumption of randomness, one would have assumed a flat distribution of movement destinations for all object positions. One would then have compared obtained with expected results. On a random basis, the expected value for a given position out of five would not be 20 percent. On a random hypothesis, there is no reason to assume only the positions selected by an experimenter to be sampled. The baseline value would depend on the accuracy of observation. The infant can move its hands to any destination in a 180° arc. If one's observations are accurate to 5°, that means that the expected value for any given position on a random hypothesis is 5/ 180 × 100, equal to just under 3 percent. If one is accurate to 10° then the expected value on a random hypothesis would be 5.5 percent. To arrive at an expected value of 35 percent, one would have to reduce one's accuracy of observation to around 60°. I give this last figure of 35 percent because that is the value obtained in Ruff and Halton's reaching study, a value that they interpret as showing that activity is not directed, but is, rather, random. It is quite clear that Ruff and Halton must have had standards of accuracy much higher than 60°. On their own criteria then, the movements observed could not have been random. How far they departed from randomness toward directedness, I cannot compute, since the standard of accuracy is not specified in the report of their study.

The above discussion is predicated on the assumption that the null hypothesis of neonate reaching is that the movements are completely random. The above two experiments would appear to eliminate that possibility. A more sophisticated null hypothesis would have a slightly different form. Suppose we assume that the infant orients its head and eyes toward a visible object. Suppose further that we assume that arm movements tend to make the hands go wherever the eyes are pointed. We could thus have directedness that did not signify reaching. The infant, excited by the sight of an object, thrashes around excitedly, its hands going where its eyes point, resulting in spurious directionality. There are two ways of eliminating this hypothesis. One depends on extending the definition of reaching to include intent to contact. On a randomness hypothesis, what should happen if the infant contacts the presented object? Since contact is no part of the intended movement, the infant should be surprised by this untoward event. Suppose the opposite hypothesis, that the movements are reaching movements. There should be no surprise on contact since that was the "aim" of the movement and some surprise on noncontact with a virtual object, an object visible but intangible (see Chapter 4, Figure 4.21). No one has ever reported that a neonate was surprised when its hand contacted a real object. Bower et al. (1970b), however, found that the infant was surprised by noncontact with a virtual object.

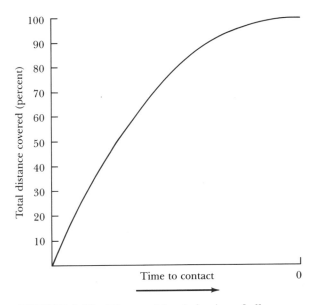

FIGURE 6.12   The reaching behavior of all
primates shows a pattern in time characterized by
high initial acceleration followed by deceleration as
the hand approaches the object.

A second way of eliminating this hypothesis is to compare movements in the presence of objects with movements in the absence of
objects. This has been done by Trevarthen et al. (1975) and Brazelton
et al. (1974), who agree that movements in the presence of objects,
the directed movements at issue, are quite different from movements
in the absence of objects. Difference does not prove that the directed
movements are reaching movements, however. To do that, we have
to assume that the reaching movements of newborns would be like
the reaching movements of all other primates, that they would have
the form shown in Figure 6.12. Bower et al. (1970b) did not have the
resources to do this. It either requires split-screen photography or
sensors in the object sensitive to hand position. Later studies (Bower,
1978) found that the form of the neonate reach was like that shown
in Figure 6.13. While this is an empirical correspondence, it is hard
to see, on any randomness hypothesis, why an infant's hand would
progressively slow as it approached an object. Surely, only if the object
were the anticipated terminus of the act, would such slowing occur.

    It seems to me that neonate reaching is bound to remain contro-
versial for some time. I do feel that the balance of the evidence sup-

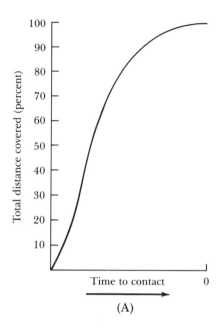

(A)

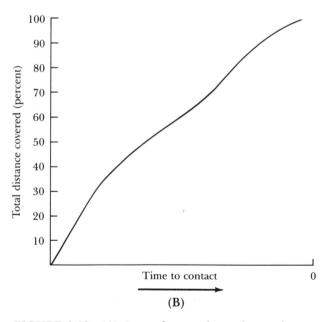

(B)

FIGURE 6.13 (A) As can be seen here, the reach
of a neonate shows the pattern illustrated in Figure
6.12. (B) A successful two-stage reach by the same
infant. (Two-part reaches are, however, fairly rare in
the neonate period.)

ports the reality of the phenomenon. While my reading of the evidence is doubtless biased, it seems to me that failures should be treated with more caution than successes. There is nothing easier than to demonstrate that a newborn will *not* do something. The difficulty of newborn investigation has been mentioned by many investigators over the years. I have outlined the problems with reaching in numerous publications and the problems are attested to by the quotation from Butterworth (1978) above. A consensual reason for accepting the validity of the phenomenon is that it makes some kind of sense of the rest of the development of reaching.

In British and American infants studied cross-sectionally, reaching behavior is very hard to elicit after the age of 4 weeks. The behavior recurs around 20 weeks, at which time it is less posture-specific and more accurate; hit rates of 80 percent are common. Reaching is still primarily one-handed, although the proportion of two-handed reaches has increased, and two-handed reaches are made toward objects in any position. Again, some reaches are clearly anticipatory, the hand opening before contact and closing as contact is made—too rapidly for the closure to be tactually released.

At 20 weeks, the behavior is still adjusted to the size of objects and still anticipates tactile consequences when the hand reaches object locations. In other words, there seems to be little to choose between the neonate reaching and 20-week-old reaching, save for changes in the quantitative parameters of the performance. There are three main quantitative changes.

For one, behavior can be elicited in a wider variety of postures. It is about twice as accurate, although still not perfect. It seems to show somewhat less anticipation, as measured by hand behavior during approach to an object. This last measure is the most surprising. It can hardly reflect a loss of knowledge that seen objects are tangible, since the virtual-object presentation still produces just as much, if not more, upset. Nonetheless, on at least one measure of anticipation, anticipation declines. This particular measure involved timing the interval when the hand closed on an object after it had reached a position where it could do so. In practice, this measure is easily obtained, since the hand and arm are always stationary for some time at the end of a reach. One can thus determine when the hand as a whole stops moving. Taking that as a zero point, one can find when the fingers close down on the object. With perfect anticipation, the offset time should be zero. The hand should close just as it reaches the object— no earlier and no later. Figure 6.14 shows the distribution of offsets

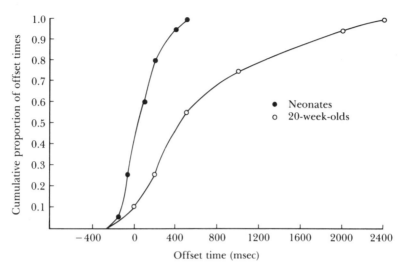

FIGURE 6.14 Distribution of offset times in neonates and in 20-week-old infants. Note the increased offset time in the older group.

in neonates and 20-week-old infants. As can be seen there, offset increases steadily until, by 20 weeks of age, the reaching component and the grasping component are temporally quite separate. The mean offset time in newborns is, in fact, zero. In 20-week-old infants, the mean offset time is greater than zero—about 450 msec on average.

How is one to interpret these quantitative changes? At first sight, they would seem to support the sort of theory proposed by Humphrey. The behaviors seem identical, and the quantitative differences could be accounted for by certain assumptions. It would be plausible to assume, for example, that cortical function is more precise than subcortical function and that, until growth is complete, we must expect some desynchronization. However, examination of the performance of older infants, around 26 weeks of age, suggests a completely different interpretation. These older infants, as noted in Chapter 5, are much less upset by the virtual object than are younger infants. Their reaching is 100 percent accurate, and two-handed reaches to all positions are common. Last, and most significant, in the virtual-object situation these infants do not grasp at all. Visual control of grasping has disappeared, and reaching can occur without grasping. In other words, it seems that the process of development—rather than coalescing reaching and grasping—has differentiated them, converting a single act (reach-to-grasp) into two acts (reach, then grasp) (see also

Bower 1979c; Bruner et al., 1971; Bruner, 1973; White and Held, 1966).

Why this differentiation? This question can be answered in several different ways. First, we can look at what it implies for future development. Once the infant can reach and then grasp, it should be possible for the infant to grasp and then reach; since grasping followed by reaching is characteristic of tool use, the importance of this possibility cannot be overestimated. As long as reaching and grasping are coalesced into a single act, tool use is not possible.

Another obvious and important payoff of differentiation is that it permits more *successful* reaching and grasping. If the offset time is intended to be zero, the coordination of the reach and grasp components must be perfect; otherwise, the fingers will close too soon, and the object will be lost. With a long offset time, this cannot happen. Reaching and grasping will thus become more successful.

If this is the case, does the dissociation alone produce the greater accuracy seen in older infants? Are they more accurate simply because they have grasping in a more functional relationship with reaching, or is something else involved? There is evidence that something else is involved. If one checks to see what happens when a newborn or a 20-week-old infant misses a target object, one observes retraction of the hand, often completely out of the visual field, followed by a second reach. In older infants, by contrast, the hand may start off on a miss path, but it is brought onto a hit path as soon as it enters the visual field. The hand is not withdrawn to begin again but rather alters its trajectory in flight. There is correction within the act, rather than correction between acts. This has been clearly brought out in a series of experiments using deviating prisms. Older infants are far better able than younger ones to make in-flight correction of misreaches produced by prisms (McDonnell, 1975). Indeed, there is a strong possibility that infants under 20 weeks of age cannot correct in-flight at all (Dunkeld and Bower, 1981) (see Figure 6.15).

Reaching thus develops from a unitary reach-grasp pattern that is visually initiated into two separate, recombinable acts—reaching and grasping—that are visually initiated and visually guided. How are we to explain this pattern of development? Is this simply the result of neural growth, or are there critical environmental inputs that produce and channel the growth? One critical period for the neural-growth theory is the "silent" period, when no reaching occurs. The neural-growth theory offers an account of this period in terms of the growth of inhibitory connections. A Piagetian position might argue that the

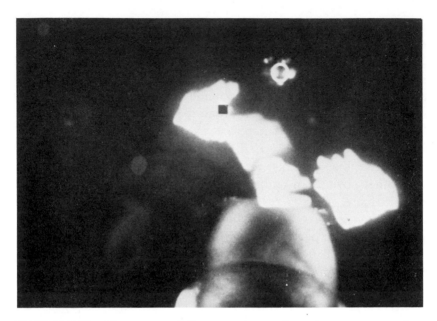

FIGURE 6.15 These young infants wearing wedge prisms are attempting to grasp a stationary object that is actually in their midline plane. The perceived position of the object, however, is to the left of its true position. Each picture is a multiple exposure, showing the path of the hand during the reach. Each infant misses and seems unable to correct its reach. (Photographs by Jennifer Wishart.)

silent period results from lack of use. This controversy is easily re-solved. One simply gives newborn infants objects to reach for every day and observes what happens. This has been done in two studies (Bower, 1973, 1979c) and the results were quite clear. Infants who had an object to reach for every day from birth demonstrated no decline in reaching at all. The decline in reaching that is normally observed must therefore result from lack of use of the behavior, rather than from inevitable neural-growth processes.

How then does the behavior change as described above? If one observes infants longitudinally, one can observe the behavior chang-ing. Reaching without grasping becomes more common. The infants begin to touch objects without grasping them (see Figure 6.16). This process is accelerated if the infants are given an object that is not rigidly fastened down. It is difficult for the infants to grasp such an object with their unitary reach–grasp action. Apparently, the grasp

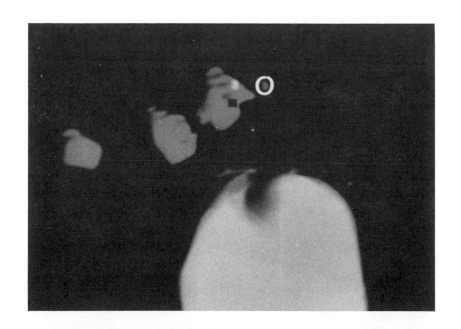

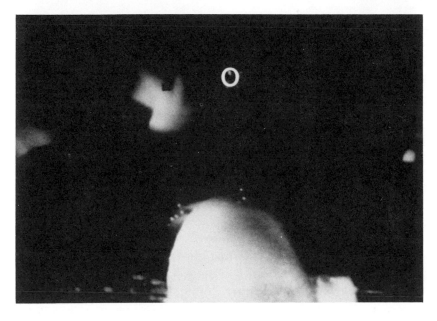

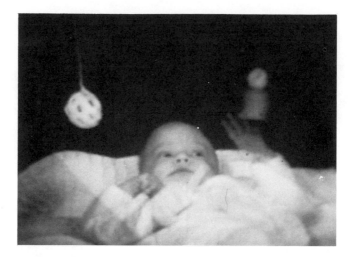

FIGURE 6.16   A 9-week-old infant reaching to touch an object without attempting to grasp it. (Photograph by Jennifer Wishart.)

component, which is rarely successful in this situation, dies away while the reaching component, which produces interesting object movement at least, predominates. Infants given rigidly tethered objects to reach for do not show the dissociation so early (see Figure 6.17). Meantime, of course, both groups are engaging in tactually elicited grasping—at their clothes, their cribs, their mothers, or anything that touches their hands.

During this period, visually initiated reaching is reinforced; visually initiated grasping is not always reinforced, but tactually initiated grasping is. On any simple learning-theory model, we would thus expect visually initiated reaching to continue, whereas visually initiated grasping should decline and be replaced by tactually initiated grasping. This, in fact, is what happens. In the virtual-object situation, younger infants grasp at the virtual object; older infants bring their hands to the object but do not close their hands in the absence of tactile input. In normal reaching, younger infants close their hands on a seen object as soon as the hand reaches it; older infants touch an object before grasping it. This can be seen with the naked eye. It is revealed more precisely by comparing the pressure pattern applied to an object in the visually initiated grasping of younger and older infants. Younger infants apply a full-force grasp straight away; older infants touch the object and then grasp it. During all of this, the

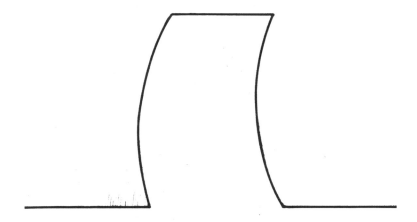

FIGURE 6.17   A polygraph tracing of pressure applied by an
infant given only rigidly tethered objects to reach for. Note the
unitary touch and grasp.

anticipatory hand shaping that occurs under visual control is not lost;
the hand remains adjusted to the size and shape of the object prior
to contact. However, the visual expectation of graspability no longer
controls grasping; that has become the province of tactile input.

None of this says anything about the shift from visual initiation to
visual control of reaching. There is a strong temptation to interpret
hand regard as a precursor to visual control. If hand regard is a
precursor to visual control, then it is another maturationally determined precursor. Every infant goes through a stage of looking at its
hand as it moves the hand to and fro. The blind infant has even been
observed to track its hand to and fro, in and out, keeping its unseeing
eyes firmly fixed on the place where the hand was (Freedman, 1964;
Urwin, 1973). This behavior degenerated and disappeared in time,
but its very occurrence is enough to rule out many interpretations of
the function of the behavior. Since the behavior occurred without
visual input, it could hardly serve to produce coordination between
the seen and the felt hand. Indeed, that coordination must be built
in for the behavior to have occurred at all in a blind infant. Does the

behavior serve to dissociate the seen hand from the felt hand? It is hard to see why this would necessarily be the case. Does the behavior help to produce visual dominance over the joint information that specifies hand location? It might, but there is no evidence that it does.

One could continue indefinitely with such speculations. It is more profitable to look at what happens when reaching has become visually controlled. When that state is reached, the infant can correct its reaching movements as they occur. In the Dunkeld and Bower (1980) experiment, where an illusion is created, one can clearly see the hand movement change direction to home in on the object. This is what we mean by visual control. Younger infants, by contrast, continue after once starting on a miss path, making their corrections between reaches rather than within reaches. This is what we refer to as visually initiated reaching. Developmentally, visually initiated reaching precedes visually guided reaching. Does this mean, then, that visually initiated reaching is replaced by visually guided reaching? Does the infant lose the ability to launch its hand toward an object without continuous visual guidance? Is continuous visual monitoring *necessary* for successful reaching in older infants, or is it merely *available* when required? There is evidence that it is not necessary.

If infants of around 5 months of age are shown an object and the lights are then extinguished, the infants can reach out in total darkness and grasp the object with very high accuracy. If reaching at this stage required visual control, this would not be possible (Bower and Wishart, 1972). Thus, visual control is available but not necessary. How then would hand regard serve to make visual control available? I do not think that hand regard could serve this function. Visual control requires the infant to attend simultaneously to the object and to its hand. Attention to two objects must be more difficult than attention to one. The change that is needed to attain double attention is precisely the kind of change produced by the maturation of processing capacity (see Chapter 5). The only function hand regard might have is to familiarize the infant with its "visual" hand; this would minimize the attentional capacities needed to register the hand. Certainly, the sight of the hand during reaching is initially disruptive. The eyes shift away from the object to the hand; this interrupts the reach, which is then stopped while the infant looks at its hand. Presumably, when the hand has been looked at for a while, it becomes boring; the object is then reengaged and reaching begins again. Bruner (1968) has pointed out how some infants at least develop strategies to avoid compulsive attention to the hand, strategies that include looking away during reaching, closing the eyes during reaching, and the like. The strategies are characteristic of middle-aged rather than younger or older infants—further support, surely, for the view that visual control of reaching only becomes possible with growth.

According to this view, hand regard could result from growing attentional capacity that allows the infant to notice its hand as the hand goes toward an object. Hand regard disappears as growing attentional capacity allows for simultaneous registration of hand and object. Thus, in this view, hand regard is an epiphenomenon—an accidental consequence of the other processes—rather than a direct precursor of later behavior. One could presumably obliterate hand regard by presenting objects that preclude attention to the hand, without retarding the development of later visually guided reaching.

Thus far, the following model of the development of reaching has been presented: The development of the behavior relies on a maturational process producing growth in attention span, plus simple learning effects of the sort known to occur in infants. Growth in attention span, extinction of visually elicited grasping, and reinforcement of tactually elicited grasping are enough to account for the development thus far—given the perceptual tuning we have considered in other chapters.

One thing that has been left in the air, however, is the hand regard observed in a blind infant. If hand regard is an epiphenomenon, why did it occur in the blind infant at all? This topic cannot be considered apart from the whole problem of the development of reaching in blind infants. This segment of development has been described in a series of papers (Fraiberg, 1968; Fraiberg and Freedman, 1964; Fraiberg et al., 1966) that show a rare combination of clinical sympathy with systematic experimentation. The development of reaching in the blind is not a problem of mere academic interest. Many blind children apparently fail to develop reaching ability at all. As Fraiberg and Freedman say:

> The child may be two years old, five years, nine, or even thirteen years old and the picture is almost unvarying. Typically the deviant child spends hours in bed or in a chair or lying on the floor, absently mouthing an object. There is no interest in toys or any objects that are not in themselves satisfying or stimulating to the mouth. Contact with human objects is often initiated by biting and even more often by a primitive clutching and clawing with the hands. For all these children the mouth remains the primary organ of perception. New objects are brought to the mouth and are rarely explored manually.
> The behavior of the hand is striking. While many of the children can

use the hand for self-feeding and can even use spoons and forks, the hand appears to have no autonomy of its own. It can serve the mouth; it can bring objects to the mouth; but it is not employed for examination or manipulation of objects. Discrimination of objects remains centered in the mouth; however, as already seen, objects are important not for their own characteristics but for their qualities in stimulating the mouth. [Fraiberg and Freedman, 1964]

Blind children as old as 12 or 13 years will hold their hands in a stereotyped shoulder-high position, while they engage in stereotyped finger and hand movements quite unrelated to events in the external world. Reaching and grasping simply have not developed in these children—a tragically restricting consequence of their loss of sight.

A careful analysis of how one blind infant developed reaching and grasping can be found in the papers of Fraiberg et al. (1966). When tested between 23 and 28 weeks of age, the infant made no attempt to reach out after an object that had been removed from his hands. When a noise-making toy was presented, he made no attempt to reach out for it. Indeed, the infant did not even turn toward it. During the next stage, 27 to 36 weeks, he made some hand movements after an object was withdrawn from his hand. These hand movements were not particularly oriented at this stage, but they did occur. Presentation of a noise-making toy still produced no reaching, although some head orientation occurred. During the next stage, 37 to 48 weeks, the infant was able to reach after a removed object in a way that showed he had registered its direction of movement. He could also find objects left in a familiar place. Sound alone still produced no attempt to reach the object; however, toward the end of this period, sound did produce finger movements without reaching—a behavior that could index some awareness that sound can signify something to be grasped. Finally, at 49 weeks, the infant searched for objects that had been taken away, and he also attempted to reach and grasp a sound-making object.

This brief summary has done little justice to the detail of Fraiberg's extremely careful and systematic report. Nevertheless, as much as I admire the study, I must quarrel with its theoretical interpretation. The authors state that the absence of vision is the reason that the coordination of hearing and prehension takes so long. They imply that the coordination should develop much earlier in the sighted infant. Two studies on auditory–manual coordination in the sighted infant have been done up to this time; in these studies, the sighted infant seemed to have no advantage over the blind infant studied by

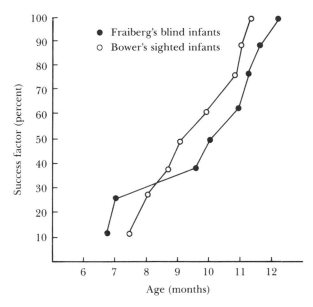

FIGURE 6.18 Comparison of success in obtaining an object specified by sound alone in sighted and in blind infants, using Fraiberg's criteria.

Fraiberg and her associates. In these studies (Bower and Wishart, 1973; Wishart et al.,1978), the sighted infant was placed in darkness, where it could see no objects nor any part of its own body. In this respect then, the sighted infant was in the same state as was the blind infant in its normal testing situation. A sound-making object was then introduced. The behavior of the infant was recorded on videotape, using an infrared sensitive camera. If we look at the results of the sighted infants over 28 weeks of age, we find that on average they too did not look nor reach out for a sound-making object presented in darkness. They did not reach or look until the age of 44 weeks—no better than the blind infants studied by Fraiberg (1968) (see Figure 6.18). It thus seems that vision does not link audition and prehension in sighted infants either.

The picture changes somewhat if we look at the behavior of sighted infants less than 28 weeks old. These younger infants (up to 20 weeks of age) have a far greater ability to reach out and grasp audible objects than do infants between 20 and 40 weeks of age. Looking at the frequency with which sighted infants can grasp an audible object

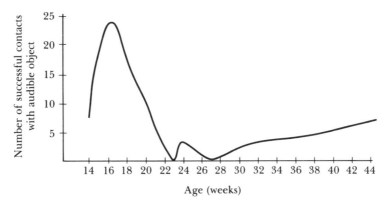

FIGURE 6.19   Success of infants in obtaining an audible object presented in darkness.

presented in darkness, we see that the success rate begins quite high, increases up to the age of 16 weeks, and then declines precipitously until 28 weeks; after 28 weeks, it gradually recovers (see Figure 6.19).

There are two sets of observations on blind infants, however, that can perhaps be taken as indicative of general development. The observation that a blind infant seemed to "look" at her hands has already been mentioned. Another observation was made when the infant was 16 weeks old; at that age, she would turn her eyes to "look" at a source of sound (Freedman, 1964). The researcher emphasizes that the eyes turned. This was not mere aural centering; rather, the unseeing eyes turned to look at the sound source. Shortly after 16 weeks, this behavior disappeared. By the age of 6 months, this infant would no longer turn her eyes toward a sound source. Urwin (1973) has made more striking observations on an infant born with no eyeballs. This infant, at 16 weeks, would reach out to grasp noise-making objects. The behavior disappeared by the age of 6 months, despite considerable reinforcement and practice, and had not reappeared by the age of 10 months.

Although these changes were only seen in two blind infants, they are strikingly similar to the behavior change seen in sighted infants tested in darkness. Because of this, I would argue that both blind and sighted infants begin life with some degree of auditory–manual coordination; this initial auditory–manual coordination is then lost during the early months of development. We have already argued that auditory–visual coordination is present at birth. Wertheimer (1961) showed that a newborn infant will turn to look at a source of sound. This coordination is not acquired through experience. Indeed, experience in the environment seems to degrade the coordination. We have argued that visual–manual coordination is built in and declines with age, rather than improves. The experiment cited above showed that sighted infants would reach out to an audible object presented in darkness. Taken together, these observations suggest that the object-specifying properties of audition decline after birth, to be reconstructed toward the end of the first year.

Why does audition lose its ability to elicit reaching? Since the phenomenon occurs in both blind and sighted infants, it is not possible that vision takes over the functions of audition. It must be that audition loses its properties by itself. The pattern of disappearance followed by reappearance is familiar to us; and, as we know, there is a well-articulated theory of neural growth to explain such a pattern. However, in the cases of walking and reaching, we have found reasons to substitute functional explanations for the growth theory. This might suggest that we attempt a functional explanation here as well.

One explanation stems from the nature of the information provided by auditory stimulation. As we saw before, audition can only specify the radial direction of objects. During locomotion, there is a kind of "auditory expansion pattern" that could specify distance, but it is not available to immobile infants. The only way audition can specify distance, as long as we talk about sound-emitting objects, is through familiarity with the characteristic loudness of an object at specified distances. Such familiarity is certainly not built in; young infants reaching on sound cue alone must misreach in depth most of the time. Such continuous failure could well explain the decline in reaching toward sound sources. Acquired familiarity with the characteristic loudness of sound-making objects might also explain the recovery of reaching toward sound sources. Echo location, discussed in Chapter 4, might also account for recovery. Indeed, studies of echo location in young blind infants point to a subtle environmental effect that may explain the initial decline. To understand it, we must consider an experiment done not on human infants but on animals. The experiment was one of many carried out by Richard Held (see e.g., Held, 1965). The subjects in the experiment were kittens that were connected together by the apparatus shown in Figure 6.20. One kitten, the active one, could move voluntarily anywhere within the limits of the apparatus. If it saw something interesting, it could move toward it. If it saw something unpleasant, it could move away. This kitten

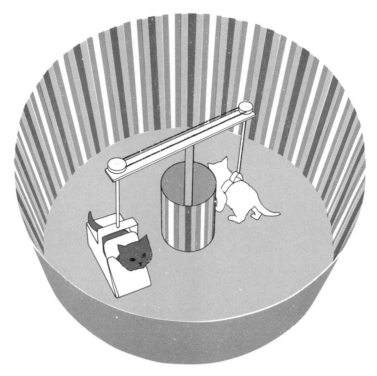

FIGURE 6.20   The kitten carousel used in Held's (1965) experiment. (After "Plasticity in Sensory-Motor Systems" by R. Held. Copyright © 1965 by Scientific American, Inc. All rights reserved.)

could use visual stimulation to control its movements and could use its movements to control the input coming to its eyes. The kitten encased in the gondola had no such interactive relationship with its visual world. It could not walk around or even touch the ground with its feet. The passive kitten saw only what the active kitten allowed it to see. When the kittens were removed from the apparatus and given a series of visual tests, the active kitten was essentially normal. The passive kitten, by contrast, simply did not react to visual inputs. It could see; its visual system was normal; but it had lost the capacity to act in a visual context. Forced to be passive in the experimental situation, it had become passive in all situations.

Now consider the situation of the blind infant. The auditory stimulation it gets is delivered to it by others. The infant does not determine what stimulation it gets, cannot shut its ears if it dislikes the sound or make the sound continue if it likes it. With the sounds produced by noise-making objects, the blind infant is in exactly the same situation as that of the passive kitten in Held's experiment. Is it any wonder, then, that the blind infant is unresponsive in the presence of auditory stimuli that are thrust on it from outside? At this point, it is worth mentioning an observation frequently made about the temperament of blind infants. They are very "good" infants, quiet, undemanding, even-tempered—in a word, passive. Is it too much to suppose that the sensorimotor passivity spreads to become a generalized personality characteristic, a generalized attitude toward the world, an habitual learned helplessness?

Thus far, we have seen that the development of reaching can be described as the result of maturational processes, with sharpening due to simple learning effects. These processes could be fitted into the Piagetian model of development. The simple learning effects could be described as changes in accommodation; the greater success resulting from these changes could be described as a greater degree of equilibration. Whether or not this formulation accomplishes anything substantial is not at all clear.

The development of reaching is far from over at this point. The infants we have been concerned with (up to about 6 months of age) can reach out and grasp objects in any direction from any posture. This is a considerable advance, as we have seen, but the behavior is still far from the adult level of competence. The behavior is equilibrated as far as the size and shape of objects are concerned. It is not yet equilibrated with respect to the weight of objects (Mounoud and Bower, 1974). That is to say, prior to actual contact with the objects, infants do not yet adjust the force of their grip or the tension of their arms in accordance with the weight of objects.

This can be shown by analyzing the grasping patterns consequent to contacting an object. A 6- or 7-month-old infant grips an object as tightly as possible, regardless of the weight of the object. The grasping force varies between infants; the point is that, in an individual infant, the force is constant and independent of the weight of the object being grasped. At this age, there is some accommodation of arm tension to object weight, although it is not yet anticipatory. The infant of this age can bring an object to its mouth; it does so with a tremor at the beginning, which indicates changes in the tension exerted. When an infant of this age is handed an object, invariably its arm initially drops under the weight of the object (see Figure 6.21). Tension is adjusted very quickly, and the object is pulled back up to the desired

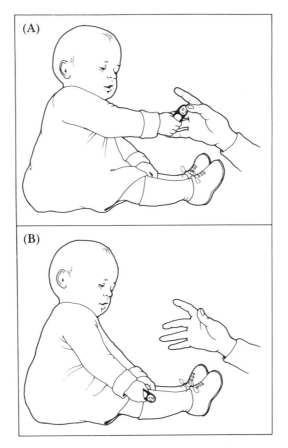

FIGURE 6.21   (A) The position of the arm on taking the object. (B) The position of the arm at the end of its first excursion. It is clear that the arm falls as the infant takes the object. (After video records.)

position. The initial hand drop indicates lack of anticipation of the weight of the object. Even on repeated presentations, the hand drop continues, indicating that anticipatory behavior cannot be built in at this stage.

Around 9 months of age, behavior begins to change. The force of grasp is adjusted to the weight of the object presented, although this still does not happen until after the object has been grasped (see Figure 6.22). The hand continues to drop on presentation of an object, even after repeated trials. At this point, both grasping and arm tension have differentiated to produce accommodation to different weights

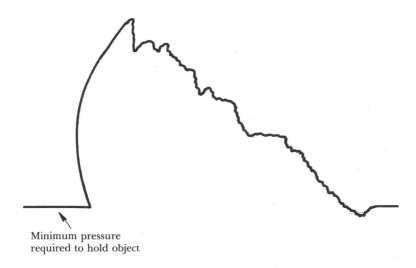

Minimum pressure
required to hold object

FIGURE 6.22   This polygraph tracing shows that the infant adjusts
the force of grasp to the weight of the object, but this adjustment is
still not made until *after* the object has been grasped.

of objects. However, the accommodation is still after the fact; there
is no anticipation of weight, even after the same object has been
presented several times.

Around the age of 1 year, a significant advance toward equilibration
occurs. On repeated presentations of an object, the errors in force of
grasp and in arm tension decline to zero. Indeed, shortly after this
pattern appears, the errors will disappear on the second presentation
of any given object. The force needed to hold an object is discovered
on the first presentation. The same force is applied instantaneously
on the second trial. Likewise, the required arm tension is discovered
during the first trial, and it is applied straight away on the second trial
(see Figure 6.23).

This amount of anticipation represents a considerable advance, but
the behavior is still very restricted. Suppose that an infant can reach
out, grasp, and transport an object with just the right force for successful holding and just the right arm tension for smooth transport.
If that infant is then given another object, say twice as long and twice
as heavy as the first, its response to that object is just as erroneous as
it would have been if the infant had had no prior information about

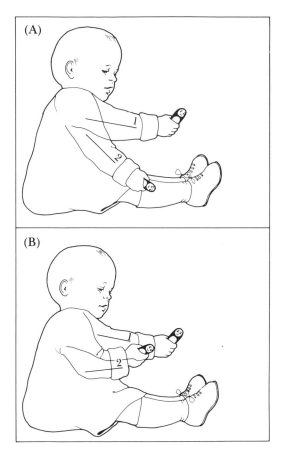

FIGURE 6.23 Each picture shows two arm positions superimposed: (1) the position on taking the object, and (2) the position of the arm at the end of its first excursion. On comparing A and B, we can see that the information about the weight of the object gained in the first presentation is applied immediately on the second presentation of the same object. Note the greatly diminished arm excursion. (After video records.)

the weight of the new object. In this stage, therefore, equilibration can be attained—but only for single objects. The responses are sufficiently differentiated to permit adjustment; however, there is as yet no predictive rule that permits anticipatory adjustments for new objects. The only predictive rule we could infer from the behavior would be something like: "The same objects weigh the same every time they are picked up." Some such rule must be in use to produce the instantaneous adjustments seen on repeated presentations of the same object.

Toward 18 months of age, the behavior changes once again; at this age, there is anticipation of the weight of objects that have not yet been grasped. If one presents an infant with a series of objects, graded according to length and weight, the infant is seemingly able to predict the weight from the perceived length. Suppose we have a series of lengths—say, 1, 2, 3, 4, and 5. Each constant increase in length is correlated with a constant increase in weight. If the infant is given object number 1, its initial grasp force and arm tension will probably be wrong. The second presentation of object 1 will elicit no error; there is nothing new in this. However, the *first* presentation of object number 2 likewise elicits no error; nor does the first presentation of objects 3, 4, and 5. The infant now seems able to *predict* the weight of objects, prior to actual interaction with them. The rule controlling the infant's behavior now seems to be: "The longer an object is, the heavier it will be when picked up." Paradoxically, this rule can lead the 18-month-old infant to make mistakes that a younger infant would never make. Suppose we add to our series a trick object—of length 6 and weight 3. The infant will overestimate the weight of the object, gripping it too hard and applying too much arm tension. The result is that the infant's arm will fly up, as shown in Figure 6.24. The opposite will happen if an object of length 2 and weight 5 is presented; the object will probably be dropped. The existence of these errors shows that accommodation is now anticipatory for all objects that can be serially ordered in some visible dimension that covaries with weight.

The stages in the development can now be summarized into four stages:

Stage I. No differential response to objects of different weight.

Stage II. Differential response to objects of different weight after grasping.

Stage III. Differential response after grasping with anticipation that the same object will weigh the same on repeated presentations.

Stage IV. Differential response after grasping with anticipation that the same object will weigh the same on repeated presentations, and anticipation that objects graded in length will be correspondingly graded in weight.

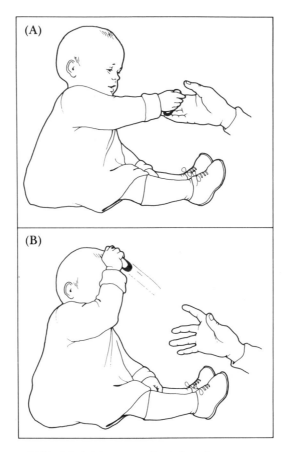

FIGURE 6.24   Here the infant has overestimated the weight of the object, and the arm flies up. (After video records.)

The critical steps in the development so far are the differentiation of responses and the emergence of anticipation. We can only speculate about the mechanisms that produce differentiation. It is possible, indeed plausible, that experience with different objects is required to produce the differentiation of behavior. In the absence of relevant experiments, no conclusions can be drawn. If such experience is necessary, then one should be able to demonstrate acceleration effects by introducing an assortment of weights. Infants given different objects should display differentiated behavior earlier, if the behavioral differentiation is environmentally mediated. If it is not so mediated, then the environmental modification should produce no effect.

One must also wonder about the nature of the sequence leading from differentiated behavior to anticipation. Is it simply a sequence, or must differentiation precede anticipation? What is it that produces anticipation? We have, at this moment, no answers to questions like these. It is difficult to say why this development should occur on a learning-theory model of development. In terms of successful manipulation of objects, younger infants do as well as older infants. Their exceedingly tight grip is a safety-first procedure. It ensures that they do not make the errors characteristic of older infants. Why then should there be development? In principle, one could give a Piagetian explanation in terms of tendencies toward equilibrium. At the beginning of this segment of development, both assimilation and accommodation are undifferentiated, perhaps even from each other. There is no prediction of weight and no adjustment to weight. There is thus a kind of equilibrium. Once there are differentiated responses to different weights, however, this fragile equilibrium is lost. The range of accommodation—the number of differentiated responses—exceeds the range of differentiated instructions that can be sent out by the mechanism of assimilation. This state of disequilibrium should produce development until the range of assimilation and accommodation covary. The Piagetian model thus predicts the development of anticipation after response differentiation has taken place. It says nothing about how the development will take place. Although perhaps strained, this model, unlike other models, at least predicts that development will take place.

The development at this point is still far from complete. We have followed the infant up to a point where it can make two different kinds of anticipation. The infant anticipates that an object will be the same weight on repeated presentations. The infant also anticipates that the longer an object is, the heavier it will be. What will happen if we put the two kinds of anticipation in conflict? Suppose we present an infant with a pliable object, so that the infant can ascertain the force required to grasp it. On the second presentation, the infant should apply the same force. Suppose, though, that we elongate the object before giving it to the infant again (see Figure 6.25). What should the infant do? Since it is the same object, should the infant apply the same force? But it is also longer; should the infant therefore apply more force? How should the infant resolve the conflict? At this

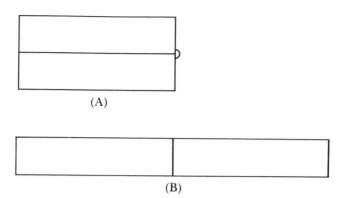

FIGURE 6.25   Object B is produced by unfolding Object A.

point, it is surely obvious that we are no longer talking about motor behavior at all—but rather about the rules that control behavior. The conflict between these rules can be resolved, as we shall see. The processes of resolution will not change the behavior, however, but the way in which the behavior is applied. With increasing age, *behavior* changes less and less, while the complexity of its *control* processes increases more and more. The study of these control processes is the subject of the next chapter.

7

Cognitive Development

In preceding chapters, we have already given an indication of the subject matter of this chapter. In Chapter 4, it was pointed out that there comes a stage in development when infants ignore perceptual information and rely on other kinds of information, such as that supplied by memory, consistency, or other nonperceptual processes. In Chapter 6, we discussed how a behavior may develop to a peak of perfection without development necessarily being over; the rules for the application of the behavior must still be elaborated. In development, there is thus a progression away from dependence on immediate stimulus input toward dependence on rules that combine perceptual information with information from memory. This progression—cognitive development—is the subject of this chapter.

Piaget has described the processes and details of infant cognitive development in his famous trilogy, *The Origins of Intelligence in Children* (1936), *The Construction of Reality in the Child* (1937), and *Play, Dreams and Imitation in Childhood* (1946). The breadth and originality of these works dwarf all of the other essays in this field. It would seem impossible to summarize these books within the compass of the present work. Indeed, they depend on an interplay between observation and theory that defies summarization. Instead of attempting a summary of the whole trilogy, I shall select one or two topics to describe in full, in the hope that a detailed analysis of selected topics will illuminate the processes at work in cognitive development.

The choice of a topic is not easy, for the whole range of topics is fascinating and important. There is one topic that stands out, however, and that is the development of the *object concept*. Piaget refers to this segment of development as the prototype of cognitive development; he describes the attainment of the object concept as the most precocious expression of processes that will eventually generate mathematical reasoning and logical thinking in adults. Other authors are equally convinced of the importance of the object concept. Elkind and Sameroff (1970) refer to it as Piaget's most significant discovery—no mean attribution when one considers how many revolutionary discoveries Piaget made.

What then is the object concept and how does it develop? According to Piaget, the main landmarks of the development are best seen by studying the infant's reaction to an object that has vanished or been hidden. Initially, as Piaget describes it, there is no special behavior toward a vanished object. This description, as we shall see, must be qualified. In terms of gross searching behavior, there is nothing to be seen at this early stage. The infant does not reach out or crawl after an object that has left its field of view; this, perhaps, is not a surprising result since the infant we are discussing is under 4 months of age. The infant in the second half of this period (2 to 4 months) will look after an object that has moved out of its field of view. The infant in the first half (zero to 2 months—referred to as Stage I) does not even do this. During Stage II, head and eye tracking and looking after an object that has moved out of view do occur. By Stage III, the infant can reach out to pick up an object that it sees. If presented with a

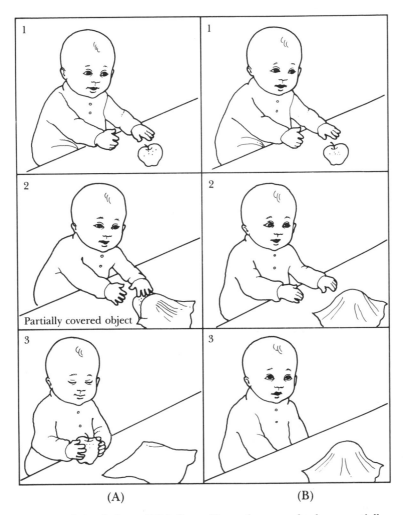

FIGURE 7.1 A Stage III infant will reach out and take a partially covered object (A) but is unable to obtain an object that has been completely covered by a cloth (B).

partially covered object, the infant can reach out and take it (see Figure 7.1). If the object is completely covered with a cloth or a cup, the Stage III infant makes no attempt whatsoever to get the object. The infant pulls back from the object and its cover and makes no attempt at all to remove the cover. Indeed, the infant acts as if the object no longer existed. Many authors have interpreted this behavior as evidence that the infant of this age (4 to 6 months) in fact believes that an object no longer exists when it is out of sight.

When the infant can recover an object that has been hidden under a cloth, this third stage ends. The Stage IV infant, though, still seems to have a peculiar concept of objects. The infant will look for an object if the object is hidden under a cloth. If, however, the infant is allowed to find an object under the same cloth two or more times, and then the object is hidden within the infant's view but under a different cloth in a different place, the infant will look for the object in its original place under the first cloth—totally ignoring the actual location of the object. This happens even if the hidden object is quite large; the infant will still pick up the flat cloth that had previously covered the object (see Figure 7.2). This error implies that the infant does not yet really understand that an object that has been covered by a cloth is under the cloth. The infant seems to think that an object that has been hidden will always be found in the same place. This place error is characteristic of the Stage IV infant. The error is usually overcome around the age of 10 to 12 months.

By the age of 10 months, we might think that the object concept was fully developed. However, the infant of this age can still be confused by some methods of hiding objects. Suppose we place two cloths on a table; we put an object under one of them and then transpose the position of the cloths, as shown in Figure 7.3A. The Stage V infant will pick up the cloth on the side where the object was first placed, ignoring the cloth that is actually concealing the object. At this point, the infant seems to believe that an object will be found where it was hidden; the infant does not take into account invisible displacements of the object even when the displacements of the thing covering the object are fully visible. Figure 7.3B illustrates a similar failure in a related task. Eventually, the infant succeeds in even these tasks; this normally occurs somewhere around 18 months of age. For future reference, these stages are summarized in Table 7.1.

These then are the main behavioral landmarks in the development of the object concept. But a summary of this sort tells us little about the meaning of the infant's failures and successes. Our interpretation of the behavior is critical, and many different interpretations have been made. Consider the behavior that is characteristic of the infant in Stage III; if an infant is presented with a desirable toy that is then covered while the infant is watching, the infant will make no attempt to remove the cover. One interpretation—the standard one—is that the infant thinks that the object no longer exists when it is under the cover. According to this interpretation, once the object is out of sight,

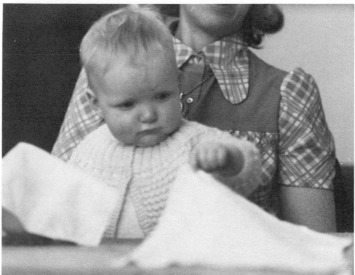

FIGURE 7.2 Stage IV place error. The infant thinks that an object that has been hidden will always be found in the same place. Even when the hidden object is quite large, the infant will still go to the place where the object was previously hidden. (Photographs by Jennifer Wishart.)

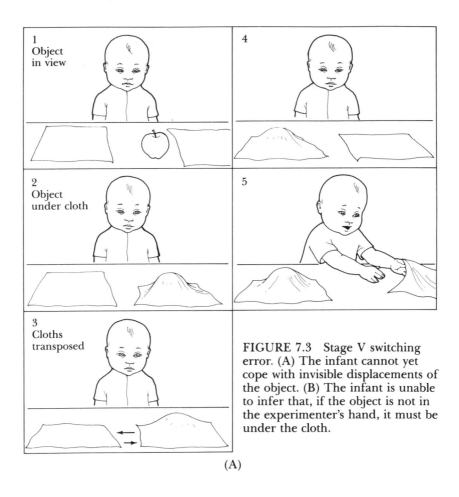

FIGURE 7.3 Stage V switching error. (A) The infant cannot yet cope with invisible displacements of the object. (B) The infant is unable to infer that, if the object is not in the experimenter's hand, it must be under the cloth.

(A)

the infant thinks it is no longer to be found anywhere and, therefore, makes no attempt to search for it.

This explanation certainly accounts for the observed behavior. If the infant thinks the object no longer exists, we could hardly expect the infant to pick up the cover. However, there are other possible alternative explanations. Suppose the infant doesn't pick up the cloth because it simply doesn't have the motor skill to pick up cloths? It is surely possible that the infant knows that the object is under the cloth but doesn't know how to remove the cloth; in this case, of course, the

1	Object is in experimenter's hand.	4	. . . removes hand, leaving object under cloth.
2	Experimenter closes hand . . .	5	Infant looks in experimenter's hand.
3	. . . puts hand under cloth. . .	6	Obviously upset, infant quits.

(B)

same lack of behavior would ensue. These two explanations are obviously quite different ways of accounting for the same behavior. Nothing we have said so far allows us to decide between these explanations; however, the relevant sorts of experiments are not too hard to do. What we need is some measure—other than search behavior—to indicate whether an infant thinks that an out-of-sight object still exists. Startle measures could obviously be useful in this account.

Suppose we present an infant with an object and then drop a screen over the object so as to make it vanish. We then remove the screen,

TABLE 7.1   Stages of development

Stage	Age (Months)*	Success	Fail
I	0–2	No particular behavior shown in response to hiding event.	
II	2–4	Infant will track a moving object that goes behind a screen. Infant can learn to track an object from place to place.	Infant continues to track a moving object after it has stopped. Infant will look for an object in its familiar place even when the infant sees the object moving to new place.
III	4–6	Infant no longer makes tracking errors of Stage II. Infant recovers an object that has been partially covered by a cloth.	Infant cannot recover an object that has been fully covered by a cloth.
IV	6–12	Infant can now recover an object that has been completely hidden under a cloth.	Infant searches for an object in the place where it was previously found, ignoring the place where it was seen to be hidden.
V	12–15	Infant no longer makes place error of Stage IV.	Infant cannot cope with invisible displacements of an object.
VI	15–18	Complete success— infant can find object no matter where or how hidden.	

*These ages are approximate; there may be considerable individual differences.

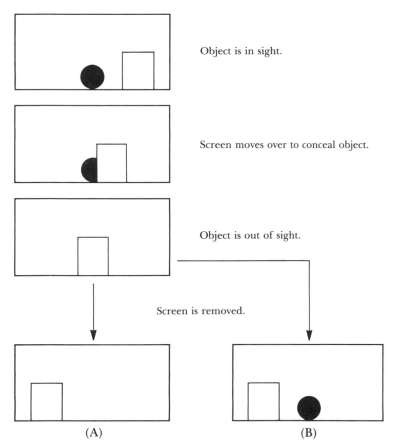

FIGURE 7.4   How will a Stage III infant respond to these two events? (A) The object has disappeared. (B) The object is in sight again.

either revealing the object or revealing an empty place where the object had been (see Figure 7.4). What responses would be predicted by the two alternative explanations? If the infant indeed thinks that an object no longer exists when it is out of sight, the infant should hardly expect to see the object again when the screen is removed. Following this logic, the infant should be more surprised by the reappearance sequence than by the nonreappearance sequence. On the contrary, if the infant believes that the object is still there, hidden behind the screen, then the infant should be more surprised by nonreappearance than by reappearance. Experiments of this kind have been done by Bower (1966c) and Charlesworth (1966).

In my own experiment, change in heart rate was used as a measure of surprise. I found that the infant too young to be able to pick up a cloth was more surprised by nonreappearance than by reappearance. The indication is that the infant did believe that the hidden object still existed even though it was out of sight. If heart rate change can be taken as a fair measure of cognitive upset, it would seem that this is a clear disproof of the standard explanation of Stage III behavior. If the infant subject actually does believe that an object still exists after it has been covered by a screen, then the belief should also manifest itself in other behaviors. If presented with a moving object that can be tracked, the infant should be able to track the object and anticipate its reappearance when the object goes behind a screen. In other words, if an infant sees an object move behind a screen, the infant should expect the object to come out on the other side of the screen—provided the infant really believes that the object continues to exist when it is out of sight. Experiments like this have also been done (Gardner, 1971; Bower et al., 1971). The results indicate quite clearly that the infants as young as 8 weeks of age will anticipate the reappearance of an object that has gone behind a screen. That is to say, the infant will turn its eyes to reach the exit side of the screen just before, or just as, the moving object emerges from behind the screen. It is not the case that the object is looked at after it emerges. Rather the infant's eyes are at the exit point just as, or just before, the object appears. This indicates anticipation of emergence rather than reaction to emergence.

This result, together with data on infants' surprise at nonreappearance, would seem to prove conclusively that quite young infants— infants still in the age range of Piaget's Stage II—know that objects still exist after they have been occluded by a screen. The infants can manifest this knowledge in their eye movements but not in hand and arm movements. Clearly, the implication is that the Stage III deficit is really a deficit in the motor system—not a deficit in the infant's knowledge of the world. However, that implication can only be admitted if we accept that the eye-movement behavior unambiguously indexes a belief in the continued existence of hidden objects. Such a belief could produce the observed behavior. However, the behavior could also be generated in other ways.

The simplest possible reason for the behavior would be inability to arrest an ongoing head movement. If the infant were moving its head and eyes in pursuit of the moving object and were unable to stop its moving head, then the infant would continue to "track" the object even if it thought the object no longer existed after it had disappeared behind the screen. Simple inability to arrest an ongoing head movement could thus result in apparent anticipatory behavior with no real anticipation or belief that the object was still moving behind the screen.

This counterexplanation was easily tested; infants were presented with an object that moved toward a screen but stopped before it reached the screen (Bower et al., 1971). If the infant were "anticipating" because of an inability to stop its head movements, the infant should also "anticipate" in this situation. Indeed, this is just what happened. The infant who was presented with a moving object that stopped while still in sight continued to look along the path the object had been traveling; the infant ignored the stationary object sitting there in full view. This kind of result obviously casts doubt on any statement that the young infant believes in the continued existence of objects that have gone out of sight; yet it is a result that does not fit with the surprise data gathered with stationary objects. Those data could hardly be accounted for by supposing some inability to arrest an ongoing action.

Closer analysis of the tracking data showed that the continuation of tracking did not in fact result from inability to arrest head and eye movements. A frame-by-frame analysis of videotape records showed that every infant—even the youngest (12 weeks)—stopped tracking when the object stopped; and then, after an interval of a few hundred milliseconds, the infant continued to move its eyes along the path the object had been following before it stopped (Bower and Paterson, 1973). In other words, the infant could arrest its head movements, but, after doing so, again began to "track," ignoring the visible, stationary object.

There are several possible explanations for these bizarre behaviors. For example, one could argue that the infant has learned something to the effect: "A movement on one side of a screen will be followed by movement on the other side of a screen." The infant might well have learned that movement of an object toward a screen is usually followed by movement of an object away from the other side of the screen. This kind of learning would explain the bizarre continuation of tracking behavior, as well as the seemingly intelligent anticipation behavior. Unfortunately for this explanation, continuation of tracking after the tracked object has stopped occurs when there is *no* screen in the visual field at all. An infant between 12 and 20 weeks of age, if presented with a moving object that stops, will continue to track along the path that the moving object was following—even if the infant had stopped momentarily with the stopped object and even if there is no screen in the visual field. This odd continuation of tracking behavior is thus not peculiar to the screen situation but rather represents a general response to moving objects.

What is it that produces this seemingly aberrant behavior? One possible explanation is that the infant does not realize that the object, once stopped, is the same object that had been moving. The infant might think that the object that stops is a new stationary object; the infant then continues to look for the moving object that it had been tracking. This sort of explanation at least makes sense of the continuation behavior. We are saying that the infant does not realize that a moving object is the same object when it becomes stationary. If this is true, then the converse must also be true; the infant should fail to recognize that a stationary object that begins to move is still the same object after it starts moving. In other words, the infant should see the moving object as a new object.

If this is the case, what behaviors might we expect to see? We might expect the infant to continue staring at the place where an object had been resting before it started to move. Piaget reports that this is indeed the case. However, such observations cannot be conclusive, for one could always argue that the infant is merely slow to respond to movement. One might also expect that an infant who is tracking a moving object will look back to where the object had been—a behavior analogous to the continued "tracking" of an object that has stopped moving. This kind of behavior has also been observed; it is not reliable, however, perhaps because a moving object is intrinsically more interesting to an infant than is a stationary object.

A more complicated experiment was done to test the predictions (Bower and Paterson, 1973). Infants were presented with an object (a toy train bedecked with flashing lights); the train remained stationary in one place (A) for 10 seconds before moving to another place (B), where it stopped for 10 seconds before returning to A, where it stopped for 10 seconds before moving off again to B. This A-B-A-B sequence was repeated a number of times. How would an infant see this sequence if it did not know that a stationary object is the same object when it moves, and vice versa? The infant should see initially an object stationary at A. After 10 seconds, this object will disappear, and a new moving object will appear. The moving object will then disappear, and a new stationary object will appear at B. After 10 seconds, that object will also disappear, and yet another moving object will appear. It in turn will disappear, and the stationary object will reappear at A, and so on. The infant who is presented with this kind of sequence between 12 and 16 weeks of age initially shows continuation of tracking after the object has stopped. However, within a few trials, the infant settles down to track the object from A to B and back again with no overshooting beyond the place where the object actually stops. The infant looks as if it is indeed tracking an object from place to place. If the analysis given above is correct, the infant is really looking at four objects, largely ignoring the moving ones and concentrating on the stationary ones. Rather than having learned to track a single object from place to place, the infant has learned something of this sort: "An object at place A will disappear and an object at place B will appear; the object at place B will disappear, and the object at place A will appear." This kind of learning would also produce the smooth tracking that is actually observed.

Suppose now that the object stationary at A, instead of going off to B, moves to a new location, C. What should the infant do in this situation? If the infant is in fact tracking a single object from place to place, the infant should simply track the object to its new location. If, on the contrary, the infant is operating with the rule "Object at A disappears; object at B appears," then the infant should not track the object to C, but rather should look for it in its familiar location, B. This is what actually happens. The infant ignores the clearly visible object at location C and looks steadfastly for it at B—often looking surprised and puzzled that the object is not to be seen at B (see Figure 7.5).

It thus would seem that the infant fitting into Piaget's Stage II does not identify a stationary object as being the same object when it moves; nor does the infant identify a moving object with itself when it becomes stationary. The question that immediately springs to mind is: how does the infant in this age range identify objects? Under what conditions does such an infant think that an object remains the same object? This is a different problem from the one we have been considering so far. The problem up till now has been to specify whether an infant thinks that an object still exists after it has been occluded from view. We are now asking under what conditions an infant thinks that an object is the same object. It seems that the transitions from being stationary to assuming motion, and vice versa, are enough to make an infant believe that it is dealing with two objects. Is it the case, then, that an infant thinks that an object is the same as long as it stays in the same place? And, similarly, does the infant think that an object is the same as long as it continues on the same path of movement?

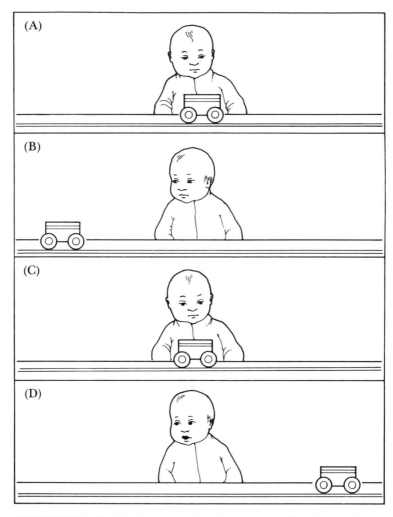

FIGURE 7.5 (C–D) On the catch trial, instead of looking to the left, where the train is now sitting, the infant typically looks to the right, where the train had stopped on all previous trials (A–B). (After "The Object in the World of the Infant" by T. G. R. Bower. Copyright © 1971 by Scientific American, Inc. All rights reserved.)

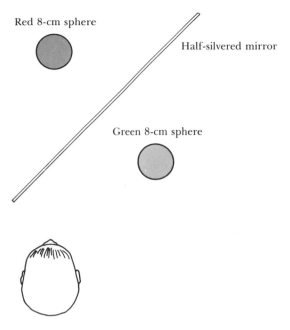

FIGURE 7.6 When the green 8-cm sphere is in darkness, the subject sees only the red 8-cm sphere on the mirror. If the illumination is changed simultaneously to the green 8-cm sphere (leaving the red 8-cm sphere in darkness), it is seen to appear at the place where the red object was on the mirror, and it looks as if the red object has turned into a green object.

We are really asking for the infant's definition of object identity. There seem to be two possible definitions: an object is the same object as long as it stays in the same place; and an object is the same object as long as it continues on the same path of movement.

How can we test whether the infant actually uses these definitions? Fortunately, similar problems have been tested in adults. Michotte (1967) presented adults with an object of some given size, shape, and color—let's say a red 8-cm sphere in a particular place. After some time, the object was changed, this time becoming a green 8-cm sphere. The way in which this was done is shown in Figure 7.6. Subjects were then asked to describe what had happened. They usually said that the object had been changed, but was still the same object. Further one-step changes (into a green 8-cm cube) elicited the same response. In fact, subjects would watch a red 8-cm sphere turn by stages (see Figure

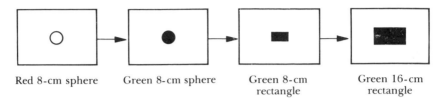

Red 8-cm sphere   Green 8-cm sphere   Green 8-cm   Green 16-cm
                                          rectangle   rectangle

FIGURE 7.7   On seeing this sequence of transformations, adults maintain that they have seen only one object that has undergone a series of changes.

7.7) into a green 16-cm cube, while maintaining that they had seen only one object undergo a series of changes. If two aspects were changed at the same time (a red 3-cm sphere became a green 16-cm sphere while staying in the same place), subjects were likely to say that the original object had been *replaced* by *another* object. If three aspects were changed (a red 8-cm sphere became, in one step, a green 16-cm cube), subjects said unanimously that the object had been replaced by another object. Continuity of place is thus not enough to produce object identity in adults, although place is still important.

In another set of experiments, the object disappeared from one place, and an identical object appeared in a different place. Subjects agreed that it was the same object that had moved. If, however, the object that appeared in the different place differed in one other aspect—say, size—subjects were more likely to say that the original object had been replaced by another object in a different place. Adults thus seem to define identity by some kind of addition of place, size, shape, and color. If there is overlap in any three of these features, subjects will say that no new object has been introduced. If any two features are changed, subjects will tend to say that some kind of substitution has taken place. Place therefore has no privileged part to play in the adults' definition of identity.

Michotte has done similar experiments with a moving object. In his experiments, an object moved behind a screen and then reemerged on course but with some of its features changed. Some of the transformations he used are shown in Figure 7.8. Movement appears to be a more powerful determinant of identity than is place, since more extreme changes could be tolerated by subjects before they would say that a new object had been introduced. With the more extreme changes, however, the subjects gave peculiar responses such as: "It looks as if it is the same object that has changed, but I *know* that you must have introduced another object somehow." In other words, it

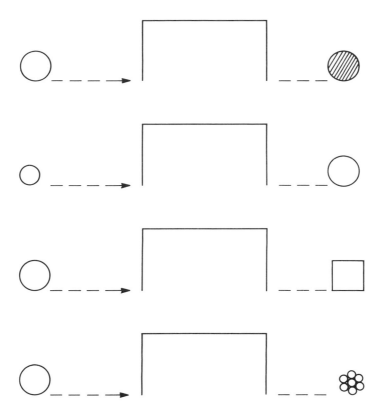

FIGURE 7.8 Transformations used in Michotte's experiment: four examples of the object reemerging from behind the screen with some of its features changed.

seems as if these subjects had a cognitive criterion of identity that could override the evidence of their senses.

These experiments depend heavily on verbal reports that are, of course, not available from infants. However, one can use other indicators. Bower et al. (1971) performed an experiment that was directly modeled on the movement experiments of Michotte. Infants watched an object approach and then move behind a screen. When the first object should have reemerged from behind the screen, a different object came out and continued along the original path at the original speed. The apparatus used to accomplish this is shown in Figure 7.9. The infants' eye movements were observed. It was thought that, if the infants saw the new object as a new object, their tracking might be disrupted as they looked back for the original object. This change in

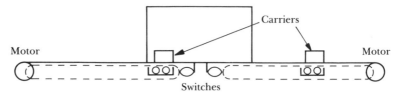

FIGURE 7.9   The carriers on the two track segments were driven
by two independent, separately controlled motors. Two solid-state
timers provided precise control of the intervals between movements.
The center segment was screened by a 15-cm white screen. The
background was black velvet. (After "The Development of the
Object Concept as Manifested by Changes in the Tracking Behavior
of Infants Between 7 and 20 Weeks of Age" by T. G. R. Bower, J.
M. Broughton, and M. K. Moore. *Journal of Experimental Child
Psychology,* **11,** 182–193, 1971.)

looking pattern was seen in infants of about 20 weeks of age or more.
The younger infants, however, continued to track as if nothing had
happened—even when the transformation was as gross as that shown
in Figure 7.10. A gross change in size, shape, and color made no
difference to those infants.

One might argue that the response demanded too much from the
younger infants, and they could not organize a looking-back response.
However, these responses were observed in the same infants in a
different experimental condition. In that condition, two identical objects were used. One object disappeared behind the screen, and a
second one emerged immediately from the other side of the screen.
The second object emerged much sooner than the original object
could have emerged while maintaining its original speed. The object
that did appear was identical to the first in all of its features; however,
it was on a different path of movement. In this condition, the infants
typically made a rapid eye movement to catch the new object but then
went back to the exit point; they then jump-tracked to catch the new
object again and then returned again to the exit point. The younger
infants would typically refuse to look at more than one or two presentations of this sequence—evidence that they found it odd and
disturbing.

Lest one think that the observed behavior was a function of the
screen, the experiments were repeated, using an enlarged tachisto-
scope to change objects (see Figure 7.11). The results were exactly the
same. As long as the object continued on the same path of movement—
even though all of its features were changed—the infants were not

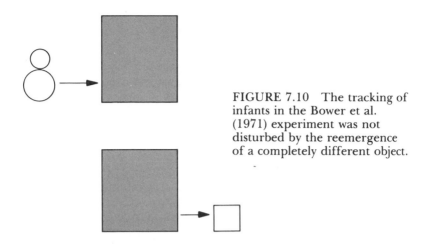

FIGURE 7.10 The tracking of infants in the Bower et al. (1971) experiment was not disturbed by the reemergence of a completely different object.

disturbed, and their tracking was not affected. As soon as the movement path was changed—even though everything else was left the same—the smooth tracking disappeared, and the infants gave some evidence of disturbance. It thus seems that 3- to 4-month-old infants define the identity of a moving object solely in terms of movement. The other features are not taken into account. We know from work described in Chapter 5 that infants of this age can tell that there has been a change. However, the change is interpreted as a change in the object—not as the introduction of a new object. The behavior of the older infants, by contrast, indicated that they took other features into account—not just movement.

Attempts to demonstrate the existence of a place criterion for identity have also been made. It would seem that the same response measure could be used. If one object is substituted for another, and the infant perceives this as a substitution rather than as a change occurring in the same object, then we might expect the infant to look for the object that has been replaced. If, on the other hand, the infant perceives a change in the same object, then we would not expect to see any searching behavior at all. Experiments have used tachistoscopic devices to produce event sequences with objects retaining the same place but changing in every other way or with objects changing place while retaining all their other features (Bower, 1968). The results were less clear than were the results from infant tracking. When an object changes place, the younger infant (3 to 4 months old) does look back and forth between the two locations. This behavior is not seen in the 5- to 6-month-old infant. If the substitute object is put in the same

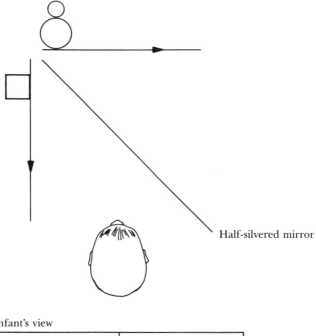

Half-silvered mirror

Infant's view

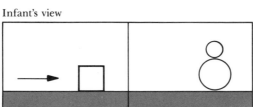

FIGURE 7.11 Both objects move at the same speed, starting from the same point on the track. If only the small object is illuminated, when the illumination is switched to the large object, the small object appears to have changed into a large object on the same path of movement. (See also Figure 7.6.)

place as the original object, the younger infant does not look for the original object but continues to stare at the place where the original object was. The older infant—even up to 1 year of age—also shows this concentration on the place where the object is put (for most objects). If a very significant object such as the infant's mother is used, however, the 5- to 6-month-old infant will look for her after a re-placement object has appeared in the place where she was. The younger infant does not show this behavior. Thus, on the criterion of looking for an object (provided that the object is as significant as the mother), place loses its exclusive role in defining the identity of stationary objects around the time when movement loses its privileged role for moving objects.

The infant roughly between the ages of 12 and 20 weeks equates an object with its place or with its path of movement. The infant seems to think that an object will remain in its place—even after the object has been occluded by a screen. Likewise, the infant's response indicates an awareness that the path of movement continues behind the occluding screen. The infant does not seem to be aware that place and movement are linked—that a single object can move from place to place without becoming a whole series of different objects. By the end of this period (around 20 weeks), the infant's behavior has changed, indicating that the infant has coordinated place and movement. When presented with a moving object that stops, the 20-week-old stops tracking and remains stopped. When presented with a stationary object that proceeds to move, the 20-week-old can follow it no matter where it moves or has moved. The infant seems to be aware that an object can go from place to place along movement paths. The infant also seems to know that movement links spatially disparate places. We are arguing then that the infant has learned the coordination between place and movement; this argument explains the change in the tracking behaviors already described.

Coordination is an inference or a construct to explain something else. However, Mundy-Castle and Anglin (1974) have done an experiment that seems to show the coordination directly. The experimental setup is shown in Figure 7.12. Mundy-Castle observed the eye movements of the infant as it looked at his display. The infant around 12 weeks of age showed a simple side-to-side, place-to-place tracking. The infant was able to anticipate the appearance of the object in each porthole, but this was done by simple eye movements in the horizontal plane. Sometime later, a completely new behavior appeared. The infant began to interpolate a trajectory between the two portholes: rather than going directly from one porthole to the other, the infant began to go up and over, *as if following the trajectory it thought the object must have been following to get from one place to the other.* This trajectory interpolation is visible evidence of the coordination of place and movement within the mind of the infant. The trajectories that are interpolated reveal a surprising degree of knowledge about the world. Thus, if the interval between disappearance from one porthole and subsequent reappearance in the other porthole is long, the interpolated trajectory is high and rather steep. If the interval is short, the

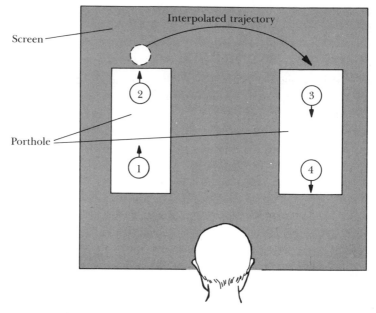

FIGURE 7.12 The apparatus in the Mundy-Castle and Anglin (1969) experiment.

interpolated trajectory is low and rather flat. This shows that the infant knows not only that objects move from place to place along trajectories, but also *how* they must move to get from one place to another at a particular speed. Indeed, this is a degree of sophistication we would not have dreamt of attributing to infants a few years ago (see also Bundy and Mundy-Castle, 1981).

Coordinating place and movement responses has obvious advantages for the infant. It will markedly improve the success of tracking. However, this advance will also create new problems for the infant— most obviously in the realm of object identity. The infant at around 12 weeks of age seems to think that an object is the same object as long as it is in the same place and that all objects in the same place are the same object, or that an object is the same object as long as it continues to move on the same path of movement and that all objects on the same path of movement are the same object. It follows that the infant thinks that a single object seen in different places is, in fact, a number of different objects. This error should disappear after place and movement are coordinated.

FIGURE 7.13 Multiple "mothers." A very simple optical arrangement allows one to present infants with multiple images of a single object.

Indeed, this does occur for at least one object, and it can be demonstrated with a simple optical arrangement that allows one to present infants with multiple images of a single object (Bower, 1971) (see Figure 7.13). If one presents the infant with a multiple image of its mother—say, three "mothers"—the infant of less than 5 months of age is not disturbed at all but will in fact interact with all three "mothers" in turn. If the setup provides one mother and two strangers, the infant will preferentially interact with its mother and still show no signs of disturbance. However, past the age of 5 months (after the coordination of place and movement), the sight of three "mothers" becomes very disturbing to the infant.* At this same age, a setup of one mother and two strangers has no effect. I would contend that this in fact shows that the young infant (less than 5 months old) thinks that it has a multiplicity of mothers, whereas the older infant knows that it has only one. That one mother can no longer be identified merely by a place or a movement. Her other features must also have become critical.

Identification by features is no problem in the case of the mother, since the mother is unique. However, most objects in the world are

---

*The same phenomenon apparently occurs in Japan (personal communication, Shiomi, Kyoto University, 1978).

TABLE 7.2   Conceptual development from birth to 5 months of age (as observed in tracking, Mundy-Castle, and multiple-mother experiments)

Prior to 5 Months	After 5 Months
An object is a bounded volume of space in a particular place. An object is a bounded volume of space in motion.	An object is a bounded volume of space that can move from place to place.
Two objects cannot be in the same place at the same time.	Two objects cannot be in the same place *simultaneously*.
Objects in the same place are the same object. Identical objects seen in different places are different objects.	Identical objects seen in different places *simultaneously* are different objects.

not unique in terms of their features. Thus, if the infant were to rely on features alone, it would identify many different objects as one object. There is evidence that identification of objects remains a problem for a long time after infancy (Piaget, 1946). There is no problem so long as an object stays in one place or is seen to move from one place to another. If the movement is unobserved (an invisible displacement), the infant then has a problem. How is the infant to know whether this is the same object that has moved or a new object that has just appeared? Obviously, this is a problem that cannot be solved in any deductive fashion. The best anyone can do—even an adult— is make an educated guess. As we shall see, the infant's guesses become progressively better as it grows up.

The tremendous conceptual development that has gone on in these first five months is summarized in Table 7.2. At this point in time, the infant, as judged by its eye movements and startle responses, knows a great deal about objects. The infant knows that objects exist when occluded by a screen. The infant also knows how to identify objects by their features as well as by their location. The infant knows that seen objects are tangible and can infer how an object gets from one place to another. Still, the infant at this age cannot solve the standard object-permanence problem: when presented with a desirable object that is covered with a cup or cloth, the infant makes no attempt to obtain the object. The infant acts as if the object no longer existed; and yet we have learned from the infant's eye movements and startle responses that it knows that out-of-sight objects are still there, behind the occluding object, the screen. Surely this can only mean that they are lacking in motor skill.

Some time ago, I tested this hypothesis by selecting infants who had failed the standard object-permanence test with opaque cups and retesting them with transparent cups (Bower, 1967b). When the transparent cup is used, the infant can see the object inside the cup. Thus, there can be no reason to believe that any failure to obtain the object is due to lack of information about its whereabouts; and the motor skills required to remove a transparent cup are exactly the same as those required to remove an opaque cup. If an infant fails to remove the opaque cup because of lack of motor skill, then the same lack should produce failure with the transparent cup. The initial results were very promising. All of the infants tested sat helplessly before the transparent cup, just as they had before the opaque cup. Since the object was clearly visible inside the transparent cup, their behavior could only have been due to a motor difficulty. Unfortunately for the hypothesis, the results did not hold up when a longer time was given to obtain the object (Bower and Wishart, 1972).

Subsequent results have complicated the picture. The most interesting studies are those of Neilson (1977). She tested infants of various ages with both opaque and transparent cups. Some of the infants were at Stage III, some at Stage IV, some at Stage V, and some at Stage VI. The interesting result was that the performance of most infants with opaque cups was identical to their performance with transparent cups (see Table 7.3). Obviously, an infant in Stage V no longer has motor problems; that infant can manipulate cups very well. The objects to be found are visible in the transparent cup case, and yet the infant still makes errors. Clearly, neither motor-skill problems nor the lack of visible information as to the object's location can account for such data (see also Bower and Wishart, 1972; Butterworth, 1977).

These data also contradict one other possible explanation of object-permanence problems, that they reflect a failure of memory. In the case of the opaque cup, it could be possible that, in the time taken to organize a response, the infant forgets what is under the opaque cup and so loses the goal of its response. In transparent-cup tests, however, there cannot possibly be any problem of memory, since the object is clearly visible inside the transparent cup. Indeed, common observation should warn us against such an hypothesis. The memory span of a 5- to 6-month-old infant is much greater than that required for object-permanence tasks.

TABLE 7.3   Results of the Neilson (1977) study. (22 out of 27 infants proved to be in the same stage when tested with transparent cups as when tested with standard opaque cups)

Stage with Transparent Cups

		III	IV	V	VI
Stage	III	2	1		
with	IV		4	1	
Opaque					
Cups	V			12	3
	VI				4

The infant, then, has problems with objects inside transparent cups, objects that are clearly not out of sight. Recall, too, the data presented in Chapter 5 that an object will "disappear" for an infant if simply placed upon another object (Bresson et al., 1977; Piaget, 1937). The precise psychophysics of disappearance in adults and children have been studied by Michotte (1962). Both Piaget, who originally made this observation, and the later investigators restricted their test situations to a single object on a single platform, a situation analogous to Stage III of object-concept testing. More recent studies have extended this analogy, presenting the infant with a platform equivalent of the Stage IV–V task (Wishart, 1979). Thus, the infant is shown a toy that is placed on platform A; if the infant retrieves the toy, it is replaced on platform A; if it is again retrieved, it is then placed on platform B. Although the toy is then completely visible, an infant of the right age will go to the wrong platform. Indeed, it has been shown that under some circumstances the infant is as likely to go to the wrong platform in this test as it is to go to the wrong cup in a conventional object-permanence test.

Both transparent cups and platforms then elicit behavior identical to that produced by opaque cups. Is there a common factor? Is it possible that "out of sight" is not the critical determinant we have assumed? There are several studies that point in this direction. Bower and Wishart (1972) and Wishart et al. (1978) studied the behavior of infants coping with objects made to vanish by a whole room being

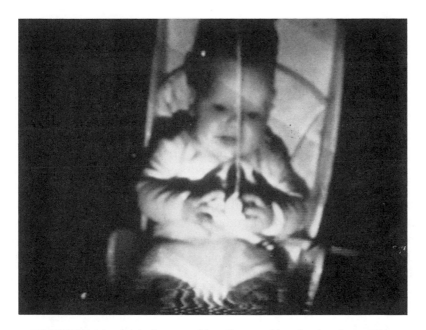

FIGURE 7.14   An infant reaching for an object in the dark. This
infant has failed the standard object-permanence test; yet he was
able to reach out and grasp the object that he had seen but could
no longer see. Apparently, the nature of the transition to "out of
sight" determines the infant's success or failure. (Photograph by
Jennifer Wishart.)

plunged into darkness. This was no problem for even the youngest
infant studied (see Figure 7.14). The same infants could not cope with
"out of sight" produced by placing an object in a cup. It was the *nature
of the transition* from "in sight" to "out of sight" that determined
whether or not the infant would successfully retrieve the object.

It thus appears that "out of sight" is not at all critical. What then
is the problem that induces the errors we see in object concept testing?
Let us recall two items of knowledge that we have attributed to the
infant. In Chapter 5 we proposed that, for the young infant, an object
is a bounded volume of space, located in up–down, near–far, and
right–left coordinates. In this chapter we have argued that the 5-
month-old infant believes that two objects cannot be in the same place
simultaneously. What then is the infant to make of a presentation in
which one object is placed on top of another? The object has lost one
of its boundaries, its bottom boundary. According to the first rule, it
then no longer exists as an object in its own right. Indeed, application

of both rules would lead the infant to believe that both object and platform had disappeared and had been replaced by a new object, the object-and-platform. Suppose we place an object inside another. Exactly the same problems will arise, perhaps in a more exacerbated form, since an object inside another has lost its top–bottom, front–back, *and* right–left boundaries. The same analysis predicts difficulty with any spatial relation between objects that involves a sharing of boundaries. Thus, de Schönen and Bower (1978) found that placing an object in front of another object produced difficulties, but only if the two objects were in contact so that a boundary was shared. Similarly, placing an object behind another object produced difficulties only if it involved a sharing of boundaries. Virtually identical results were obtained by Neilson (1977). It is noteworthy that the tracking tasks described earlier that had one object go behind another all used a sufficient spatial separation between screen and object that no sharing of boundaries occurred. Overall, these results suggest that object permanence is no problem for the young infant, that the infant may indeed have more generous criteria for continued existence than adults do.

On this hypothesis, development after 5 months is development of understanding the spatial relations that involve common boundaries. The main landmarks of the development have been sketched out already. One question is: do we gain anything from placing the burden of development on comprehension of spatial relations? I think we do, although the evidence is far from systematic. At the end of Stage III, before the infant begins to remove cloths and cups from objects, the infant will often lift the cloth and object together. If we are lucky, we can then observe the infant's reaction if the object falls out of the cloth. The reaction is one of stunned amazement, with prolonged orientation to the object and the cloth in the hand; this may last for many seconds before the object is picked up (see Figure 7.15).

This kind of observation can be interpreted as the infant's accepting object-with-cloth as a new object. When the object-with-cloth turns into object *and* cloth, the infant is surprised—hardly an amazing result considering the conceptual knowledge the infant can bring to the situation. It is possible to set up a similar situation more easily if one covers a toy with a cup that is intrinsically attractive. The infant will pick up the toy by itself or the cup by itself, and play with either. If, however, the cup is used to cover the toy and the cup is then picked up, the sight of the toy is surprising enough that neither may be played with for a long time.

FIGURE 7.15   Having picked up the object and the cloth together, the infant is amazed when the object falls out of the cloth. The infant does not pick up the object for some time. (Photograph by Jane Dunkeld.)

Of course, the infant eventually reaches the stage where it will routinely remove a cup or a cloth that covers a desirable toy. This does not imply that the infant necessarily understands the spatial relation involved. It is much more likely that the infant has learned an S–R rule of the sort: "When one object replaces another, pick up the replacement object, and the original object will reappear." There is no causality in such a rule—no comprehension of the spatial relationship involved. In fact, this rule is far too specific to describe the behavior of the Stage IV infant. The infant can find an object that has been hidden in view. If, however, the infant is allowed to find an object in one place after having watched while it was hidden there, the infant will look for the object again in that same place even after seeing the object hidden somewhere else.

This second behavior—which we will refer to as the *place error*— could not be accounted for by the rule just outlined. This behavior would require a rule such as: "When a desired object is not in sight, search for it where it has previously been found." This is a bizarre rule, and we must wonder where it came from. Even though we can only speculate, there are nonetheless some pointers in our previous discussion of identity. The problem posed by invisible displacements has been mentioned. If an object moves or is moved while the infant is looking away from it, and is out of sight when the infant looks back to the place where it was, what can the infant do to retrieve the object? The infant has no perceptual information at all about the location of the object.

The infant under 6 months of age in fact shows no attempt at retrieval. Over this age, we do see behaviors that include looking for an object where it has been found before (Bower, 1968). The behavior is a perfectly valid answer in this context. Where there is no perceptual information about the location of an object, it makes sense to look for it in places where it has been seen before. If we are correct in saying that covering one object by another is a totally mysterious transition to a Stage IV infant, then perhaps it is not surprising that place errors also appear in the standard object-permanence test, where looking at an original object site is a completely inappropriate behavior.

These two behaviors (removing a cup or cloth and the place error) characterize Stage IV. At the end of Stage IV, they are amalgamated so that the infant seems to have a conditional pairing of responses. If an object is seen to disappear when its place is taken by another object, the infant will pick up the replacement object to obtain the original object. If the original object disappears, but is not seen to disappear, then the infant will look for the object where it has previously been found. This pair of behaviors leads naturally to the errors as well as the successes characteristic of Stage V. Consider the following observation from Piaget:

> OBS. 55. At 1;6 (8) Jacqueline is sitting on a green rug and playing with a potato which interests her very much (it is a new object for her). She says "po-terre" and amuses herself by putting it into an empty box and taking it out again. For several days she has been enthusiastic about this game.
>
> I. I then take the potato and put it in the box while Jacqueline watches. Then I place the box under the rug and turn it upside down thus leaving the object hidden by the rug without letting the child see my maneuver, and I bring out the empty box. I say to Jacqueline, who has not stopped looking at the rug and who has realized that I was doing something under it: "Give papa the potato." She searches for the object in the box, looks at me, again looks at the box minutely, looks at

the rug, etc., but it does not occur to her to raise the rug in order to find the potato underneath.

During the five subsequent attempts the reaction is uniformly negative. I begin again, however, each time putting the object in the box as the child watches, putting the box under the rug, and bringing it out empty. Each time Jacqueline looks in the box, then looks at everything around her including the rug, but does not search under it.

II. At the seventh attempt, I change the technique. I place the object in the box and the box under the rug but leave the object in the box. As soon as I remove my empty hand Jacqueline looks under the rug, finds and grasps the box, opens it and takes the potato out of it. Same reaction a second time.

III. Then I resume the first technique: emptying the box under the rug and bringing it forth empty. At first Jacqueline looks for the object in the box, and not finding it there searches for it under the rug. Hence the attempt has been successful. This occurs a second time but from the third attempt on, the result becomes negative again, as in I. Is this due to fatigue? [Piaget, 1937]

What are we to make of this sequence? At first the infant searches for the object in the box where the potato disappeared. When it is not there, she has no information about its location—not even information about its usual place because the only place the object has been found before is in the box. During the second procedure, the object is "given" a location where it has been found, so that as soon as the third part begins the infant can apply the appropriate behavior—that is, look for an object that has vanished in places where it has been found before. This behavior still shows no comprehension of the spatial relation involved, as is made clear by other behaviors. One behavior that can be observed in infants of this age and that seems particularly bizarre occurs after the infant has found an object several times under the same cup. If the object is then placed to one side of the cup in full view, the infant will still pick up the cup, examine it, and shake it, as if expecting objects to pop out. The cup is seen as a cornucopia rather than as a container—something that objects can emerge from without first having to go into. The same lack of comprehension produces the error we have taken as most typical of this stage—the *switching error*. If the infant sees an object hidden under one of two cups and the cups are then transposed, the infant will search for the object at the place where it was last seen, ignoring the transposition. There is thus no awareness that the object is out of sight *inside* the cup. Eventually, of course, the relationship is discovered. The infant becomes aware that two objects can be in the same place— provided that they bear a spatial relationship to each other that involves the sharing of common boundaries. At this point, the development of the object concept (as this is conventionally understood) is almost over. What is still to be attained is the arrangement of all of the information acquired up to this point into a coherent whole. This allows the infant in some circumstances to deduce the location of an object that has been invisibly displaced. Piaget has described the classic circumstance:

> OBS. 59. Lucienne at I; I (4) finds a watch chain in my fist. I then replace the chain in my hand and slip this hand under a pillow. I leave the chain under the pillow and bring my hand out closed.
> I. First attempt: Lucienne looks in my hand, then finding nothing, looks at me, laughing. She resumes searching, then gives up.
> Attempts 2–5: Same reactions. I use the watch instead of the chain to increase her interest; same difficulty.
> Sixth attempt: This time, sudden success. Lucienne opens my hand as soon as I take it out from under the pillow. After having examined it a moment she stops, looks around her, then suddenly looks under the pillow and finds the watch.
> Subsequent attempts: Same reaction.
> II. Then I resume the experiment with a quilt which is on the child's right. Lucienne begins by looking in my hand which I have removed closed from under the quilt. After having opened and explored it for a moment Lucienne searches under the quilt without hesitation.
> Subsequent attempts: Same success. [Piaget, 1937]

The infant here has seen the object disappear into the hand; she has seen the hand with the object inside it (as she now understands) move under a cloth and come out again. She has inspected the hand and found nothing there. Her success reflects an ability to order these facts and deduce that the object that was in the hand *must* be under the cloth.

The sequence of development is laid out in Table 7.4, which incorporates the observed sequence of behavior and the hypothetical rules and concepts that are supposed to underlie it. One must remember that these rules and concepts *are* hypothetical. Since there are as many rules as there are observed behaviors, it is no more economical at this point to talk of rules than it is to talk of behaviors.

The rule–concept terminology can only be justified if it illuminates the process of development. One may ask whether it is necessary here. There are a variety of ways to account for the development of the object concept. If we go back to the earliest stages of development (development of tracking behaviors), we can see that there are ways to account for the development that do not rely on hypothetical internal mechanisms. The 12-week-old infant will continue to track along the path of a moving object after the object has stopped moving;

TABLE 7.4   Hypothetical sequence of development

Stages I and II	
Rules	1. An object is a bounded volume of space. (See Chapter 5.) 2. All objects in the same place are the same object. (See text.) 3. Two objects cannot be in the same place. (See text.) 4. All objects on the same path of movement are the same object. (See text.) 5. Two objects cannot be on the same path of movement. (See text.)
Behavior	To find a stationary object, search for it in the place where it usually is. To find a moving object, search for it along its path of movement.

Stage III	
Rules	1. An object is a bounded volume of space that can move from place to place along trajectories. 2. Two objects cannot be in the same place simultaneously. 3. Objects are identified by their size, shape, color, and location.
Behavior	If an object is replaced in the same place by an object of a different size, shape, and color, do nothing.

Stage IV	
Rules	Same as Stage III.
Behavior	Same as Stage II, plus: If an object is replaced in the same place by an object of a different size, shape, and color, search for the original object where it has been seen before.

Stage V	
Rules	Same as Stage IV.
Behavior	Same as Stage II, plus: If an object is replaced by another object, search for the replaced object where it was last seen.

Stage VI	
Rules	Same as Stages III–V, except that rule 2 becomes: Two objects cannot be in the same place simultaneously, unless they bear a spatial relationship to each other that involves the sharing of common boundaries.
Behavior	See text.

the same infant will look in the place where a stationary object had been resting before it was moved—ignoring the seen movement of the object. We interpreted this as the result of a conceptual failure—a failure to identify a moving object with itself when stationary and vice versa. When these errors disappeared, we interpreted it as the removal of the conceptual block. Even though this argument seemed to be a plausible one, it is not necessarily the explanation.

The development could be generated in other ways: the change in one case is a change from continuing along the object's path of movement after the object stops moving. Even from the very beginning of this segment of development, the infant can stop when the object stops. Eventually, by the end of the segment, the infant stops with the object and does not continue. This change has been explained in terms of a coordination of two hypothetical rules: "An object is the same object as long as it stays in the same place," and "An object is the same object as long as it continues on the same path of movement." Obviously, it is not necessary to speak of coordination. Each of the two behaviors could develop independently through learning with reinforcement. Thus, the infant could cease to follow the path of an object after the object had stopped simply because (1) there is no reinforcement of the following behavior and (2) there is reinforcement for stopping with the object. Continued tracking means losing sight of the object, whereas maintaining the stop fixation means maintaining sight of the object. If sight of an object is taken as reinforcement, then a very simple learning model could account for the development. A similar learning model could be used to account for development from looking for an object where it has previously been seen to looking for an object in the direction it has been seen to move. Both behaviors are in the repertoire of the youngest infants studied, but only the latter behavior will be likely to lead to the behavior of keeping an object in view. The former behavior, in fact, will quite often lead to failure. It is no wonder that the latter behavior should replace the former behavior in the course of development.

Is there any good reason to abandon this simple learning model? The learning model proposes two independent learning processes underlying the two observed changes in behavior. The pattern of change in both behaviors is in fact exceedingly similar, however, which might lead one to believe that a single process underlies both sets of behavior changes (see Figure 7.16). The similarity, of course, could be dismissed as coincidence; but how would we then explain the Mundy-Castle trajectory-interpolation effect (see Figure 7.12)? We

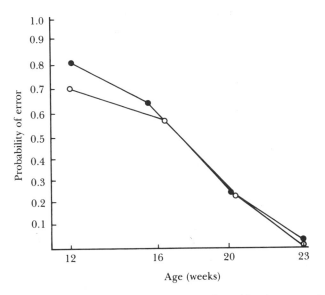

● = Probability of continuation when object has stopped moving
○ = Probability of searching for a stationary object that has moved
   in the place where it has been

FIGURE 7.16   The pattern of development in both
tracking tasks is very similar. This might be taken as a
suggestion that a single process underlies both of them.

have argued that this effect reflected the same change process as that
which reduced the tracking errors to zero. Obviously, if two independent learning processes account for the reduction of the tracking
errors, nothing can be said about the Mundy-Castle effect. It must
remain on the sidelines, as a curious effect that has nothing to do with
learning or reinforcement; certainly, no reinforcement theory could
explain why the useless trajectory is interpolated in that situation.

What alternative account of the change process can we offer? We
have talked about development as the coordination of rules or concepts, but we have not specified any mechanisms to explain what
produces the coordination. The major virtue of the learning model
is that it does offer an explanation of the processes producing change,
rather than give a mere description of the effects of the processes.

Piaget's dynamic model for development also has these virtues, but
it is quite different from a simple learning model. The key concept
in Piaget's model is the idea of *conflict* or *contradiction*. Piaget proposes
that cognitive development occurs only when the infant is made aware

TABLE 7.5   An example of the equilibration process

	Conflict		
Concept	An object is a place.	vs.	An object is movement.
Rule	To find an object, look in its usual place.	vs.	To find an object, look along its path of movement.
Behavior	Place error.	vs.	Continuation of tracking.

	Amalgamation
Concept	An object is a *thing* that can move from place to place along trajectories.
Rule	To find an object that has been seen to move, follow the path of movement; to find a moving object that no longer moves, look for it stationary.
Behavior	Cessation of place and movement errors and incorporation of Mundy-Castle trajectory interpolation.

of a conflict between two rules, concepts, or modes of coping with the world when applied to the same situation. The rules for maintaining contact with stationary objects characteristic of the 12-week-old contradict its rules for maintaining contact with moving objects. Indeed, the concepts underlying these rules are fundamentally incompatible and must result in conflict whenever they are applied to any situation involving objects that move or stop. As long as place and movement are not coordinated, a conflict must be generated whenever a stationary object moves or a moving object stops. This kind of conflict between two partially valid rules or concepts is the necessary condition for cognitive development. The existence of such a conflict triggers processes aimed at resolving the conflict or contradiction. These processes are (confusingly) labeled *equilibration* processes. The end product of equilibrium is the formulation of new concepts and rules that amalgamate the elements in the conflict. Thus, the conflict for the 3-month-old infant can be resolved by the amalgamation shown in Table 7.5. According to Piaget, equilibration itself must be a regulated process so that—given the elements of a conflict—one should be able to predict the outcome of the amalgamation. Unfortunately, the rules for equilibration are not well specified; prediction is possible in principle, but it is not yet possible in practice.

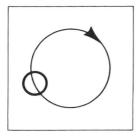

FIGURE 7.17   Circular training.

This theory and the simple learning model could hardly be more different. The learning model assumes that there is development within a single behavior. Piaget's model asserts that development is not possible until there is conflict between behaviors or between the rules controlling the behaviors. The learning model asserts that development is specific to a behavior. Piaget predicts that development occurs in all behaviors generated by a concept or rule, including behaviors that may never have appeared before.

The differences between these theories can produce differential predictions, particularly about the effect that special experience has on development. The learning model clearly cannot predict any transfer from one tracking task to another. Piaget, by contrast, predicts that any equilibration sufficient to improve performance on one task will also improve all of the other tasks employing that same concept. This was tested in a specific training experiment. Two groups of infants were matched for age, sex, and initial performance on the Mundy-Castle task. Mean age at the beginning of the experiment was 80 days, so it was not surprising that the average performance was reactive looking from side to side, with little anticipation and no interpolated trajectories. One group of infants was given intervening practice in following an object moving in a circular trajectory, as shown in Figure 7.17. The extremes of its arc were the same distance apart as the portholes used in the Mundy-Castle situation. The eye movement required to track the object would have counted as a trajectory interpolation, if elicited in the Mundy-Castle situation. The object was never seen as stationary by the infant, so the situation did not elicit any conflict. It provided training in circular tracking with no conflict. According to Piaget's view, then, it might be expected to improve the actual process of circular tracking; but it should not produce any conflict and, therefore, should produce no development of trajectory

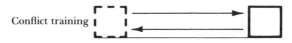

FIGURE 7.18   Place-to-place training.

interpolation or place–movement amalgamation. Since the movement at the horizontal ends of the arc are similar to the movements seen in the portholes in the Mundy-Castle task, one might strain the learning model to predict some kind of generalization of the circular tracking behavior from one situation to the other.

The other group of infants was exposed to a simple place-to-place movement of an object in the horizontal plane (see Figure 7.18). The object was stationary in one place first and then moved to the other location, where it stopped for a while before returning to its original location. The cycle was repeated several times. This situation is a rich conflict situation in Piagetian terms. Every time the object begins moving or stops moving, it induces a conflict between the two partial object concepts that the infant has. Exposure to this situation should therefore produce development on a wide front, including development of trajectory interpolation in the Mundy-Castle situation. This is the last thing one could expect on a simple learning model, since there is no basis for stimulus generalization and no commonality of response between this situation and the Mundy-Castle situation. The results most definitely favored the Piagetian hypothesis. Infants shown the conflict situation produced four times as many trajectory interpolations as did the infants trained in the circular tracking situation. The situation that elicited the conflict also elicited the development— a result entirely in accord with Piaget's predictions.

Further support for Piaget's hypothesis can be found in studies on the age when training can produce development. In the development of tracking ability, an *asynchrony* usually takes place between the two modes of coping with objects that stop and start; these modes are later amalgamated. Usually, though not always, anticipatory responses to a moving object appear sooner than do anticipatory responses to a stationary object seen in different places at different times. Thus, it is possible to present the infant with a training situation where only one behavior can be applied. The alternative behavior is not yet in the infant's repertoire and so cannot be brought into conflict with the first behavior. The situation looks like this: if the infant in this stage is presented with an object that moves from place to place, no conflict will be induced, since the response to movement is the only one in the infant's repertoire.

Would the presentation of this situation lead to accelerated development of the behavior in question, or must there be conflict before development is possible? According to the learning theory model of development, the shaping of a behavior could begin at any time after the behavior appears. Thus, if an infant continues to follow the trajectory of an object that stops, the subsequent lack of contact with the object should lead to extinction of the behavior.

A test was made by comparing two groups of infants on just that task. One group began at 8 weeks, the other at 12 weeks. Each was tested weekly for a response to an object that moved in a circular path and stopped occasionally. At 16 weeks, neither group made any errors to speak of. Neither group continued tracking after the object had stopped. However, after the 8-week-old group had had four weeks of training, they did worse on the test than did the naive group—not in errors but in terms of successful following. The experienced group would not track the target object; indeed, they seemed to find the situation aversive. Apparently, then, if experience is introduced to correct a behavior at a time when there is no alternative way of coping, the experience does not lead to improved behavior, but rather to its complete extinction—a result quite in accord with Piaget's theory but wholly in contradiction to any simple learning model.

Another way that Piaget's model differs from simple learning models concerns the issue of *stages* in development. Piaget explicitly describes development as proceeding through a series of stages. A stage is defined as a period during which development is stationary for a period—one stage terminating when a new stage begins, with no intermediate periods. This concept is quite contrary to the standard predictions of learning theory. Learning theory standardly predicts that behavior change is cumulative and gradual. Piaget's stage theory predicts that behavior change is all or none: the infant responds in a way typical to one stage or in a way typical to the next stage—with no intermediate modes of response. Normally, learning theory would claim that performance on a task improves gradually. Stage theory, by contrast, would predict no improvement in a task until errors simply disappear—all at once, with no slow change.

The stage is a very controversial concept. Indeed, the idea of sudden discontinuities in development upsets our standard ideas of how these processes occur. Perhaps because physical growth is so obviously continuous, we find it very difficult to think of mental growth as pro-

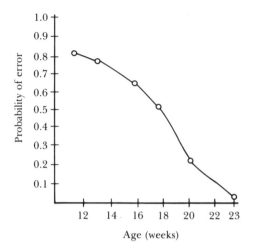

FIGURE 7.19 Smooth change in average performance on a tracking task of infants between 12 and 23 weeks of age. If, however, we look at each individual record, performance in terms of reduction of errors is much more likely to be discontinuous than a smooth decline.

ceeding by way of a series of discontinuities. Certainly, there are enormous problems in establishing the hypothesis that development is stagelike. If, for example, the performance of a number of infants at the same age is averaged and then a range of ages is compared, one usually obtains a smooth change in average performance with age, like that shown in Figure 7.19. If one examines an individual infant, one is much less likely to observe such a smooth change and more likely to see discontinuities. However, the question that is always asked is whether these discontinuities are genuine.

Suppose one sees an infant at age 20 weeks and the infant makes 100 percent errors. Suppose one then sees the same infant at 21 weeks of age, and performance is 100 percent correct. Does this change indicate a discontinuity? It might, but there might, on the other hand, have been a gradual change in the intervening week. The same argument can be applied if the interval between tests is only a day or even an hour. In order to demonstrate a discontinuity, there must be a gap between tests, and it is impossible to prove that an intermediate level of performance would not have been observed had one tested during the gap.

Fortunately, this need not be a barrier to using the concept of a stage. There are other ways to demonstrate that development is stagelike. Let us again use the transition of the object concept from Stage II to Stage III. Piaget would argue that the transition is accomplished by the amalgamation of rules governing responses to stationary objects and rules governing responses to moving objects. Prior to this amalgamation, the infant can respond to a moving object or to a stationary object but cannot respond to an object that moves and stops. Presented with an object that moves and stops, the infant can deal with it either as a moving object, (which leads to one type of error) or as a stationary object (which leads to another type of error). Either mode of response is possible; in a situation where both are possible, we should not expect one mode of response to predominate completely. (We would never expect to find 100 percent errors of any one kind.) Thus, in a situation where an object is moving and then stops, we can expect continuation of tracking if the infant is using the movement strategy of coping. If the infant is using the place strategy, then we would not expect a "continuation of tracking" error.

We might ask what determines which strategy will be used at any particular instant. If the strategies are equally probable, then a random process will decide which strategy is employed at any arbitrary point in time. If the strategies are not equally probable, then the more probable strategy is, of course, more likely to be employed. All this is banal enough. It nevertheless allows us to make very precise predictions on the stage theory and to contrast them with predictions from the continuous-learning model. Suppose the infant is at a stage where each strategy is equally probable. The movement strategy has a probability of occurrence of 0.5, and the place strategy has a probability of occurrence of 0.5. Thus, when presented with a moving object that stops, the infant might employ its strategy for dealing with moving objects; in this case, the infant will continue tracking after the object has stopped, thereby making an error in this situation. On the other hand, the infant might employ the strategy for dealing with stationary objects; in that case, the infant will stop and remain stopped with the object, making no error in the situation. We would thus expect the error rate in this situation to be 50 percent, reflecting the strategy probabilities.

The converse of this is true in the case of the transition between stationary places. How will the error rate change during the transition to Stage III? According to Piaget's theory, it will not change at all. Performance will not improve but will remain at a level determined by the strategy probability (0.5) until it changes completely. Then the single strategy probabilities will drop to zero, and the amalgamated

TABLE 7.6   Expected and obtained distributions of
errors in last error trial of tracking task

N Errors	f Expected	f Obtained
1	0.38	1
2	1.32	4
3	2.63	2
4	3.28	2
5	2.63	0
6	1.32	2
7	0.38	0
8	0.05	1

$$\chi^2 = 1.32 \qquad 0.3 > p > 0.2$$

strategy will be applied whenever the infant has to cope with an object
that changes position. On a continuous learning model, the probability
of movement errors and place errors should decline continuously.
The latter condition has never been found in any experimental investigation. Table 7.6 shows the distribution of results obtained from
a group of infants in a tracking task. The session shown was the last
session on which any of the infants showed any errors. On the next
and all succeeding sessions, performance was without error. On this
last session with errors, performance was exactly as predicted by Piaget: the error probability was 0.5 on average, and there was no indication of any decline at all.

It thus seems that Piaget's dynamic model of contradiction and
equilibration has even more going for it—at least as a description of
the transition of the object concept from Stage II to Stage III. Conflict
can accelerate development; practice without conflict does not produce development; and development is discontinuous—a conceptual
revolution rather than a gradual evolution.

Can Piaget's model similarly illuminate the later stages of object
concept development? I have suggested elsewhere (Bower, 1967b) that
conflict is necessary to generate the beginnings of search for objects
that have vanished incomprehensibly, whether under cups or in some
other way. The infant of 5 months has begun to identify objects by
their features rather than by their position in space. This means that
the infant can recognize an object as being the same when seen in
different places at different times—even if the infant has no idea how

the object got from place to place. When an infant younger than 5 months is presented with an incomprehensible disappearance, the infant genuinely acts as if the object no longer existed. The infant makes no attempt to look for the object. When the object is presented again, the infant acts as if it were a new object, as gauged by latency-of-response data and the like. Adults presented with similarly incomprehensible disappearances (Michotte, 1962) tended to say: "It looks as if it has vanished into thin air but I know it must be somewhere." The young infant has not yet acquired the "but." However, soon after the appearance of identification based on features, the infant does begin to search for an object that has vanished incomprehensibly. The search is not well guided—How could it be?—but it is a search. When the object reappears, it is treated as the same object. I have previously argued that the new behavior was produced by conflict between the two original responses—the response to disappearance ("The object has vanished into thin air and no longer exists anywhere") and the response to reappearance ("This is the same object as that which vanished"). The conflict induced by these two strategies can only be resolved by introducing a new rule: "An object that has vanished still exists somewhere." This is a rule that produces the poorly oriented search behavior characteristic of the stage.

The main outlines of an argument supporting the importance of conflict in generating the transition from Stage IV to Stage V behavior have already been sketched. The infant in Stage IV seems to have two "magical" rules for finding an object that has vanished incomprehensibly "Look for it at the place where it was last seen," and "Look for it where it usually is." If simultaneously available to the infant, these two rules would necessarily produce a conflict every time the infant was presented with an incomprehensible disappearance. Direct evidence is not yet available on this point since no one as yet has attempted to produce acceleration of development by maximizing the conflict. However, two other predictions from Piaget's theory have been tested and confirmed. These are that development is discontinuous and that the mean probability of application of either rule stays at 0.5 until amalgamation of the rules occurs (Bower and Paterson, 1972). Table 7.7 shows the results of the last session of testing prior to the beginning of errorless performance. As can be seen, the pattern of errors is very close to that predicted on the assumption of stationary performance with a 0.5 probability of adopting an erroneous strategy. Such data are in accord with Piaget's theory. Thus, even though con-

TABLE 7.7   Expected and obtained distributions of errors on last error trial of Stage IV to Stage V transition test (table shows the distribution of errors on the last day on which infants made an error and the expected distribution based on the assumption of random responding; as can be seen, the difference was not significant)

N Errors	ƒ Expected	ƒ Obtained
6	0	1
5	5	6
4	13	14
3	18	14
2	13	12
1	5	7

$$\chi^2 = 2.09 \qquad 0.90 > p > 0.75$$

Source: Bower and Paterson, 1972.

flict has not been established here as the driving force in development, the pattern of development fits with the conflict theory of cognitive growth.

What about the last major transition, from Stage V to Stage VI? We have argued that this transition is accomplished by the amalgamation of the concepts of spatial relations with the general object concept. How does the infant acquire this last? For one spatial relation, "inside," Piaget has described the sequence of development. Piaget's observations suggest that the "inside" relation is highly mysterious even to a 1-year-old. The relationship between the goal ("one object inside the other") and the means for obtaining it are obviously not clear to the infant until well after the requisite motor skills have been attained. Four of Piaget's observations may show this.

OBS. III. From 1;2 (28) to 1;3 (6) Lucienne systematically puts grass, earth, pebbles, etc., into all the hollow objects within reach: bowls, pails, boxes, etc.

At 1;3 (6) her finger explores the surface of a spade and discovers that the metal handle is hollow: she puts her finger inside and immediately looks for grass to put in the opening.

The same day she puts bowls (of identical dimensions) inside each other; she does it delicately, carefully examining the interrelations of objects.

At 1;3 (7) she has four or five pebbles before her. She puts them into a bowl one by one and takes them out in the same way. Then she empties them from one bowl into the other, still one by one.

At 1;3 (9), on the other hand, she discovers the possibility of emptying the entire contents of a receptacle at one stroke; she piles into a basket the metal molds she has at hand, some stones, blades of grass, etc., then turns the whole thing upside down.

At 1;3 (12) she puts her five molds into a big strainer and takes them out one by one. Sometimes she puts two or three in a pile, sometimes one, then she takes it out, puts in a second one, takes it out, etc.

Afterward she puts a little spade in the strainer, then lifts it up and turns it upside down until the spade falls out.

At 1;3 (14) she puts her molds in a watering can and empties the whole thing at once.

At 1;4 (11) for the first time she is presented with nested boxes. She immediately tries to take out those which are inside. Not succeeding, she purposely turns the whole thing upside down and the contents spread out on the floor. Then she tries to replace them, but hastily and naturally without order. [Piaget, 1937]

OBS. 112. At 1;3 (28) Jacqueline for the first time sees the same boxes to be nested but now scattered on the floor. She takes one of them (I), turns it in all directions, and puts her index finger inside it. She rejects it and takes a second (II), same behavior (this time she puts her whole hand inside). In throwing aside the second cube she drops it accidentally into a much larger one (III); she immediately takes it out and puts it in again. Then she takes another (IV), which she also puts into the big one (III). She takes them out and puts them both in again, several times in succession.

After this she takes a big one (V), almost as large as the one she has heretofore used as a container (III), and immediately tries to put it inside. She does not succeed and merely places it askew across the opening of the other one. Then she manages to put it in but not to take it out. It does not occur to her to reverse the big one (III) in order to make the smaller one (V) fall out. Finally she discovers an adequate procedure by sliding her finger against the inside wall of the little one.

Then she chooses a much smaller cube (VI) and puts it into the big one (III). She takes it out and puts it in again about ten times. Then she takes the big one (V) which she puts back and takes out right away. Then she takes a little one (VII) which she puts in and takes out many times.

Then comes a curious experiment: she takes one of the largest cubes (VIII) which she tries to put into a smaller one (VI); she gropes a moment and then gives up quite soon. Same reaction a second time.

Then she picks up cubes V and III and tries to put the first into the second. She succeeds in putting it in but has great difficulty in getting it out again. As soon as she has achieved her goal she repeats the procedure ten times, through functional assimilation. Finally, when cube V is in cube III, she grasps a smaller cube (IV) and puts it into V. She takes it out and puts it back in, sometimes performing this operation with her left hand, sometimes with her right. [Piaget, 1937]

OBS. 113. Around 1;2 (18) Laurent has begun to put pebbles, small apples, etc., into various pails, etc., and to turn them over. This behavior pattern becomes increasingly frequent during the following weeks. Between 1;3 and 1;6 the sight of a hollow object almost automatically arouses in Laurent a desire to fill it, to displace it, and to empty it shortly afterward. At 1;3 (17), for example, he fills a metal cup with grass and pebbles and empties it at a distance, etc. [Piaget, 1937]

OBS. 174. These kinds of apprenticeship can be further complicated by requiring the child to correct the position, not only of the object to be put in, but also of the container. So it is that at 1;1 (23) Lucienne sees me put a ring into half of a case for eyeglasses. She looks at the object inside the case, shakes the case and lets the ring fall out. She then tries immediately to replace it but the apprenticeship is accomplished on two occasions.

During a first phase, Lucienne tries four sequential maneuvers, all unsuccessful. (1) She first presses her three fingers holding the ring against the opening of the case and drops the ring. The ring falls to the side because her fingers prevent it from entering. (2) She presses the ring against the closed end of the case and lets it go. (3) She holds the case upside down and puts the ring into the opening but without tilting it up. The ring falls out at the first movement of the case. (4) She places the ring on the floor and presses both ends of the case against it, alternately, as though the ring would enter it by itself.

During a second phase, on the contrary, Lucienne learns to correct her attempts. First, she no longer places the case on the ring as though the latter would enter by itself. Then when she presses the ring against the wrong end of the case, she does not let it go but turns the case over in order to slide it into the opening. She holds the case almost vertically and, when it is too slanting, she straightens it before letting the ring go. Finally, she learns only to drop it inside the case by first sliding it to the end of her fingers instead of letting it fall when the fingers still obstruct an opening of the case.

At 1;1 (24) after having disengaged the ring from her thumb around which it fell by chance, Lucienne sees me put it around a stick. She then tries to draw it toward her without putting it along the wood. Then she shakes the stick and the ring falls. In order to put it around the stick again, she simply presses it at a certain place and lets it go. Same reaction six times in succession. Then she tries to put it on at the end, but lets it drop. That afternoon she succeeds twice in putting it on the stick but she merely presses it several times against the stick. The following days both reactions subsist without excluding each other, but the attempts to put it on the stick prevail increasingly above the others. [Piaget, 1936]

These observations suggest something of the difficulty an infant has in putting one object inside another and some of the fascination the act has for the infant once it can be accomplished. The perfection of this act is an excellent example of the assimilation–accommodation–equilibration process discussed in the last chapter, operating at a higher level. Here, the sight of one object inside another defines the end point or purpose of the schema to which the separated objects are assimilated; the infant, having seen a ring inside a box, tries to reinstate this relationship when presented with the ring and the box separately. Accommodation here consists in trying a range of possible behaviors to discover whether they can produce the desired end. Equilibrium is attained by the discovery of the appropriate means to achieve the end.

Once an infant has achieved the behavioral skills necessary to put one object inside another object, the infant has a piece of information that can correct its erroneous object concept. The infant thinks that two objects cannot be in the same place simultaneously but now knows that one object can be inside another. Somehow the infant must amalgamate these two items of information and discover that two objects cannot be in the same place at the same time unless one object is inside (or on or behind) the other. The infant must, for example, become aware that two objects—one inside the other—are like one object insofar as movement is concerned. Container and contained move as one, but they remain two objects, potentially separable into two independent objects. The discovery can be made at any time after the infant finds out how to put one object inside another, but it is not made immediately. In the case of Piaget's daughter, there was a delay of three months between the discovery of the relation "inside" and its amalgamation with the object concept.

There is at this time no explanation of how the amalgamation is accomplished. We do not know that conflict between the belief that two objects cannot be in the same place at once and the information that one object can be inside another is important. However, there is an obvious possibility of conflict, and we must agree that conflict is an important motor force in development. It seems highly likely that the potential conflict is critical in the final attainment of the object concept.

What about attaining the ability to deduce the location of an object that has vanished invisibly? Can that be fitted into the conflict model? It would seem not at first sight. Deduction becomes possible after all the information gathered during the course of development is organized into a coherent whole, with general principles that can be coordinated and applied in specific situations. In a sense, this is amalgamation, but it does not seem to require the kind of subordination typical of amalgamation after conflict. Piaget seems to argue that deduction at this level is irreducible—a basic process whose existence we must accept. Certainly, the primitive deductions of the infant seem to spring inevitably from its acquired knowledge; no further events are necessary to force deduction from this corpus of information.

The outline of development of the object concept presented thus

far makes for a relatively simple theoretical account. The infant acquires rules and behaviors to cope with specific situations. Whenever
a new situation comes along that brings existing rules and behaviors
into conflict, we will get an amalgamation of rules, generating more
abstract knowledge that can generate in turn more adequate behaviors. This hierarchical upward flow is quite in accord with generally
accepted models of development (Sameroff, 1975). However, there
are some data that would seem to contradict the model, particularly
its emphasis on the role of specific sensorimotor schemes in generating
concepts. By far the most striking instance of this is the study of
limbless thalidomide infants carried out by Gouin-Décarie (1969). She
found that the sensorimotor intelligence of these infants, tested
around the age of 2 years, was approximately normal. To perform
the tests, the infants would lift cloths with their teeth, to discover
where the experimenter had hidden the object. Such a finding must
raise the possibility of a maturational account of the development.
This is not necessary if the development we are discussing is conceptual development. The thalidomide infant, like the normal infant,
tracks objects with its eyes and so should develop normally up to Stage
IV. After that, the thalidomide infant's search behavior must diverge
from that of the normal infant. Even so, there is no reason why its
concepts should be different. The thalidomide infant's ways of testing
them, however, will be very different. Whereas the normal infant can
manipulate screens or cloths with its hand, the thalidomide infant can
only look with its eyes. The normal infant can discover "inside" in the
course of its manipulative play. The thalidomide infant can only discover "inside" by watching. However, as soon as cup feeding begins,
the thalidomide infant can hardly help observing the relation. Gouin-
Décarie's data indicate that this kind of discovery is almost as effective
as discovery through manipulation.

In terms of our previous discussion, this would seem to indicate
that specific sensorimotor schemes are not necessary for development,
that development can proceed at a conceptual level. Further evidence
to the point was obtained by Wishart (1979). Wishart gave a group
of 12-week-old infants weekly exposure to a variety of tracking tasks
involving spatial relations. Three spatial relations were used: on, in,
and behind. The object moved backward and forward along a track,
either passing over the top of a platform, through a tunnel, or behind
a screen placed in the center of the track. As soon as the infants were
old enough to reach, they were presented with the standard manual

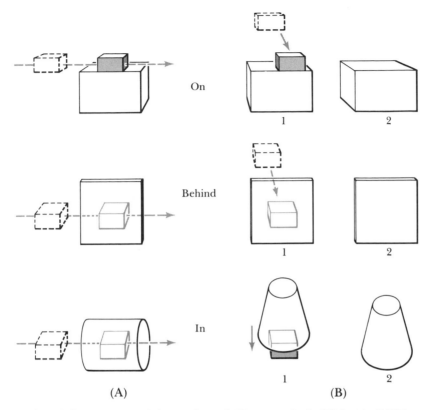

On

Behind

In

(A)   (B)

FIGURE 7.20   (A) Training tasks and (B) test tasks in Wishart's (1979) experiment. (After *Human Development* by T. G. R. Bower. W. H. Freeman and Company. Copyright © 1979.)

tests of object permanence (see Figure 7.20). The results and the implications of this study are quite fascinating. First, the infants in the study passed the manual Stage III and Stage IV tests of the object concept virtually as soon as they were tested. Indeed, they also passed the transition tests from Stage V to Stage VI well ahead of schedule. Their performance was thus amazingly accelerated, presumably as a result of the tracking experience they had had. The fact is, though, that the behaviors involved in tracking were quite different from the behaviors involved in object-concept testing. Indeed, the stimulus situations were different too. The factor underpinning the transfer—the acceleration—must therefore have been a conceptual framework, brought forward from the tracking situation to the manual test situation—a conceptual framework, moreover, derived without benefit of the sensorimotor, manipulative experience normally deemed necessary for its genesis. Indeed, within the tracking phase of the study, there was evidence that emerging conceptual frameworks generate behavior, rather than vice versa. The infants arrived in the experiment with whatever conceptual framework had been derived from their day-to-day interactions with their own environment. These frameworks produced the behaviors typical of infants of this age. Quite rapidly these particular behaviors declined and were supplemented by others; instead of checking back to the place where the object was last seen or continuing to follow its path of movement when it stopped, the infants now paid more attention to what was happening in the center of the track and would check back and forth between the two sides of the track on which the object appeared. What does this pattern of behaviors signify? The initial decline in place and movement errors could signify the emergence of the hypothesis that an object is a thing that can move from place to place along trajectories. Prior to this, the infants, believing objects to be either places or movements, produce the characteristic Stage III behavior. This form of hypothesis-testing behavior declined around 17 weeks, but further evidence of confusion reappeared again at around 21 weeks. What was the function of this second manifestation of hypothesis-testing behavior? Surely, it was to check the hypothesis that one object can go into spatial relation with another object and still exist.

This study may also help us understand the motive force underlying the processes of equilibration. Let us look at one of the tracking situations, the platform-tracking situation, as it must appear to a 12-week-old with the conceptual framework we have attributed to the average 12-week-old. That framework (Table 7.2) would produce, in the platform-tracking situation, no fewer than eight objects: a platform, a platform-plus-object, two objects moving from left to right, two objects moving from right to left, an object stationary at the right end of the track, and an object stationary at the left end of the track. In the course of a single experimental session with this situation, the infant will "see" eight objects. Suppose the infant advances to the conceptual framework represented by the identity rule "An object is a bounded volume of space that can move from place to place along trajectories." The infant will cut the number of objects it must deal with to four: the moving object on the right of the platform, the moving object on the left of the platform, the platform, and the object-plus-platform. The final stage of development, in which the infant appreciates that an object can go into a spatial relationship with another object without violation to its identity, will reduce this number to two: the object and the platform.

Each of these gains will be bought at some cost—cost in terms of the amount of information the infant must process or keep in its conceptual store. Initially, the infant must only attend to three locations and two movements. By the end, the infant must not only attend to these but also to the featural details of object and platform (Table 7.2). These gains and costs could in principle be quantified, using the techniques of information theory (Attneave, 1959). As Table 7.4 shows, the infant makes a net gain in developing from one stage to the next.

This profit-and-loss account should, I feel, be viewed as a supplement to the processes of conflict reduction emphasized before, a perhaps surprising statement given the lack of obvious conflict in the studies I have just been discussing. Can processes of conflict reduction be invoked to account for the data presented by Gouin-Décarie (1969) and Wishart (1979)? In neither study was there any possibility of behavioral-conceptual conflict of the kind discussed earlier. However, there is a possibility of purely conceptual conflict, provided the infant formulates a conceptual rule to do with *permanence*. Permanence is normally equated with "out of sight." I trust that the preceding discussion has emphasized that permanence has more to do with modes of disappearance than with disappearance per se. Nonetheless, there are modes of disappearance that seem to produce loss of existence for objects as far as the young infant is concerned, rather more for the infant than for the adult (Michotte, 1962; Bower, 1967b). The infant who has developed the second level but not yet the third level of identity rule when faced with an object moving to and fro, passing over a platform, is thus faced with four objects, two of which are not only featurally identical but also normally on the same path of movement and are never seen simultaneously. On these three criteria, the two objects are one object. What happens then to that one object when it "vanishes" on the platform? Two objects or one—a conflict of interpretation that the infant can only resolve by assuming that the object still exists *somewhere*, eventually *on* the platform. The infant's evolving criteria of identity thus generate a notion of permanence that can be refined to include spatial relations. The generation of the more advanced idea of permanence thus depends on the conflict between the output of the decision rules for permanence and the decision rules for identity, a conflict that can be produced by the purely visual presentations that were all that could be involved in the studies of both Wishart and Gouin-Décarie. Similar hypotheses about the origins of permanence have been offered by Moore (1975) and Wishart (1979).

What, then, has a cost–gain ratio to do with conflict reduction? I would propose that cost–gain ratios may determine when conflict reduction is accomplished by what we have been describing as cognitive advance and when it is accomplished by *suppression* of one of the competing hypotheses. "Conflict" is an everyday event in the lives of most humans; in adults certainly suppression of one of the competing hypotheses is more frequent than anything else (Festinger, 1957). Why is suppression less frequent in infancy and, indeed, throughout childhood? The answer, I believe, is that infants, unlike adults, have cost–gain ratios that are less than 1. Indeed, cost–gain ratios may determine when a developmental advance may take place, and thus when an acceleration program may be successful. Would the Wishart experiment have been so successful if the number of objects and hence the feature list required for identification, the cost, had been greater? We do not know but the magnitude of acceleration that can be obtained seems to support the idea that simple situations involving low cost can permit more rapid advance than can the diversified situations faced in everyday life.

There is one last point to be made about the account of a conceptual genesis of permanence offered above, a point to do with the hypothesized direction of development. The first-appearing idea of permanence is very vague; only with further experience will it become linked to specific spatial relations. We might thus expect that some practice with a specific spatial relationship—"on," say—might produce equal acceleration in tasks involving "on," "in," and "behind," provided the transfer tasks were begun before the general idea of continued existence had become specific to the "on" relation presented in training. Preliminary data supporting this notion have been gathered by Neilson (1977) and Wishart (1979).

The object, as we have analyzed it thus far, is an object in space. We have been concerned with change in the infant's responses to objects moved around in space and placed in spatial relationships with other objects. The discovery of the properties of objects in space does not exhaust the development of the object concept. The abstraction of the quantitative properties of objects is at least as important, although as yet very little studied.

By quantitative properties I mean dimensions of difference between objects, such as size or weight. Our analysis of the infant's treatment of weight, based on the work of Mounoud and Bower (1974), was begun in the last chapter. We saw how differentiated responses to different weights gradually emerged, with anticipation of weight coming later. The infant learns that the same object weighs the same each time it is picked up; this allows the infant some measure of prediction. The infant also learns that weight covaries with the visible dimensions of objects, so that (other things being equal) the longer an object is, the heavier it will be; this allows the infant an even greater degree of anticipation. In the last chapter, we left the infant facing a puzzle that brought these two behaviors into conflict. How should the infant respond to an object it has already picked up but has then seen transformed (made longer)? On the one hand, it is the same object, so it should weigh the same; on the other hand, it is longer, so it should weigh more. We might think that the infant would instantaneously solve the problem by noting that, although the object was longer, it was also narrower. This is not what happens, however. Mounoud and Bower found that the infant initially responds as if it expects the object to be heavier; conversely, if the object is compressed to become shorter (and wider), the infant responds as if it thinks the object has become lighter. Weight at this point is not an independent dimension of objects; it is equated with length. In time (in the second half of the second year), the infant is able to respond appropriately, ignoring the increased length and expecting the changed object to weigh the same. At this point, we can say that the infant has abstracted the dimension of weight from the visible properties that covary with it. This attainment does not affect the infant's ability to use dimensions correlated with weight, such as length, to predict the weight of an object that has not been handled.

Curiously enough, prediction is not in fact enhanced by consideration of dimensions other than length that covary with weight. The infant seems to know two things: that weight is correlated with length, and that weight is also simultaneously independent of length, so that an object weighs the same regardless of deformations of its shape. Thus, if the infant is presented with a series of objects such as that shown in Figure 7.21, the infant will respond to Object C entirely on the basis of its length. If the infant has previously picked up the object and then seen it bent in two (C′), the infant will ignore the new length and respond on the basis of the information acquired in its prior contact with the object. This is a perfectly satisfactory state of affairs from a practical point of view. It will be years before the child's cognitive development forces it to modify these empirical rules. For the

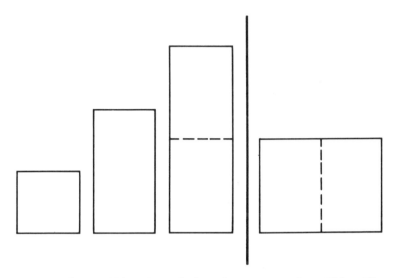

FIGURE 7.21   Object C can be bent in two to produce Object C'.

moment, the infant's inherently contradictory concept of weight as something related to, but independent of, visual dimensions serves the infant well enough.

Size is a more easily attainable dimension of objects than is weight. One might think that, by the age of 6 months, the infant has discovered all there is to know about sizes. The infant at this age can adjust its hand to the size of an object, perceive it as constant during displacements in space, identify various sizes, and so on (see Chapter 5). The discoveries of a 5-month-old are, however, very far from a concept of size. The deficiencies of the young infant's size concept is shown in a simple, ingenious experiment performed by Greenfield et al. (1972). Infants of 1 year were shown a set of objects like those shown in Figure 7.22. The experimenter showed the infant how to make a nested structure out of the cups and then left the infant to stack the objects on its own. All of the infants made some attempt at stacking but failed to do much more than get one object on top of or inside another. Having placed one smaller object on top of a larger object, the infant might then place a yet larger object on top of the previous two, undoing the whole structure. The infant aged 1 year and even 2 years simply cannot organize these objects according to their size. The infant can perceive the sizes of the objects relative to its own hand, for it can reach out and pick up the objects with perfect success. What the infant cannot do is organize the sizes of the objects *relative*

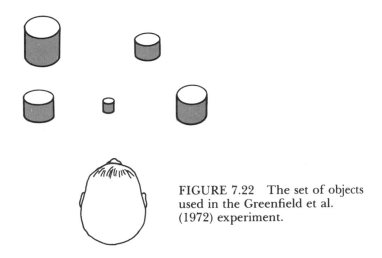

FIGURE 7.22 The set of objects used in the Greenfield et al. (1972) experiment.

to one another. "Size" at this stage is something relative to the infant; it is not yet a relation between objects. Size is still egocentric.

The first signs of development come when the infant dichotomizes objects into big and little. When this occurs, the infant consistently makes pairs of objects with a little object on top of a big one; the infant does not try to add an inappropriately sized object to the two component structures. This degree of classification does not permit a very high level of success, and it invariably leads to conflict, since the same object can be big or little depending upon whether it functions as a supporting object or a supported object. What, for example, would the infant make of the situation shown in Figure 7.23, where the center object can be big or little depending on which object it is paired with? We may speculate that this conflict produces the concept of size as a dimension along which objects may be ordered, so that they are not merely big or little, relative to the infant. Certainly, the infant's two-item structures (little object on top of big object) soon give way to ordered piles of five objects, each object progressively smaller than the one beneath it.

It must be emphasized that the concepts of size and weight thus far described are the merest beginnings of quantitative concepts. The development of true number concepts takes many years. The nature of the development has been intensively described by Piaget and his coworkers in a long series of books such as *The Child's Conception of Number* (1941), *The Child's Conception of Space* (1948), and *The Child's Conception of Geometry* (1948). These can hardly be summarized here.

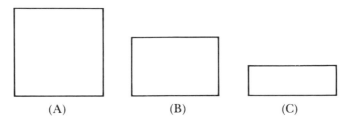

FIGURE 7.23   Object B can be big or little, depending on whether it is paired with A or C.

The major point is that the development of the concept of number begins in infancy, long before speech or formal instruction play any part. The infant is forced to generate number concepts by the requirements of its everyday activities—activities so commonplace that the fondest parent barely thinks them worthy of comment. They are worth mentioning because these are the simple beginnings from which the whole structure of mathematical thinking takes root.

Mounoud (1972) has argued that conservation and all other mathematical capacities have behavioral as well as verbal–symbolic manifestations. The behavioral symptoms of these concepts are continuous from birth onward, and it is only by studying them that we can truly grasp the continuity of the development of mathematical thought processes. Most research on the development of mathematical thinking has concentrated on the ages between 4 and 7 years and has ignored the beginnings of mathematical reasoning in the sensorimotor period. It seems to me that this is a perilous strategy. Only when we understand the beginnings of a process, when it is still simple and relatively undifferentiated, can we hope to understand its more complex manifestations.

Our discussion of cognitive development has focused on the infant over 12 weeks of age. In part this is because there is a gap in our knowledge of what goes on before, a gap only partially filled by the kinds of studies reviewed in other chapters. These other chapters were to do with perception and motor development. In truth, until the problems of the registration of information and the execution of motor acts have been resolved, it will be very hard to analyze cognition. Nonetheless, these difficulties should not stop us from looking beyond available, and potentially available, data to the very presuppositions of cognitive development. In Chapter 1, we pointed out the presuppositions of learning, the amount of information the infant had to bring to the learning situation if learning was to be possible. Here I would like to discuss the information required if cognitive development is to be possible. Obviously, there is considerable overlap. However, I have been at pains in this chapter to distinguish cognitive development from learning, an effort that implies some distinction in their prerequisites. What additional prerequisites would be required for cognitive development, on the account given here?

Before getting to that, we should look at the nature of the knowledge we have attributed to the 12-week-old. In the context of the object concept, that knowledge is summarized in Table 7.2. The infant is supposed to have in its head a variety of rules to guide behavior. These rules are in effect small-scale theories about the physical world. What can we say about the origin of such rules, or theories? They could perhaps develop as a result of maturational processes but this seems rather unlikely. The rules are empirical; they make predictions about the world the infant lives in; they do not describe invariant features of the world; they do not contain the kind of information that evolution might have selected for incorporation in the genes: evolution will only select information that is highly and universally adaptive, as these rules manifestly are not. On the other hand, rules of this kind do not seem to be typical products of learning. Learning, as conventionally understood, involves specific responses to specific stimuli. There is no such specificity in the rules we are considering. They are applied to any old object. Rules of this kind could be the products of specific learning experiences. The infant learns to behave in a specific way with a specific object; from many such learning experiences, the infant abstracts a general rule (Piaget, 1967). Figure 7.24 outlines this kind of model. It is a very powerful model, with a great deal of intuitive appeal. However, an entirely opposite model is equally plausible. The opposite model would assert that the first thing the infant picks up in any learning situation is a general rule about the situation. Suppose, for example, that we show an infant an object passing through a tunnel. At first, the presentation is totally mysterious to the infant. I would propose that, first of all, the infant decides that the object it sees on the two sides of the tunnel is the same object. Given that, the infant can deduce that, while the moving object is out of sight, it must be inside the stationary object. In other words, the infant learns that one object can be inside another. At this point, an infant confronted with the standard manual object-permanence task with cups would have no difficulty. Although the be-

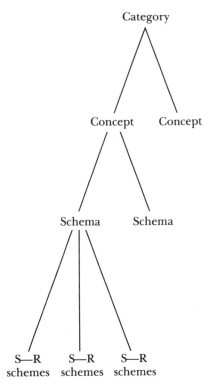

FIGURE 7.24   The outline presented here is a
possible model of development. Development
begins with S–R schemes. These are amalgamated
to form schemas from which are abstracted
concepts from which in turn are abstracted very
general categories (such as space).

havioral response appropriate to this task is different from that for
the tracking task, it nevertheless requires comprehension of the same
spatial relation. This would account for the perfect transfer found in
the experiment described above. The infant is still coping with tracking at a level abstract enough that the information derived from the
tracking task can transfer perfectly to the manual task in the object-
permanence test. Suppose, though, that the infant is given greater,
long-term exposure to the tracking task (the object passing through
the tunnel) before being presented with the manual object-permanence task. The internal description of the event would become more
and more precise, so that the infant would end up with information

of the form, "When the object disappears on the left, look for it to reappear on the right after *x* seconds." This is a very specific sensorimotor rule or schema, and very obviously would not help an infant cope with standard object-permanence tests. On the other hand, it is specific enough to insure perfect contact with the object in the tracking situation, which may explain why it replaces the abstract description of the tracking event. Some of the data supporting this as a general model of cognitive development have been reviewed earlier in the chapter. A specific experiment to test the model by de Schönen and myself (1978) gave at least tentative support to the hypothesis, as does an experiment by Nelson (1971). If the hypothesis were valid, cognitive development would look like perceptual and motor development—a process in which the general becomes specific, in which the abstract is differentiated. However, a desire for neatness should not lead us to forsake the competing specific → general hypothesis. At present, the issue is still unresolved.*

Let us now look at what happens to rules, however they arise. We have argued that, whenever conflicts arise, rules are rewritten. "Conflict" must be sensed in some fashion. As we pointed out above, behavioral conflict would provide the simplest trigger, since the infant cannot behave simultaneously in two conflicting ways.† We then need to look at the nature of the rewrite rule that is called into operation. Essentially, the rewrite rule combines two simple propositions into a more complexly differentiated proposition. I see no reason in principle why this rewrite rule should differ from those posited by linguists (e.g., Chomsky, 1976; Fodor, 1976). Current work in artificial intelligence in Edinburgh and elsewhere (Ephraim, 1977; Prazdny, 1979; Luger et al., 1981) aimed at simulating cognitive development in infancy will soon, I trust, specify the necessary rewrite rules more precisely.

Do we need to propose anything more? To account for single steps in cognitive development, I do not think we do. Developmental possibility will be determined by the perceptual analysis the infant can do and the rules the infant brings to any cognitive problem situation. The one addition I would propose is that, among the rules or theories

---

*For an extended discussion, see Bower, 1976; Bower and Wishart, 1979; Bower, 1979b.

†It is clear from the work of many psychiatrists that adults sometimes can behave simultaneously in conflicting ways. In those cases the conflict may not be realized and its resolution may be impossible (Bateson, 1972; Laing, 1959; Eisenberg, 1958).

the infant brings to any situation, there may be theories about itself in relation to the world that constrain developmental possibility. In this I am following Watson (1979), whose ideas were outlined in Chapter 1. There is some evidence that the infant formulates hypothesis about how successful it can expect to be in problem-solving situations (Watson, 1979; Wishart et al., 1978). If the infant is less successful, or, more intriguingly, more successful than it expects, the infant may well retreat from the situation. This kind of notion, as Watson (1966a) has pointed out, may well be useful in analyzing handicapping conditions, whether social or biological in origin. I certainly find it intriguing that the infant with Down's syndrome rarely shows the 100 percent confidence in its own solutions to problems that characterizes the normal infant. Down's syndrome is a genetic defect. The defect has numerous physiological effects, including sensory and motor defects that mean that very simple acts, such as looking or reaching, are rarely as successful as the same acts carried out by the normal infant. A psychological consequence of these motor defects may be a mistrust of personal efficacy on the part of the Down's infant. Such mistrust might explain the extraordinary instability of cognitive acquisitions in the Down's infant. The simplest way to understand these fluctuations is to assume normal cognitive rules, invested with less than normal confidence (Morss, 1979). Speculations of this kind will require a great deal of research, to substantiate them or to refute them. They do offer the possibility of a psychological understanding of handicap, an understanding that might lead to therapy, to an applied developmental psychology that went beyond *testing for* difference to *remedying* difference.

8

Social Development

In recent years social development has been the busiest area of research on infancy. Until this decade, few would have dissented from
the proposition that the infant is born nonsocial, interested only in
"basic" needs, such as food, liquids, warmth, and comfort. The task
of psychology was to explain how this nonsocial organism became
susceptible to the powerful social motives that so control the behavior
of adults (Milgram, 1974; Schachter, 1959). This proposition has been
under continuous attack for some years. There are now many psychologists who would argue that the infant is social from birth—indeed, that social motives are the most powerful motives operating
during development (e.g., Trevarthen, 1975).

  This change in orientation has been impelled by two forces: a re-
alization that traditional views could not account for even traditional
data, and an acceptance of the validity of new kinds of data—data

indicating that the infant is indeed social. What does "social" mean in this context? When we say that the newborn has social behaviors, what are we saying? I would propose a mixed set of criteria: on the negative side, a social behavior is a behavior that is not terminated by delivery of food, drink, warmth, or comfort; more positively, a social behavior is one that is elicited by the presence of another human and terminated by the departure of that human. More refined criteria are possible (Bower, 1979c) but these will serve as a beginning.

Does the newborn then have social behaviors thus defined? Recent research has produced strong evidence that the newborn does. One behavior that demonstrates inherent sociability appears within hours of birth. *Interactional synchrony* is a form of motor behavior seen whenever one human being speaks to another. Both speaker and listener move together in a very subtle dancelike fashion; as one moves, the other moves—the moves being made in precise synchrony with the segments of the speaker's speech. The movements are usually very small and the participants may be quite unaware of them. Evidence of interactional synchrony has been found in infants only a few hours old (Condon and Sander, 1974) (see also Figure 8.1). Interactional synchrony is a form of communicational interaction; it transmits no precise messages but indicates a degree of rapport between the participants. The behavior is specifically human and can be elicited only by human speech; no other auditory stimulus will produce it. Interestingly, the neonate will interact synchronously with *any* human speech and not only with the particular language of the community into which it has been born.

Another form of social behavior present in the neonate period is *imitation.* Imitation has traditionally been thought of as something that developed late in infancy and required an elaborate cognitive structure before it could be manifested (e.g., Piaget, 1946). However, a number of recent investigations have shown that the capacity for imitation is present in the very first weeks of life (Maratos, 1973; Meltzoff and Moore, 1977; Dunkeld, 1978). Infants have been observed to imitate adults in opening the mouth, widening the eyes, opening the hand, and protruding the tongue (see Figure 8.2).

Is this behavior specific to humans? The question has not been put in this precise form because none of the investigators have thought it a meaningful question. However, the answer must definitely be in the affirmative for the imitative behaviors that have been seen are quite specific to *parts* of humans. That may seem a pointless thing to say but consider this: the infant has been observed to imitate eye *opening,* mouth *opening,* and hand *opening;* in each case the infant

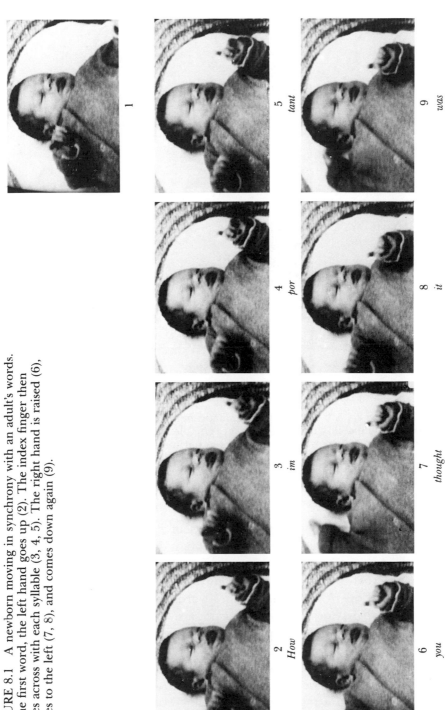

FIGURE 8.1   A newborn moving in synchrony with an adult's words. At the first word, the left hand goes up (2). The index finger then moves across with each syllable (3, 4, 5). The right hand is raised (6), moves to the left (7, 8), and comes down again (9).

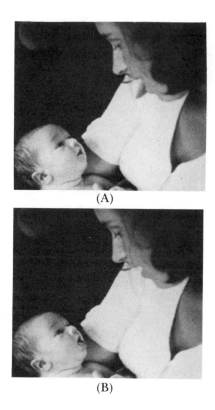

(A)

(B)

FIGURE 8.2 A 6-day-old infant imitates her mother protruding her tongue. The ability to imitate is a very complex achievement: it requires the infant to recognize that what she sees in her mother's mouth is a tongue (A) and that what she feels in her own mouth but cannot see is also a tongue. Then the infant must execute complex muscular actions required for her to protrude her own tongue (B). (Photographs by Jane Dunkeld.)

opens and closes the appropriate part of its own body. When the model opens and closes its eyes, the infant does the same. When the model opens and closes its mouth, the infant does the same. There are no cross-confusions. The infant does not open its mouth when the model opens its hand. In other words, what the infant picks up from the behavior of the model is not just "opening" but opening of a particular body part that the infant mimics with the corresponding body part. We would hardly expect to see anything at all if we presented an infant with, say, an opening and closing matchbox. The infant, from what we have seen, knows very well that no part of itself corresponds to a matchbox. The infant would not map the opening–closing matchbox onto any part of its own body and so would hardly be likely to imitate the matchbox.

Imitation appears, then, to be specific to humans and can only be elicited by humans. It surely indicates that the infant is aware that it is human. By imitating, the infant is showing us that it knows it has eyes, mouth, tongue, hands and that these parts of itself correspond to the same parts of us. I would argue that imitation is an affirmation of identity, evidence that, at some (however primitive) level, the infant knows that it is one of us. Imitation is also interaction in some sense. The infant will imitate the adult but also shows a rapt attention and an increased frequency of behavior if an adult imitates it. At the most basic level, two persons are interacting if the behavior of each influences the behavior of the other. This is certainly true in mutual imitation sessions. This interaction seems in itself to be satisfying, a way of affirming to both participants their mutual awareness of each other.

In addition to behaviors such as imitation and interactional synchrony, there is evidence that development through infancy may be affected by specific social experiences in the newborn period. Take, for example, the work of Klaus and Kennell (1974) on early separation. They compared the development of two groups of infants. One group was with their mothers continuously from birth. The others were on a more normal hospital routine, seeing their mothers at four hourly intervals, with the rest of their time spent in a nursery. This differential experience lasted only through the lying-in period, about five days. Despite the brevity of the differential treatment, there were significant differences between the two groups throughout infancy on both physical and psychological measures. The mechanism for such effects is obscure. We will return to this problem later.

In addition to such long-term effects as those described above, there is evidence that infants are immediately sensitive to changes in social aspects of their care, even though basic needs are fully met. This is shown in a study by Sander (1969). Sander studied the behavior of infants awaiting adoption and their "mothers" over the course of the first two weeks of life in a hospital. Each infant was assigned a "mother," an experienced caretaker whose sole task was to look after the infant 24 hours a day. After 10 days of living with this "mother," each infant was assigned a new caretaker. Even on the first day without its original "mother," the infant showed signs of upset. The infant cried more often and for longer periods, although it was being cared for perfectly adequately.

Let us return for a moment to the early social behaviors. What is the essence of these behaviors? First of all, they are clearly only elicited by other humans. Second, "elicited" may well be the wrong word since the infant, certainly in the imitation situation and possibly in other interaction situations, serves also as an elicitor, eliciting behavior from its mother or other adult caretaker. Furthermore, there is, even in the newborn period, some time sharing, some exchange of roles, with the infant at one time the leader, at others the follower. Thus, in the newborn period, there is at least a plan for the reciprocal, turn-by-turn communication that is the essence of social interaction. To be sure, there is not much information transmitted in these early stages, but there is some, even if only a sense of mutuality.

In the weeks after birth, there is a rapid increase in the range of information communicated between mother and infant. This can easily be seen if we look at the interactional games played by mothers and infants. The patterning of interchange becomes more complex and diverse, and also more specific to a given mother–infant pair (Trevarthen and Hubley, 1978; Abravanel et al., 1976). There are leaps in communication as the infant gains more control over expressive acts, particularly over facial expressions. The first such leap is signified by the emergence of the smile.

If one asks parents whether their infants are at all sociable, those who have an infant 6 weeks of age or more will almost unanimously answer in the affirmative and will base their reply on the fact that the infant smiles at them. An infant's smile is a wonderful thing. The effects on parents are immediate; suddenly they feel that the sleepless nights and continuous fatigue are all worthwhile. The amount of time the parents *want* to spend with the infant, as opposed to the amount of time they *have* to spend with it, goes up quite significantly once smiling has begun (Newson and Newson, 1963). It is no wonder that the smiling response has attracted so much empirical investigation, with literally hundreds of research papers addressing the problem of its genesis and control. These studies taken together show that the smile is not the straightforward social signal to other humans that it appears to be. Smiling of sorts can be observed in the first few hours after birth.* However, these very early smiles strike observers as quite incomplete, as not being real smiles. It seems that these early "false

---

*The following account is largely based on Wolff (1963).

smiles" give the impression they do because they do not reach the eyes. They do not, as real smiles do, involve the crinkling of the eyes that is caused by contraction of the muscles around them. These "smiles" fail as social behaviors simply because the average adult does not register them as smiles. Parents often put them down to wind, explaining them as grimaces of slight pain. This explanation is probably incorrect. Smiles of this sort are in fact less likely when the infant is full of wind, as they are after feeding, than at other times. During the first two weeks of life, these primitive smiles can be elicited only when the infant is not fully awake but not in a state of regular sleep either. During the first week of life, the response can be elicited by gentle stroking of the infant's skin, by not too intense changes of visual stimulation, or by presentation of low-intensity sounds. None of these stimuli, however, seems particularly effective and none of them, we should note, is specific to humans. During the second week of life, the smile retains its incomplete quality. However, it has become more specific to humans in that the human voice is a more effective stimulus than other auditory events, such as those produced by a bell, a whistle, or a rattle. During the third week of life, we see real smiles. They are shorter in duration than the smiles that will come later but they do involve the whole face. By far the most effective stimulus for this smile is the human voice, particularly a female voice. Wolff (1963) found that a female voice could elicit smiles even from an infant who was crying or feeding. The visual aspects of humans are not effective by themselves at this age, although they do increase the effectiveness of the vocal stimulus. In the course of the fifth week of life, there is a dramatic shift in the control of smiling; the voice loses its authority almost completely, and the truly effective stimuli are visual. In Wolff's study, it was the face and particularly the eyes that seemed to be most effective in eliciting smiling.

Everything we have mentioned so far would seem to indicate that smiling is a behavior that is quite specific to humans. The infant's smile is elicited by the human voice and the human face, surely indicating that humans are a special kind of stimulus in the world of the infant, eliciting its own special kind of behavior. It also seems to be a form of interaction and not just an automatic reflex that is triggered by a perception of a particular concatenation of stimuli. Thus, Ambrose (1961), for example, has found that smiling will be terminated if the infant is picked up, even though this results in presentation to the infant of all of the human-specific stimuli in even greater proximity than before. More direct evidence that smiling is an inter-active behavior comes from a study of Brackbill's (1958). Her pro-cedure was basically an operant conditioning procedure. Every time the infant smiled, the experimenter smiled back, talked to the infant, and picked it up. Not surprisingly, rate of smiling increased. However, it increased in specific ways, so that putting down the infant became a signal for smiling, since smiling led to being picked up again. The infant and the experimenter had linked their behaviors in a quite precise way—one feature of true interactive behavior.

Unfortunately for all of the above, however, more careful investi-gation has undermined both of the foundations for the claim that smiling is a truly social act in early infancy. Many investigators, for example, have tried to find out what is special about the human face. The consensus is that its special characteristics have little to do with humanness per se. It was discovered many years ago that there was no need to present a whole face to elicit smiling; a crude mask like that shown in Figure 8.3 will do. From that, it was but a short step to the discovery that a plain piece of cardboard with two eyelike blobs on it would also elicit smiling. Now, such results do not mean that the infant is not smiling at a "face" when it is smiling at a card with two dots on it. Recall the perceptual process "completion" that we dis-cussed in Chapter 5. We presented evidence that the infant is even more likely than the adult to fill in the missing parts of a stimulus and "see" the whole thing when only a part is actually present. It is possible that the infant will see a plain card with two eyes on it as a face. Only a quantitative increase in tendency to completion would be required. However, such explanations become increasingly untenable when one considers other data on early smiling. For example, it has been found that a card with six dots on it is more effective in eliciting smiles than a card with two dots on it and is even more effective than a whole, human face. "Completion" will not explain away this kind of result. Indeed, it seems that we must accept that the infant will smile at any high-contrast pair of stimulus objects, and the more pairs the better. It seems that it is not the "faceness" of a face that elicits smiling from an infant but its "contrastiness," the fact that it contains two dark shiny areas, each surrounded by a white shiny area.

The strongest evidence that smiling is not a social response in our sense comes from Watson (1973), an investigator who has focused on the interaction aspect of sociability. Watson did not set out to inves-tigate the nature of "social stimuli" in infancy. His initial concerns were the processes of, and constraints on, learning in early infancy.

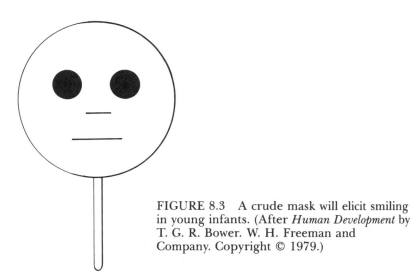

FIGURE 8.3 A crude mask will elicit smiling in young infants. (After *Human Development* by T. G. R. Bower. W. H. Freeman and Company. Copyright © 1979.)

Some of his work on learning was discussed in Chapter 1. Learning, you will remember, consists in the detection of a contingent relationship between a response of the organism and an event in the organism's environment. Watson has argued that, in the world of the Western infant, the infant is most likely to be presented with contingencies that it can detect when an adult plays with it. Watson argues that the games adults play with infants are all variants of a prototypical "game" that has as its main features presentation of clear and simple response–event contingencies. Thus, an adult may play a game with an infant in which each time the infant opens its eyes wide, the adult touches the infant on the nose; or perhaps each time the infant waves its arms, the adult pokes its tummy. The actual responses and events are not critical. What is critical is that every time the infant emits a particular behavior, the infant elicits a specific behavior from the adult. The infant thus can detect a contingency relationship in the context of the "game." Watson argues that the experience of contingency detection releases vigorous smiling in infants, and, further, that it is the detection of contingencies that is the primary cause of smiling. The bulk of the evidence for the hypothesis comes from observations of smiling in the context of contingency detection. Recall the experiments of Papousek (1969) described in Chapter 1. Papousek found that successful contingency detection was accompanied by clear smiling and cooing that were certainly not elicited by the reinforcing event that he had presented, since the infant barely even glanced at it, and did not smile when the event occurred on a noncontingent basis. Papousek's experiments were the main reason that we decided that contingency detection is its own reward in learning situations, an inherently pleasurable event.

Other investigators have also noticed smiling in the course of learning experiments. Thus, Hunt and Uzgiris (1964) observed that infants who were given mobiles that they could control showed clear smiling and cooing while controlling their mobiles. Infants who did not have control of the mobiles showed no particular smiling in the experimental situation at all. Watson himself has carried out the most systematic experiments on the role of contingency detection in the genesis of smiling. In two experiments he gave 8-week-old infants an unambiguous 100 percent contingency to detect. By moving its head, the infant could move a mobile suspended over its crib. Control groups saw a mobile that moved noncontingently, independently of their own movements. The infants had 10 minutes per day of exposure to the situation. The infants with contingent movement all began to show clear, vigorous smiling in the experimental situation on the third or fourth day, just about the point at which their patterning of head movements began to differ significantly from that shown by the group with noncontingent movement. That is, they began vigorous smiling at about the time their behavior showed that they had detected the contingency (see Figure 8.4).

In an additional study, Watson (1973) worked with an 8-month-old infant who had been characterized as a developmental failure. This infant had never shown any appreciable movement of any kind and had never really smiled at anyone or anything. Within two hours of exposure to a contingently moving mobile, this infant was showing not only increased activity but also vigorous and prolonged smiling in the contingency situation, virtually the first smiling this infant had ever shown.

These data, particularly the study of the retarded infant, strongly reinforce the hypothesis that the primitive cause of smiling in infancy is the infant's awareness of a contingency, that it is the "game" that elicits smiling, and that the reason people come to elicit smiling is that people play the game with infants and therefore become associated with the pleasure deriving from the game. As Watson succinctly puts it, "The game is *not* important to the infant because people play it, but rather people become important to the infant because they play the game." Strange as this hypothesis may sound at first, it not only is consistent with its own data but explains some rather puzzling data

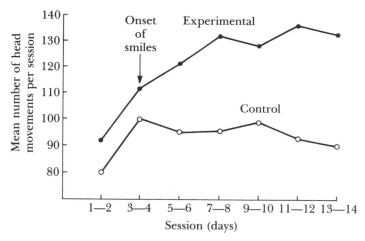

FIGURE 8.4 The subjects in this experiment began to smile at the mobile after they realized that they could control it. (Data from "Smiling, Cooing and 'The Game' " by J. S. Watson. *Merrill-Palmer Quarterly,* **18,** 323–339, 1973.)

about the effectiveness of faces as stimuli provoking smiling. Watson himself some years ago found that the orientation of a face was important in determining its effectiveness as an elicitor of smiles (Watson, 1966b). He presented infants with the same face in three different orientations: 0°, 90°, and 180° (see Figure 8.5). Now, the average Western infant sees its mother's face mostly in a 90° orientation. That is how she will be seen when she is feeding or changing her infant, and these activities do fill the greater part of the time that the mother spends with her infant. If smiling were associated with faces as a result of faces being associated with food, the average infant should smile most at the 90° face. If, on the other hand, smiling were simply elicited by high-contrast blobs, as the data reviewed above would suggest, then there should be no difference between the three orientations of the face. What in fact happens is that from about 8 weeks of age the infant smiles about twice as much at the 0° face as at either of the other two, a result that neither of the hypotheses given above could have predicted. Why does it happen? Because, says Watson, in those situations where an adult begins playing the "game" with an infant, the adult will typically make sure his or her face is at a 0° orientation relative to the infant and the infant will thus come to associate the pleasures of contingency detection with faces at a 0° orientation.

What are we to make of the smile then? On the one hand, we have

FIGURE 8.5   Different orientations of the same face are differentially effective in eliciting smiles. (After *Human Development* by T. G. R. Bower. W. H. Freeman and Company. Copyright © 1979. Data from "Perception of Object Orientation in Infants" by J. S. Watson. *Merrill-Palmer Quarterly,* **12,** 123–135, 1966.)

data like Wolff's (1963), indicating that the smile is a response, if not to people, at least to stimuli that are specific to people, such as voices and faces. Not so, says the opposition; the smile is simply a response to high-contrast stimuli, stimuli of a sort found about human faces but in no way specific to them. Not even that, say Watson. The smile reflects contingency detection and is not specific to any stimulus at all, save by association with the experience of contingency detection. Some theorists (e.g., Piaget, 1936) have attempted to bring order to this confused set of results by proposing that the smile is really a response to anything familiar. This hypothesis would seem to cover all of the instances of smiling that we have come across thus far. However, it does not cover cases of nonsmiling. Why, for instance, should the infant stop smiling in response to its mother's voice, as Wolff found the infant did at about 6 weeks of age? On the familiarity hypothesis, they should surely smile more and more as the voice becomes more and more familiar. Why did the infant in Watson's noncontingent group not smile at its mobile, which was just as familiar to it as the identical mobile was to the infant in the group that had control over the mobile and that did smile? On the familiarity hypothesis, there should have been no difference. Why indeed should a 0° orientation face elicit more smiling than the more familiar 90° face? Why has an infant never been observed to smile at its feeding bottle or crib (Bowlby, 1969)? The list could go on. But enough has been said, surely, to rule out familiarity as a general explanation of smiling.

What then are we to make of the smile? I think that most of our problems with the smile stem from our use of the term "*the* smile." The use of the definite article here is nonsensical. There are smiles, and then there are smiles. There are laughing smiles, amazed smiles, contemptuous smiles, flirtatious smiles, and all the rest. We can identify all of these smiles when emitted by adults (Eibl-Eibesfeldt, 1971). Of late, child psychologists have not even tried to find out whether the infant emits different smiles in different specific situations, although many years ago, before the story of the smile had reached its present level of complexity, Washburn (1929) did describe some of the different smiles emitted by the infant. I think it is clear that one way, possibly the only way, left open to us, to clarify the muddle over smiling is to refine what we mean by smiling, to look more closely at the actual behavior to find out whether the infant shows different specific smiles in different specific situations. Perhaps there is a specific social smile, a specific smile of amusement, and a specific smile of satisfaction, corresponding to the three types of stimuli that have been claimed to elicit smiles.

A recent experiment would seem to indicate that there are indeed different sorts of smiles in infancy (Dunkeld, 1978). Infants were presented with four stimulus situations: a contingency detection "game," a card with six large black dots on it, the mother's face, and a female stranger's face. All four elicited smiles. However, the smiles were quite different (see Figure 8.6 and Tables 8.1 and 8.2). The contingency game elicited quicker and shorter, but larger, smiles than the other three. The high-contrast dots elicited short smiles, less frequently accompanied by tongue protrusion than in the other three situations. The mother's face elicited slower smiles, lasting longer than those elicited by the dots and with accompanying movements toward the stimulus. The female stranger elicited smiles after a longer latency than with the others. These results would seem to argue that, in the infant, as in the adult, there are multiple smiles that are specific to specific situations. These different smiles communicate different information; rather than merely signaling pleasure or displeasure, the infant can signal four different kinds of pleasure.

The range of information the infant can communicate by facial expression or other gesture grows rapidly. In the second half of the first year sounds are incorporated into this repertoire of gestures, further increasing the range of information that can be communicated. Along with this growth of communication potential, there is growth in the range of topics about which there will be communica-

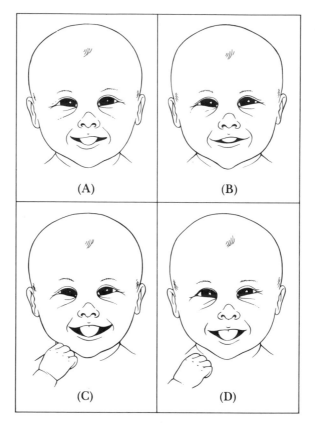

FIGURE 8.6 Different stimuli elicit different smiles even in 6- to 12-week-old infants. (A) Contingency detection. (B) High-contrast dots. (C) The infant's mother. (D) A female stranger. (After "The Function of Imitation in Infancy" by J. Dunkeld. Unpublished Ph.D. thesis, University of Edinburgh, 1978.)

tion. The very young infant will communicate little more than pain or pleasure—pain or pleasure with only self-reference. By 5 months of age, or thereabouts, the range of topics includes objects of interest to the infant and objects of interest to the adult companion. A 5-month-old, for instance, will look where an adult looks, sharing the adult's interest in whatever has caught the adult's eye (Scaife and Bruner, 1975).

The nonverbal communication of the infant eventually grows so sophisticated that, as Lenneberg (1967) pointed out, it is a mystery why the wordless infant ever bothers to acquire language, so long will it be before linguistic communication can match the efficacy of non-linguistic communication. We may be one step closer to solving the

TABLE 8.1   Data for Figure 8.6: Percent of smiles in which certain eye and mouth behaviors were observed (male and female combined in each condition)

Behavior	A	B	C	D
Eye				
1. Eyes wrinkle	94.90	61.71	90.05	92.88
2. Eyes close	21.10	7.69	33.37	43.52
3. Eyes look away	21.10	16.31	41.46	51.74
Mouth				
1. Mouth curls up on both sides	63.33	67.82	78.26	76.57
2. Grin: mouth curls up on one side	26.65	16.78	8.53	6.67
3. Mouth extends vertically	51.10	53.49	63.49	52.98
4. Mouth extends horizontally	15.55	24.47	39.48	28.03
5. Tongue to lips/protrudes	21.10	6.12	28.96	22.04
6. Hand goes to mouth	0	0	9.72	6.90

TABLE 8.2   Data for Figure 8.6

Aspect of Smile	A	B	C	D
Number of smiles	19	35	64	89
Average percent of infants who smiled	41.50	70.00	75.70	87.90
Mean latency (in sec):				
Male	23.89	75.72	26.84	40.08
Female	25.38	57.44	29.42	38.59
Mean duration (in sec):				
Male	0.93	2.45	4.35	3.23
Female	1.87	1.60	2.48	2.17

Percent of Difference Between Conditions

	Latency					Duration			
	Girls			**Boys**		**Girls**			**Boys**
	B	C	D	B	C	D	B	C	D	B	C	D
A	**	*	**	**	ns	ns	ns	ns	ns	*	**	**
B		**	**		**	**		*	ns		*	ns
C			*			ns			ns			*

* = $p < 0.025$ ** = $p < .001$ * = $p < .05$ * = $p < .005$
** = $p < .001$ ** = $p < .001$

mystery if we note that the infant's nonlinguistic communication is private to the infant and one or two privileged partners. The more complex and efficient that communication system becomes, the less easy is it for the infant to interact with a stranger—a problem that does not arise with linguistic communication. The increasing specificity of nonverbal communication may help explain two of the traditional problems of social development in infancy: the appearance of stranger fear and separation anxiety. A stranger will find it difficult, if not impossible, to enter into one of these pair-specific "conversations." If the person attempts to do so, the infant is put into a situation similar to that of an adult approached by a very large stranger speaking a foreign tongue and conveying the impression of expecting to be understood. Not surprisingly, distress ensues. The degree of distress will depend on just how articulated are the communication routines that the infant knows; the less articulated they are, the more easily should a stranger fit into them.

Considerations of this kind cannot be the whole story, however. Other factors must be involved. My warrant for saying this is an ingenious set of experiments by Lewis and Brooks (1975). Lewis reasoned that one of the strangest sights an infant can see is another infant or a young child. The average firstborn has lots of exposure to adults, familiar and unfamiliar. Other infants, other young children, are encountered much less frequently. If stranger fear then reflects a fear of the strange, the sight of an unknown young child should be far more terrifying than the sight of an unknown adult. In fact it is not. Infants who showed classic stranger fear to unknown adults showed, if anything, rather positive responses to unknown children. Size was not the critical feature, since a dwarf was treated as an adult rather than a child. What are we to make of such results? Communication *is* important in the elicitation of stranger fear. We know that because we know that an unknown adult who does not try to communicate will not arouse the fear that will be elicited by an unknown adult who does attempt communication (Schaffer, 1971). Why then is a strange child, attempting communication, not fear-inducing? The answer is suggested by some other data of Lewis's, not concerned with fear but with positive interest. Inasmuch as positive interest is the opposite side of the coin from negative interest—or fear—the topics are related. As we have already noted, Lewis found that while unknown adults are greeted with fear, unknown children are greeted with positive interest. The interest becomes yet more positive if the unknown child is of the same gender as the observing child. This latter effect is strong enough to show up in slide presentations. It would thus appear that by the time the infant is old enough to show stranger fear, the infant can discriminate child from adult, and same-sex child from opposite-sex child. The basis for positive interest appears to be the degree of resemblance the stranger has to the infant, with a same-sex child preferred to an opposite-sex child, and an opposite-sex child preferred to an adult. If the least interesting target of attention, an unknown adult of either sex, turns out in addition to be incomprehensible, it is perhaps no wonder that we see stranger fear so readily elicited.

The basis on which the infant makes the discriminations outlined above is extremely puzzling. Lewis used slides of faces in his study. The slides contained few obvious clues to gender, apart possibly from hair length and perhaps some details of the little clothing that was visible. In a replication study, Aitken (1977) presented slides of the whole body, so that both the model's clothing and toys with which he or she was playing were visible. Some attempt was made to make the latter items as gender-appropriate as possible (see Figure 8.7). This increased information resulted in improved gender identification. The next stage of the study was to swap clothing and toys around to obtain slides of baby boys dressed in a frilly dress playing with a doll and baby girls in blue jeans playing with a drum (Bower et al., 1979). These switches were enough to confuse gender identification: boys looked more at girls in boyish clothes with boyish toys; girls, more at boys in girlish clothes with girlish toys.

While clothing and toys might seem attractively simple clues to gender, the next stage in the research complicated the picture. In this stage we repeated the presentations listed above—girl baby/girl toy/ girl clothes; girl baby/boy toy/boy clothes; boy baby/boy toy/boy clothes; and boy baby/girl toy/girl clothes—only this time motion-picture presentations were used, rather than stills. Under this dynamic condition, clothes and toys did not determine response; actual gender was detected, despite contradicting clothes and toys. This hypothesis was taken one step further by making very artificial films of infants moving (Aitken et al., 1981). The infants had lights attached to each of their joints, a total of 12 in all. An example of the resulting patterns is shown in Figure 8.8. Although gender or even "humanness" is not visible in a single frame, the dynamic pattern of movement was enough to tell infants whether they were looking at a boy or a girl (see Table 8.3).

This last result indicates that the basis for gender identification, for

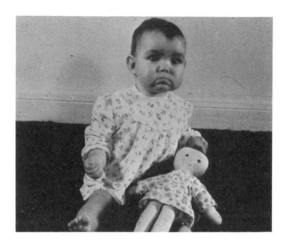

FIGURE 8.7 The gender-appropriate
clothes and toys used in Aitken's (1977)
experiment. (Photographs by Jane Dunkeld.)

identification of "like me," is the dynamic pattern of movement. The
infant's awareness of his or her own movement patterns, manifested
at birth in imitation, can be compared with the perceived movement
patterns of another, giving a match or a mismatch, with the degree
of match determining interest.

The origins of the different movement patterns are at present obscure. It is possible that parents reinforce particular patterns of movement in their infants. It is possible that the skeletal differences between
boys and girls determine different patterns of movement. In the smiling study described above, there was a suggestion that the early smiles

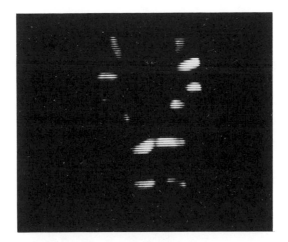

FIGURE 8.8   This figure shows a still frame from a film of infant movement patterns. (Photograph by Jacqueline Kujawski.)

TABLE 8.3   Mean duration of first look at same-sex or opposite-sex infant (sec)

Same Sex	Opposite Sex
5.29	2.88

of boys are different from those of girls (see Figure 8.9 and Tables 8.4 and 8.5), a result that could hardly result from skeletal differences but could reflect parental judgments about what is a smile. Certainly, the plasticity of gender identification in infancy (Money and Ehrhardt, 1972) would argue against any fixed biological basis. A decision must await further research.

What then is happening in social development? I would suggest that two processes go on; the infant formulates a concept of self and a concept of others. The infant is born with a very general concept of itself as a human being—a concept manifested in the early interest in all humans, the early ability and willingness to interact with anyone. This self-concept gradually differentiates to include such information as "I am a child," "I am a boy," and so on. Along with this elaborating self-concept goes a developing concept of the other, the other humans

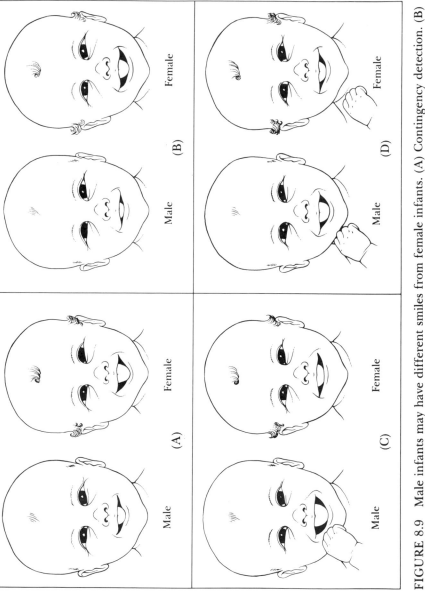

FIGURE 8.9 Male infants may have different smiles from female infants. (A) Contingency detection. (B) High-contrast dots. (C) The infant's mother. (D) A female stranger. (After "The Function of Imitation in Infancy" by J. Dunkeld. Unpublished Ph.D. thesis, University of Edinburgh, 1978.)

TABLE 8.4 Data for Figure 8.9: Percent of smiles in which certain eye, mouth, and head behaviors were observed (male and female separated in each condition)

Behavior	A		B		C		D	
	Male	Female	Male	Female	Male	Female	Male	Female
Eye								
1. Eyes wrinkle	88.90	100.00	77.27	46.15	94.40	85.71	97.67	99.09
2. Eyes close	22.20	20.00	0	15.38	38.89	28.57	34.88	52.17
3. Eyes look away	22.20	20.00	4.55	28.08	47.22	35.71	53.49	50.00
Mouth								
1. Mouth curls up on both sides	66.70	60.00	81.80	53.85	91.67	67.86	81.40	71.74
2. Grin: mouth curls up on one side	33.30	20.00	18.18	15.38	2.78	14.29	4.65	8.70
3. Mouth extends vertically	22.20	80.00	45.45	61.54	80.55	46.43	58.14	47.83
4. Mouth extends horizontally	11.10	20.00	18.18	30.77	36.11	42.86	25.58	30.49
5. Tongue to lips/protrudes	22.20	20.00	4.55	7.69	47.22	10.71	9.30	34.78
6. Hand goes to mouth	0	0	0	0	19.44	0	11.63	2.17
Head								
Moves back	0	0	4.55	0	13.89	3.57	20.93	4.35
Degree of vertical extension of mouth	1.50	2.63	1.80	2.75	2.27	2.54	2.36	2.45

Chi Square Test of Differences Between Males and Females

A	$\chi^2 = 49.96$	$df = 9$	$p < .001$	C	$\chi^2 = 73.18$	$df = 9$	$p < .001$
B	$\chi^2 = 52.34$	$df = 9$	$p < .001$	D	$\chi^2 = 39.36$	$df = 9$	$p < .001$

TABLE 8.5 Data for Figure 8.9

Aspect of Smile	A		B		C		D	
	Male	Female	Male	Female	Male	Female	Male	Female
Number of smiles	9	10	22	13	36	28	43	46
Total number of infants who smiled	40	42.9	90	50	80	71.4	90	85.7
Duration (in sec):								
Mean	0.93	1.87	2.45	1.60	4.35	2.48	3.23	2.17
S.D.	0.50	1.08	1.76	1.15	4.06	2.32	2.34	1.29

Chi Square Test of Differences
Between Mean Durations
of Males and Females

A	*
B	ns
C	*
D	**

$* = p < .025$
$** = p < .01$

in the infant's social world. Evidence for this developing concept of the other comes from one of the most discussed and disputed areas of research in infancy, research on the effects of abnormal social experience during infancy. Bowlby (1951) in particular has argued that any deviation from the normal Western pattern of mothering, a one-to-one relation between mother and infant, can produce deviations in personality development. While Bowlby's earlier conclusions now seem overdrawn (Rutter, 1972), it does appear that the infant's early social experiences can determine its later social possibilities. When the early experience precludes any opportunity for deep, one-to-one relations, it may be difficult for the individual to establish deep, one-to-one relations at any later time. Why should this be so? What has happened during infancy to produce such effects? It is at least possible that the infant who has not had one-to-one relations has formed a concept of others that defines them as untrustworthy, impermanent, fickle—a concept that has transience at its very core. Any such concept of the other would surely preclude any attempts at deep relations. Any attempt by another to pierce this barrier would be almost certain to founder, leading to even greater strength for the handicapping concept. I emphasize the word "concept." The deep, intimate relations of an 18-month-old are very different, behaviorally, from the deep, intimate relations an 18-year-old will have. The former is necessary for the latter but it is not necessary in the sense that the infant acquires specific skills that the 18-year-old needs. Rather, the infant acquires the very abstract idea that it is possible to have deep, intimate relations with people, an idea that will be translated subsequently into whatever behaviors are culturally permissible expressions of intimacy at a particular time of life.

The pattern of social development bears a strong resemblance to the pattern of conceptual development described in the last chapter, and indeed to the process of perceptual development outlined in Chapter 5. It is a process in which very general hypotheses are refined and specified to produce increasingly precise adjustment to the world the infant lives in. I emphasize that the adjustment is to the world of the infant, rather than to the "real" world. The infant who has formulated the hypothesis that people are not to be trusted will live in a world without trust, just as the blind baby will continue to live in a world without spatial order, no matter how much spatial information is presented.

Whether the resemblance between social and cognitive development extends to the very mechanisms of development is a question we

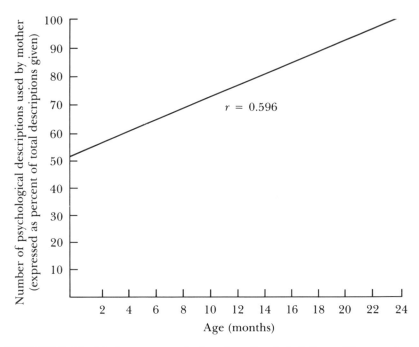

FIGURE 8.10 Mothers were asked to describe their infants. The number of psychological terms in the descriptions grows with the infant's age. (Data from "Maternal 'Theories' of Personality Development in Infancy" by R. S. Noble. Unpublished Ph.D. thesis, University of Edinburgh, 1981.)

cannot at present answer. Social development, like cognitive development, would seem to depend on internal consistency checks rather than external reinforcement, at least after the very early phase in which the infant is open to the most general forms of human experience. Whether conflicts or contradictions can play a generative role in social as in cognitive development is a question we can hardly as yet formulate, much less test.

The previous discussion has focused on the infant's developing conception of itself and others. A possibly significant factor in this development is the mother's developing conception of the infant. It is surely clear that the mother's view of the infant will affect the way she treats the infant, which in turn will affect the way the infant views itself, its mother, and the other inhabitants of its social world. Indeed, the mother's theory of the infant in general may well affect perceptual and cognitive development. It is clear that a mother who believes that infants cannot see will have no reason to give her own infant anything interesting to look at; a mother who believes that infants have no social needs will be more than likely to respond to crying with offers of food. Considerations of this kind have been invoked to explain the results of Klaus and Kennell (1974) described above. This explanation proposes that the period in the hospital was a significant learning experience for the mother, during which the behavior of the hospital staff served as a model for her own subsequent behavior. Thus, the mother subjected to the standard hospital regime would carry away the idea that the infant is to be seen every X hours, at which time it is to be fed and then put back to bed to sleep. A continuance of this regime would certainly affect the infant's development, and probably not for the good.

As yet, we know little about the theories that mothers bring to the childrearing situation. Each mother does perceive changes in her infant and does modify her view of the child. However, the changes do not coincide with obvious changes in behavior and their origin is therefore obscure (see Figure 8.10). We have a great deal to learn about the dynamics of the mother–infant relation. A great deal of research is currently focusing on the *behavioral* aspects of this relationship. It might be well worthwhile to look more at the *theories* the mother relies on to guide her behavior (Noble, 1981).

Bibliography

Abravanel, E.; Levan-Goldschmidt, E.; and Stevenson, M. B.
    1976   Action imitation: The early phase of infancy. *Child Development,*
        47, 1032–1044.

Ahrens, R.
    1954   Beiträge zur entwicklung des physiognomie—und mimiker-
        kennes. *Zeitschrift für Experimentelle und Angewandte Psychologie,* **2,**
        412–454.

Aitken, S.
    1977   Psychological sex differentiation as related to the emergence of
        a self concept in infancy. Unpublished honours thesis, Depart-
        ment of Psychology, University of Edinburgh.
    1981   Differentiation theory and the study of intersensory substitution
        using the sonic-guide. Unpublished Ph.D. thesis, University of
        Edinburgh.

Aitken, S.; Kujawski, J. H.; and Bower, T. G. R.
    1981   Gender identification in infancy. Manuscript in preparation,
        University of Edinburgh.

Alegria, J., and Noirot, E.
    1978   Neonate orientation behaviour towards the human voice. *Inter-*
        national Journal of Behavioural Development, **1,** 291–312.

Alt, J.; Trevarthen, C.; and Ingersoll, S. M.
  1973   The co-ordination of early reaching with visual fixation in infants.
          Unpublished manuscript, but see Trevarthen, 1980.
Ambrose, J. A.
  1961   The development of the smiling response in early infancy. In B.
          M. Foss (Ed.), *Determinants of Infant Behaviour.* Vol. 1. London:
          Methuen.
André-Thomas, C. Y., and Autguarden, R.
  1953   Les deux marches. *La Presse Médicale,* **61,** 582–584.
André-Thomas, C. Y., and Dargassies, St. A.
  1952   *Études Neurologiques sur le Nouveau-Né et le Jeune Nourrisson.* Paris:
          Masson.
Aronson, E., and Rosenbloom, S.
  1971   Space perception in early infancy: Perception within a common
          auditory–visual space. *Science,* **172,** 1161–1163.
Attneave, F.
  1959   *Applications of Information Theory to Psychology.* New York: Holt,
          Rinehart and Winston.
Ball, W., and Tronick, E.
  1971   Infant responses to impending collision: Optical and real. *Science,*
          171, 818–820.
Bateson, G.
  1972   *Steps to an Ecology of Mind.* New York: Ballantine.
Bechtold, A. G., and Salapatek, P.
  1976   Research reported in Annual Report of Institute of Child De-
          velopment, University of Minnesota, 1976–1977.
Békésy, G. von.
  1969   *Sensory Inhibition.* Princeton: Princeton University Press.
Berkeley, G.
  1923   Essay towards a new theory of vision. In *Theory of Vision and Other
          Writings by Bishop Berkeley.* London: Dent. (Originally published
          in 1709.)
Boring, E. G.
  1942   *Sensation and Perception in the History of Experimental Psychology.*
          New York: Appleton-Century-Crofts.
Bower, T. G. R.
  1965a   Stimulus variables determining space perception in infants. *Sci-
          ence,* **149,** 88–89.
  1965b   The determinants of perceptual unity in infancy. *Psychonomic
          Science,* **3,** 323–324.
  1966a   The visual world of infants. *Scientific American,* **215,** 80–92.
          Offprint No. 502.
  1966b   Heterogeneous summation in human infants. *Animal Behaviour,*
          14, 395–398.

1966c   Object permanence and short-term memory in the human infant. Unpublished manuscript.

1967a   Phenomenal identity and form perception in infants. *Perception and Psychophysics,* **2,** 74–76.

1967b   The development of object permanence: Some studies of existence constancy. *Perception and Psychophysics,* **2,** 411–418.

1968   Reality and identity in the development of the object concept. To appear in J. Mehler (Ed.), *Handbook of Cognitive Psychology.* Englewood Cliffs, N.J.: Prentice-Hall.

1971   The object in the world of the infant. *Scientific American,* **225,** 30–38. Offprint No. 539.

1972   Object perception in infants. *Perception,* **1,** 15–30.

1973   The development of reaching in infants. Unpublished manuscript.

1974   *Development in Infancy,* 1st ed. San Francisco: W. H. Freeman and Company.

1976   Concepts of development. Paper presented at International Congress of Psychology, Paris, July. Published in *Proceedings of the 21st International Congress of Psychology.* Paris: Presses Universitaires de France, 1978.

1977a   *A Primer of Infant Development.* San Francisco: W. H. Freeman and Company.

1977b   Blind babies see with their ears. *New Scientist,* **73,** 255–257.

1978   La préhension chez les bébés aveugles-nés. Paper presented at Institut National de la Santé et de la Recherche Médicale, Paris, April.

1979a   Visual development in the blind child. In V. Smith and J. Keen (Eds.), *Visual Handicap in Children: Clinics in Developmental Medicine,* No. 73. London: Heinemann Medical Books. Philadelphia: Lippincott.

1979b   The origins of meaning in perceptual development. In A. Pick (Ed.), *Perception and Its Development: A Tribute to E. J. Gibson.* Hillsdale, N.J.: Lawrence Erlbaum Associates.

1979c   *Human Development.* San Francisco: W. H. Freeman and Company.

Bower, T. G. R.; Broughton, J. M.; and Moore, M. K.

1970a   Infant responses to approaching objects: An indicator of response to distal variables. *Perception and Psychophysics,* **9,** 193–196.

1970b   Demonstration of intention in the reaching behaviour of neonate humans. *Nature,* **228,** 679–681.

1970c   The coordination of vision and touch in infancy. *Perception and Psychophysics,* **8,** 51–53.

1971   The development of the object concept as manifested by changes in the tracking behavior of infants between 7 and 20 weeks of age. *Journal of Experimental Child Psychology,* **11,** 182–193.

Bower, T. G. R.; Dunkeld, J.; and Wishart, J. G.
    1979   Infant perception of visually presented objects. *Science,* **203,** 1137–1138.

Bower, T. G. R., and Paterson, J. G.
    1972   Stages in the development of the object concept. *Cognition,* **1,** 47–55.
    1973   The separation of place, movement and time in the world of the infant. *Journal of Experimental Child Psychology,* **15,** 161–168.

Bower, T. G. R.; Turnbull, J. D.; and Wishart, J. G.
    1979   The effects of infant research toward understanding families. In T. B. Brazelton and V. C. Vaughan (Eds.), *The Family: Setting Priorities.* New York: Science and Medicine Publishing Co.

Bower, T. G. R., and Wishart, J. G.
    1972   The effects of motor skill on object permanence. *Cognition,* **1,** 28–35.
    1973   Development of auditory–manual co-ordination. Unpublished manuscript.
    1979   Towards a unitary theory of development. In E. B. Thoman (Ed.), *Origins of the Infant's Social Responsiveness.* Hillsdale, N.J.: Lawrence Erlbaum Associates.

Bowlby, J.
    1951   *Maternal Care and Mental Health.* Geneva: World Health Organisation.
    1959   *Attachment and Loss.* Vol. 1. London: Hogarth Press.

Brackbill, Y.
    1958   Extinction of the smiling response in infants as a function of reinforcement schedule. *Child Development,* **29,** 115–124.

Brazelton, T. B.; Koslowski, B.; and Main, M.
    1974   The origin of reciprocity in the mother–infant interaction. In M. Lewis and L. Rosenblum (Eds.), *The Effect of the Infant on Its Care-Giver.* New York: Wiley.

Bresson, F.; Maury, L.; Le Bonniec, G. P.; et al.
    1977   Organisation and lateralisation of reaching in infants: An instance of asymmetric functions in hands collaboration. *Neuropsychologia,* **15,** 311–320.

Bruner, J. S.
    1968   *Processes of Cognitive Growth: Infancy.* Worcester, Mass.: Clark University Press.
    1973   Organization of early skilled action. *Child Development,* **44,** 1–11.

Bruner, J. S.; May, A.; and Koslowski, B.
    1971   *The Intention to Take.* Film, Center for Cognitive Studies, Harvard University.

Bruner, J. S.; Olver, R. R.; Greenfield, P. M.; et al.
    1966   *Studies in Cognitive Growth.* New York: Wiley.

Brunswik, E.
 1956   *Perception and the Representative Design of Psychology Experiments.*
        Berkeley: University of California Press.
Bullinger, A.
 1976   La découverte du soi. Paper presented at International Congress
        of Psychology, Paris, July. Published in *Proceedings of the 21st In-
        ternational Congress of Psychology.* Paris: Presses Universitaires de
        France, 1978.
Bundy, R., and Mundy-Castle, A.
 1981   Looking strategies in Nigerian infants: A cross-cultural study. In
        The Developing Child: A Nigerian Perspective. London: Routledge
        and Kegan Paul, in press.
Butterworth, G. E.
 1977   Object disappearance and error in Piaget's Stage IV task. *Journal
        of Experimental Child Psychology,* **23,** 391–401.
 1978   A review of "A Primer of Infant Development." *Perception,* **7,**
        363–364.
Butterworth, G. E., and Castillo, M.
 1976   Coordination of auditory and visual space in newborn human
        infants. *Perception,* **5,** 155–160.
Caron, A. J.; Caron, R. F.; and Carlson, V. R.
 1978   Do infants see objects or retinal images? Shape constancy revis-
        ited. *Infant Behavior and Development,* **1,** 229–243.
Carpenter, G.
 1975   Mother's face and the newborn. In R. Lewin (Ed.), *Child Alive.*
        London: Temple Smith.
Changeux, J.-P., and Danchin, A.
 1976   Selective stabilisation of developing synapses as a mechanism for
        the specification of neuronal networks. *Nature,* **264,** 705–712.
Charlesworth, W. R.
 1966   Persistence of orienting and attending behavior in infants as a
        function of stimulus–locus uncertainty. *Child Development,* **37,**
        473–491.
Chomsky, N. A.
 1976   *Reflections on Language.* London: Temple Smith, in association
        with Fontana.
Cohen, L. B.
 1976   Habituation of infant visual attention. In R. J. Tighe and R. N.
        Leaton (Eds.), *Habituation: Perceptives from Child Development, An-
        imal Behavior and Neurophysiology.* Hillsdale, N.J.: Lawrence Erl-
        baum Associates.
 1977   Habituation of attention in infants. In B. B. Wolman and L. R.
        Pomeroy (Eds.), *International Encyclopedia of Neurology, Psychiatry,
        Psychoanalysis and Psychology.* New York: Aesculapius Pubs., Inc.

Cohen, L. B., and Gelber, E. R.
 1975   Infant visual memory. In L. B. Cohen and P. Salapatek (Eds.), *Infant Perception: From Sensation to Cognition*, Vol. 1. New York: Academic Press.

Condon, W. S., and Sander, L.
 1974   Neonate movement is synchronized with adult speech: Interactional participation and language acquisition. *Science*, **183**, 99–101.

Cornell, E. H., and Strauss, M. S.
 1973   Infants' responsiveness to compounds of habituated visual stimuli. *Developmental Psychology*, **9**, 73–78.

Cotzin, M., and Dallenbach, K. M.
 1950   "Facial vision": The role of pitch and loudness in the perception of obstacles by the blind. *American Journal of Psychology*, **63**, 485–515.

Cruikshank, R. M.
 1941   The development of visual size constancy in early infancy. *Journal of Genetic Psychology*, **58**, 327–351.

Curti, M. W.
 1930   *Child Psychology*. Philadelphia: Longmans Green.

Day, R. H., and McKenzie, B. E.
 1973   Perceptual shape constancy in early infancy. *Perception*, **3**, 315–326.

Dennis, W.
 1940   The effect of cradling practices upon the onset of walking in Hopi children. *Journal of Genetic Psychology*, **56**, 77–86.

Dittrichova, J.
 1969   Social smiling: General discussion of Wolff's paper. In R. J. Robinson (Ed.), *Brain and Early Behavior*. New York: Academic Press.

Dodwell, P. C.; Muir, D.; and Di Franco, D.
 1976   Response of infants to visually presented objects. *Science*, **194**, 209–210.

Duncker, K.
 1938   Induced motion. In W. H. Ellis (Ed.), *Source Book of Gestalt Psychology*. London: Routledge and Kegan Paul. New York: Harcourt Brace.

Dunkeld, J.
 1978   The function of imitation in infancy. Unpublished Ph.D. thesis, University of Edinburgh.

Dunkeld, J., and Bower, T. G. R.
 1981   The effect of wedge prisms on the reaching behaviour of infants. Manuscript in preparation, Department of Psychology, University of Edinburgh.

Eibl-Eibesfeldt, I.
 1971   *Love and Hate*. London: Methuen.

Eisenberg, L.
    1958   School phobia: A study in the communication of anxiety. *American Journal of Psychiatry,* **114,** 712–718.
Elkind, D., and Sameroff, A.
    1970   Developmental psychology. *Annual Review of Psychology,* **21,** 191–238.
Engen, T.; Lipsitt, L. P.; and Kaye, H.
    1963   Olfactory responses and adaptation in the human neonate. *Journal of Comparative Physiology and Psychology,* **56,** 73–77.
Ephraim, G. W.
    1977   Babel: A computer simulation of infant ontogeny. Unpublished manuscript, Department of Psychology, Leavesden Hospital, Watford, England.
Fagan, J. F.
    1977   An attention model of infant recognition. *Child Development,* **48,** 345–359.
Fantz, R. L.
    1961   The origin of form perception. *Scientific American,* **204,** 66–72. Offprint No. 459.
Festinger, L.
    1957   *A Theory of Cognitive Dissonance.* Stanford, Calif.: Stanford University Press.
Field, J.
    1976   Adjustment of reaching behavior to object distance in early infancy. *Child Development,* **47,** 304–308.
    1977   Coordination of vision and prehension in young infants. *Child Development,* **48,** 97–103.
Fishman, M. C., and Michael, C. R.
    1973   Integration of auditory information in the cat's visual cortex. *Vision Research,* **13,** 1415–1419.
Fodor, J. A.
    1976   *The Language of Thought.* Hassocks, England: Harvester Press.
Fraiberg, S.
    1968   Parallel and divergent patterns in blind and sighted infants. *Psychoanalytic Study of the Child,* **23,** 264–299.
Fraiberg, S., and Freedman, D. A.
    1964   Studies in the ego development of the congenitally blind infant. *Psychoanalytic Study of the Child,* **19,** 113–169.
Fraiberg, S.; Siegel, B. L.; and Gibson, R.
    1966   The role of sound in the search behavior of a blind infant. *Psychoanalytic Study of the Child,* **21,** 327–357.
Freedman, D. G.
    1964   Smiling in blind infants and the issue of innate versus acquired. *Journal of Child Psychology and Psychiatry and Allied Disciplines,* **5,** 171–184.

Gardner, J. K.
   1971   The development of object identity in the first six months of
           human infancy. Unpublished Ph.D. thesis, Harvard University.
Gardner, J., and Gardner, H.
   1970   A note on selective imitation by a six-week-old human infant.
           Child Development, **41,** 1209–1213.
Gesell, A., and Amatruda, C. S.
   1941   *Developmental Diagnosis.* New York: Hoeber.
Gesell, A., and Thompson, H.
   1929   Learning and growth in identical infant twins: An experimental
           study by the method of co-twin control. *Genetic Psychology Mon-
           ographs,* **6,** 1–124.
Gesell, A.; Thompson, H.; and Amatruda, C. S.
   1934   *Infant Behavior: Its Genesis and Growth.* New York: McGraw-Hill.
Gibson, E. J.
   1969   *Principles of Perceptual Learning and Development.* New York: Ap-
           pleton-Century-Crofts.
Gibson, E. J., and Walk, R. D.
   1960   The "visual cliff." *Scientific American,* **202,** 64–71. Offprint No.
           402.
Gibson, J. J.
   1950   *The Perception of the Visual World.* Boston: Houghton Mifflin.
Gouin-Décarie, T.
   1969   A study of the mental and emotional development of the tha-
           lidomide child. In B. M. Foss (Ed.), *Determinants of Infant Behav-
           iour.* Vol. 4. London: Methuen.
Graham, C. H.; Bartlett, N. R.; Brown, J. L.; et al.
   1965   *Vision and Visual Perception.* New York: Wiley.
Gratch, G., and Breitmeyer, B. G.
   1978   Visions of the wee "Wunderbairn." *Contemporary Psychology,* **23,**
           724–725.
Greenfield, P. M.; Nelson, K.; and Saltzman, E.
   1972   The development of rulebound strategies for manipulating ser-
           iated cups: A parallel between action and grammar. *Cognitive
           Psychology,* **3,** 291–310.
Gregory, R. L.
   1966   *Eye and Brain.* New York: World University Library.
Gregory, R. L., and Zangwill, O. L.
   1963   The origin of the autokinetic effect. *Quarterly Journal of Experi-
           mental Psychology,* **15,** 252–261.
Griffin, D. R.
   1960   *Echoes of Bats and Men.* London: Heinemann (Educational).
Guilford, J. P., and Dallenbach, K. M.
   1928   A study of the autokinetic sensation. *American Journal of Psychol-
           ogy,* **40,** 91–93.

Gunther, M.
  1961   Infant behaviour at the breast. In B. M. Foss (Ed.), *Determinants of Infant Behaviour.* Vol. 1. London: Methuen.

Harris, C. S.
  1965   Perceptual adaptation to inverted, reversed, and displaced vision. *Psychological Review,* **72,** 419–444.

Hay, J. C.
  1966   Optical motions and space perception: An extension of Gibson's analysis. *Psychological Review,* **73,** 550–565.

Hebb, D. O.
  1949   *The Organization of Behavior.* New York: Wiley.

Held, R.
  1965   Plasticity in sensory-motor systems. *Scientific American,* **213,** 84–94. Offprint No. 494.

Held, R., and Bauer, J. A.
  1967   Visually guided reaching in infant monkeys after restricted rearing. *Science,* **155,** 718–720.

Held, R., and Hein, A.
  1963   Movement-produced stimulation in the development of visually guided behavior. *Journal of Comparative and Physiological Psychology,* **56,** 872–876.

Helson, H.
  1933   The fundamental propositions of Gestalt psychology. *Psychological Review,* **40,** 12–32.

Hofsten, C. von.
  1976   Binocular convergence as a determinant of reaching behaviour in infancy. *Perception,* **6,** 139–144.

Humphrey, T.
  1969   Postnatal repetition of human prenatal activity sequences with some suggestions of their neuroanatomical basis. In R. J. Robinson (Ed.), *Brain and Early Behavior.* New York: Academic Press.

Hunt, J. McV., and Uzgiris, I. C.
  1964   Cathexis from recognitive familiarity: An exploratory study. Paper presented at American Psychological Association, Los Angeles, September.

James, W.
  1890   *The Principles of Psychology.* Vol. 2. New York: Holt.

Jirari, C.
  1970   Form perception, innate form preference and visually mediated head turning in the human neonate. Unpublished Ph.D. thesis, University of Chicago.

Johansen, M.
  1957   The experienced continuations. *Acta Psychologica,* **13,** 1–26.

Katz, D.
  1911   Die erscheinungsweisen der farben. *Zeitung Psychologie Erbildung,* **7.**

Klaus, M. H., and Kennell, J. H.
  1974   Maternal behavior one year after early and extended post-par-
          tum contact. *Developmental Medicine and Child Neurology,* **16,**
          172–179.
Kohler, I.
  1964   The formation and transformation of the perceptual world. *Psy-
          chological Issues,* **3,** No. 4, Monograph No. 12.
Laing, R. D.
  1959   *The Divided Self.* London: Tavistock.
Lashley, K. S., and Russell, J. T.
  1934   The mechanism of vision: A preliminary test of innate orga-
          nization. *Journal of Genetic Psychology,* **45,** 136–144.
Lasky, R. E.
  1973   The effect of visual feedback on the reaching of young infants.
          Unpublished Ph.D. thesis, University of Minnesota.
Lee, D. N.
  1974   Visual information during locomotion. In H. L. Pick and R. B.
          McLeod (Eds.), *Essays in Honor of J. J. Gibson.* Ithaca, N.Y.: Cornell
          University Press.
Lee, D. N., and Lishman, R.
  1977   Visual control of locomotion. *Scandinavian Journal of Psychology,*
          18, 224–230.
Le Grand, Y.
  1967   *Form and Space Vision.* Bloomington: Indiana University Press.
Lenneberg, E. H.
  1967   *Biological Foundations of Language.* New York: Wiley.
Lewis, M., and Brooks, J.
  1975   Infant's social perception: A constructivist view. In L. B. Cohen
          and P. Salapatek (Eds.), *Infant Perception: From Sensation to Cog-
          nition.* Vol. 2. New York: Academic Press.
Lipsitt, L.
  1969   Learning capacities of the human infant. In R. J. Robinson (Ed.),
          Brain and Early Behavior. New York: Academic Press.
Luger, G. F., Bower, T. G. R., and Wishart, J. G.
  1981   A model of the development of the early infant object concept.
          Paper presented at Artificial Intelligence and Simulation of Be-
          haviour Meeting, Sheffield, April.
Lyons-Ruth, K.
  1977   Bimodal perception in infancy: Response to auditory–visual in-
          congruity. *Child Development,* **48,** 820–827.
McDonnell, P. M.
  1975   The development of visually guided reaching. *Perception and Psy-
          chophysics,* **19,** 181–185.
Macfarlane, A.
  1977   *The Psychology of Childbirth.* London: Open Books. Cambridge,
          Mass.: Harvard University Press.

McGraw, M. B.
    1940   Neural maturation as exemplified by the achievement of bladder control. *Journal of Pediatrics,* **16,** 580–590.

McGurk, H.; Turnure, C.; and Creighton, S. J.
    1977   Auditory–visual coordination in neonates. *Child Development,* **48,** 138–143.

Mach, E.
    1959   *The Analysis of Sensations.* New York: Dover Publications. (Originally published in 1885.)

Mack, A., and Bachant, J.
    1969   Perceived movement of the after-image during eye-movements. *Perception and Psychophysics,* **6,** 379–384.

McKenzie, B. E., and Day, R. H.
    1972   Object distance as a determinant of visual fixation in early infancy. *Science,* **178,** 1108–1110.

Mann, I. C.
    1928   *The Development of the Human Eye.* Cambridge, England: Cambridge University Press.

Maratos, O.
    1973   The origin and development of imitation in the first six months of life. Unpublished Ph.D. thesis, University of Geneva.

Meltzoff, A. N., and Moore, M. K.
    1977   Imitation of facial and manual gestures by human neonates. *Science,* **198,** 75–78.

Mendelson, M. J.
    1975   The relation between audition and vision in the human newborn. Unpublished Ph.D. thesis, Harvard University.

Mendelson, M. J., and Haith, M. M.
    1976   *The Relation Between Audition and Vision in the Human Newborn.* Society for Research in Child Development Monographs, **41** (4).

Michotte, A.
    1962   *Causalité, Permanence et Réalité Phénoménales.* Louvain, Belgium: Publications Universitaires.

Michotte, A.; Thines, G.; and Crabbé, G.
    1964   *Les Compléments Amodaux des Structures Perceptives.* Louvain, Belgium: Publications Universitaires.

Milgram, S.
    1974   *Obedience to Authority.* New York: Harper and Row. London: Tavistock.

Mills, M., and Melhinsh, E.
    1974   Recognition of mother's voice in early infancy. *Nature,* **252,** 123.

Money, J., and Ehrhardt, A. A.
    1972   *Man and Woman, Boy and Girl.* Baltimore: Johns Hopkins University Press.

Moore, M. K.
  1975   Object permanence and object identity: A stage-developmental
          model. Paper presented at Society for Research in Child Devel-
          opment, Denver, April.
Morss, J. R.
  1979   A comparative study of the cognitive development of the infant
          with Down's syndrome and the normal infant. Unpublished Ph.D.
          thesis, University of Edinburgh.
Mounoud, P.
  1972   Développement des systèmes de représentation et de traitement
          chez l'enfant. *Bulletin de Psychologie Scolaire et d'Orientation,* **25,**
          5–7.
Mounoud, P., and Bower, T. G. R.
  1974   Conservation of weight in infants. *Cognition,* **3,** 29–40.
Mundy-Castle, A. C., and Anglin, J.
  1974   Looking strategies in infancy. In L. J. Stone, H. T. Smith, and
          L. B. Murphy (Eds.), *The Competent Infant.* London: Tavistock.
Munn, N. L.
  1965   *The Evolution and Growth of Human Behavior.* Boston: Houghton
          Mifflin.
Murata, K.; Cramer, H.; and Bach-y-Rita, P.
  1965   Neuronal convergence of noxious acoustic and visual stimuli in
          the visual cortex of the cat. *Journal of Neurophysiology,* **28,**
          1223–1240.
Neilson, I. E.
  1977   A reinterpretation of the development of the object concept.
          Unpublished Ph.D. thesis, University of Edinburgh.
Nelson, K. E.
  1971   Accommodation of visual-tracking patterns in human infants to
          object movement patterns. *Journal of Experimental Child Psychology,*
          12, 182–196.
Newson, J., and Newson, E.
  1963   *Infant Care in an Urban Community.* London: Allen and Unwin.
Noble, R. S.
  1981   Maternal "theories" of personality development in infancy. Un-
          published Ph.D. thesis, University of Edinburgh.
Papousek, H.
  1965   The development of higher nervous activity in children in the
          first half-year of life. In P. H. Mussen (Ed.), *European Research
          in Cognitive Development.* Society for Research in Child Develop-
          ment Monographs, **30,** (2).
  1967   Experimental studies of appetitional behavior in human new-
          borns and infants. In H. W. Stevenson, E. H. Hess, and H. L.
          Rheingold (Eds.), *Early Behavior.* New York: Wiley.

1969   Individual variability in learned responses in human infants. In R. J. Robinson (Ed.), *Brain and Early Behavior.* New York: Academic Press.

Peiper, N.
1963   *Cerebral Function in Infancy and Childhood.* New York: Consultations Bureau.

Piaget, J.*
1936   *The Origins of Intelligence in Children.* London: Routledge and
[1953]   Kegan Paul.
1937   *The Construction of Reality in the Child.* London: Routledge and
[1955]   Kegan Paul.
1946   *Play, Dreams and Imitation in Childhood.* New York: Norton.
[1951]
1948   *The Child's Conception of Space.* London: Routledge and Kegan
[1956]   Paul.
1954   *Origins of Intelligence.* New York: Basic Books.
1961   *Les Mécanismes Perceptifs.* Paris: Presses Universitaires de France.
1967   *Biologie et Connaissance.* Paris: Éditions Gallimard.

Piaget, J.; Inhelder, B.; and Szeminska, A.
1948   *The Child's Conception of Geometry.* New York: Basic Books.
[1960]   Piaget, J., and Szeminska, A.
1941   *The Child's Conception of Number.* New York: Humanities Press.
[1952]

Prazdny, S.
1980   A computational study of a period of infant object-concept development. *Perception, 9,* 125–150.

Prechtl, H. F. R.
1965   Problems of behavioral studies in the newborn infant. In D. S. Lehrman, R. A. Hinde, and E. Shaw (Eds.), *Advances in the Study of Behavior.* New York: Academic Press.

Rice, C. E., and Feinstein, S. H.
1965   Sonar systems of the blind: Size discrimination. *Science,* **148,** 1105–1107.

Rock, I.
1966   *The Nature of Perceptual Adaptation.* New York: Basic Books.

Rock, I., and Harris, C. S.
1967   Vision and touch. *Scientific American,* **216,** 94–104. Offprint No. 507.

Rock, I., and McDermott, W.
1964   The perception of visual angle. *Acta Psychologica,* **22,** 119–134.

*The first date given is that of the original French edition.

Royce, J. R.; Stayton, W. R.; and Kinkade, R. G.
  1962   Experimental reduction of autokinetic movement. *American Journal of Psychology,* **75,** 221–231.
Ruff, H. A., and Halton, A.
  1978   Is there directed reaching in the human neonate? *Developmental Psychology,* **14,** 425–426.
Rutter, M.
  1972   *Maternal Deprivation Reassessed.* Harmondsworth, England: Penguin Books.
Salapatek, P.
  1969   The visual investigation of geometric pattern by the one- and two-month-old infant. Paper presented at American Academy for the Advancement of Science, Boston, December.
Sameroff, A. J.
  1975   Early influences on development: Fact or fancy? *Merrill-Palmer Quarterly,* **21,** 267–294.
Sander, L. W.
  1969   Regulation and organization in the early infant-caretaker system. In R. J. Robinson (Ed.), *Brain and Early Behavior.* New York: Academic Press.
Scaife, M., and Bruner, J. S.
  1975   The capacity for joint visual attention in the infant. *Nature,* **253,** 265–266.
Schachter, S.
  1959   *The Psychology of Affiliation.* Stanford, Calif.: Stanford University Press.
Schaffer, H. R.
  1971   *The Growth of Sociability.* Harmondsworth, England: Penguin Books.
Schaffer, H. R., and Parry, M. H.
  1969   Perceptual–motor behaviour in infancy as a function of age and stimulus familiarity. *British Journal of Psychology,* **60,** 1–9.
  1970   The effects of short-term familiarisation of infants' perceptual–motor coordination in a simultaneous discrimination situation. *British Journal of Psychology,* **61,** 559–569.
Schönen, S. de, and Bower, T. G. R.
  1978   The understanding of spatial relations. Paper presented at Biannual Round Table on Cognitive Development in Infancy, Paris, March.
Schweizer, G.
  1909   *Über das Sternschwanken.* Referred to in H. F. Adams, The autokinetic sensations. *Psychological Review Monograph Supplement,* **14,** 1–45.

Scott, B. L.
    1979   Speech as patterns in time. In R. A. Cole (Ed.), *Proceedings of the 14th Annual Carnegie Symposium on Cognition, June 1978.* Pittsburgh: Carnegie–Mellon University Press.

Siqueland, E. R., and Lipsitt, L. P.
    1966   Conditioned head-turning in human newborns. *Journal of Experimental Child Psychology,* **3,** 356–376.

Sperry, R. W.
    1959   The growth of nerve circuits. *Scientific American,* **201,** 68–75.

Stevens, J. K.; Emerson, R. C.; Gerstein, G. L.; et al.
    1976   Paralysis of the awake human: Visual perception. *Vision Research,* **16,** 93–98.

Stevens, S. S., and Newman, E. B.
    1936   The localization of actual sources of sound. *American Journal of Psychology,* **48,** 297–306.

Stoper, A. E.
    1967   Vision during pursuit movement: The role of oculomotor information. Unpublished Ph.D. thesis, Brandeis University, Waltham, Mass.

Supa, M.; Cotzin, M.; and Dallenbach, R. M.
    1944   Facial vision–perception of obstacles by the blind. *American Journal of Psychology,* **57,** 133–183.

Teuber, H.-L.
    1960   Perception. In J. Field (Ed.), *Handbook of Physiology,* Vol. 3. Washington, D.C.: American Physiological Society.

Trevarthen, C.
    1974   The psychology of speech development. In E. H. Lenneberg (Ed.), *Language and Brain: Developmental Aspects.* Neurosciences Research Program Bulletin, **12,** 570–585.

    1975   Early attempts at speech. In R. Lewin (Ed.), *Child Alive.* London: Temple Smith.

    1980   Basic patterns of psychogenetic change in infancy. In T. Bever (Ed.), *Dips in Learning.* Hillsdale, N.J.: Lawrence Erlbaum Associates.

Trevarthen, C., and Hubley, P.
    1978   Secondary intersubjectivity: Confidence, confiding and acts of meaning in the first year. In A. Lock (Ed.), *Action, Gesture and Symbol: The Emergence of Language.* New York: Academic Press.

Trevarthen, C.; Hubley, P.; and Sheeran, L.
    1975   Les activités innées du nourrison. *La Recherche,* **6,** 447–458.

Tronick, E.
    1971   Stimulus control and the growth of the infant's visual field. Unpublished manuscript, Center for Cognitive Studies, Harvard University.

Tronick, E., and Clanton, C.
    1971   Infant looking patterns. *Vision Research,* **11,** 1479–1486.
Turkewitz, G.; Birch, H. B.; Moreau, T.; et al.
    1966   Effect of intensity of auditory stimulation on directional eye-movements in the human neonate. *Animal Behaviour,* **14,** 93–101.
Urwin, C.
    1973   The development of a blind baby. Paper presented at University of Edinburgh, January.
Waddington, C. H.
    1957   *The Strategy of the Genes.* London: Allen and Unwin.
Walk, R. D.
    1969   Paper presented at Eastern Psychological Association, Philadelphia, March.
Wallach, H.
    1968   Informational discrepancy as a basis of perceptual adaptation. In S. Freedman (Ed.), *The Neuropsychology of Spatially-Oriented Behavior.* Homewood, Ill.: Dorsey Press.
Walls, G. L.
    1942   *The Vertebrate Eye and Its Adaptive Radiation.* Cranbrook Institute of Science Bulletin 19 (whole issue).
Washburn, R. W.
    1929   A study of smiling and laughing of infants in the first year of life. *Genetic Psychology Monographs,* **6** (5–6).
Watson, J. S.
    1965   Evidence of discriminative operant learning within thirty seconds by infants 7 to 26 weeks of age. Paper presented at Society for Research in Child Development, Minneapolis, March.
    1966a   The development and generalization of "contingency awareness" in early infancy: Some hypotheses. *Merrill-Palmer Quarterly,* **12,** 123–135.
    1966b   Perception of object orientation in infants. *Merrill-Palmer Quarterly,* **12,** 73–94.
    1967   Memory and "contingency analysis" in infant learning. *Merrill-Palmer Quarterly,* **13,** 55–76.
    1973   Smiling, cooing and "the game." *Merrill-Palmer Quarterly,* **18,** 323–339.
    1979   Perception of contingency as a determinant of social responsiveness. In E. B. Thoman (Ed.), *Origins of the Infant's Social Responsiveness.* Hillsdale, N.J.: Lawrence Erlbaum Associates.
Werner, H.
    1947   *The Comparative Psychology of Mental Development.* Chicago: Follett.
Wertheimer, M.
    1961   Psychomotor co-ordination of auditory–visual space at birth. *Science,* **134,** 1692.

White, B. L.
   1963   Development of perception during the first six months. Paper presented at American Association for the Advancement of Science, December.
   1971   *Human Infants: Experience and Psychological Development.* Englewood Cliffs, N.J.: Prentice-Hall.
White, B. L.; Castle, P.; and Held, R.
   1964   Observations on the development of visually directed reading. *Child Development,* **35,** 349–364.
White, B. L., and Held, R.
   1966   Plasticity of sensory-motor development in the human infant. In J. F. Rosenblith and W. Allinsmith (Eds.), *The Causes of Behavior,* 2nd ed. Boston: Allyn and Bacon.
Wishart, J. G.
   1979   The development of the object concept in infancy. Unpublished Ph.D. thesis, University of Edinburgh.
Wishart, J. G.; Bower, T. G. R.; and Dunkeld, J.
   1978   Reaching in the dark. *Perception,* **7,** 507–512.
Wolff, P. H.
   1963   Observations on the early development of smiling. In B. M. Foss (Ed.), *Determinants of Infant Behaviour.* Vol. 2. London: Methuen.
   1969   Motor development and holotelencephaly. In R. J. Robinson (Ed.), *Brain and Early Behavior.* New York: Academic Press.
Yonas, A., and Pick, H. L.
   1975   An approach to the study of infant space perception. In L. B. Cohen and P. Salapatek (Eds.), *Infant Perception: From Sensation to Cognition.* Vol. 2. New York: Academic Press.
Zelazo, P. R.; Zelazo, N. A.; and Kolb, S.
   1972   "Walking" in the newborn. *Science,* **176,** 314–315.

Index